STRUGGLING FOR ORDINARY

CRITICAL CULTURAL COMMUNICATION
General Editors: Jonathan Gray, Aswin Punathambekar, Nina Huntemann
Founding Editors: Sarah Banet-Weiser and Kent A. Ono

Struggling for Ordinary

Media and Transgender Belonging
in Everyday Life

Andre Cavalcante

NEW YORK UNIVERSITY PRESS
New York

NEW YORK UNIVERSITY PRESS
New York
www.nyupress.org

References to Internet websites (URLs) were accurate at the time of writing. Neither the author nor New York University Press is responsible for URLs that may have expired or changed since the manuscript was prepared.

Library of Congress Cataloging-in-Publication Data
Names: Cavalcante, Andre, author.
Title: Struggling for ordinary : media and transgender belonging in everyday life / Andre Cavalcante.
Description: New York : New York University Press, [2018] | Series: Critical cultural communication | Includes bibliographical references and index.
Identifiers: LCCN 2017034137 | ISBN 9781479881307 (cl : alk. paper) | ISBN 9781479841318 (pb : alk. paper)
Subjects: LCSH: Transgender people—Social aspects. | Social media.
Classification: LCC HQ77.9 .C398 2018 | DDC 306.76/8—dc23
LC record available at https://lccn.loc.gov/2017034137

New York University Press books are printed on acid-free paper, and their binding materials are chosen for strength and durability. We strive to use environmentally responsible suppliers and materials to the greatest extent possible in publishing our books.

Manufactured in the United States of America

10 9 8 7 6 5 4 3 2 1

Also available as an ebook

CONTENTS

Introduction

I Felt Like I Was Going to Explode

"I don't know what drew me to the cover of the book, but I looked at it and went, 'Oh my god!' I'm like this! Everything changed after that," explained Margie. Etched into her memory, Margie recalled that pivotal moment she first encountered a transgender representation in popular media. As a teenager strolling through the aisles of her local drugstore, the book that caught her eye chronicled the life of Christine Jorgensen. Jorgensen was a former American soldier who had undergone a sex change in the 1950s, and whose story garnered international attention. When Margie came across Jorgensen's story in paperback, she experienced a jolt of self-recognition. "I was a teenager, and I was at a local drugstore that had magazines and paperbacks. I saw the Christine Jorgensen story . . . I took it home and I read it. I was just flabbergasted. I was like, this is me. I knew, 'hey there's one other person in the world like me.' Reading those pages gave me comfort." For Margie, that book served as a kind of mirror. She saw herself in Jorgensen's life story, and the act of reading helped her realize that gender transformation was possible, and even more, that changing sex did not mean foregoing a successful and fulfilling life. Feelings of solace and encouragement washed over her. She no longer felt so alone.

Margie is a 59-year-old white transgender woman and a small-business owner who lives in the Detroit suburbs. She is a grandmother, a Detroit Tigers fan, and an avid viewer of Fox News. Raised as a boy in a close, conservative Michigan community, Margie grew up in a media and information environment that had little to offer in terms of transgender visibility and discourse. "I grew up in the 1950s and 1960s and there just wasn't anything," she explained, "I think probably in the 1970s magazines were important because we didn't have the Internet. I'd search through magazines sometimes. But the things I found in magazines were always from a pornographic point of view because there wasn't anything else. I did search, but there just weren't any options." Margie remembers feeling alienated in the suburbs and facing unrelenting pressure from family, friends, and teachers to fit in and to convincingly portray masculinity. Despite this she recalled, "I knew I was different . . . I felt that I should be a girl." As a young person, even though she lacked the self-awareness, vocabulary, and social support to fully come to terms with what she called "her situation," Margie cross-dressed in private. In her bedroom, she cautiously experimented with her identity, because, as she admitted, "My parents had very specific ideas about what you were going to be and about what roles you were allowed to be in. My parents were strict. Very loving, but I tried very hard to please them." So, as a teenager Margie kept that drugstore paperback about Christine Jorgensen, her precious resource, hidden from sight in her room, reading it every chance she could get beyond her parents' watchful eyes. Armed with the new and liberating perspective she gleaned from the book, Margie imagined becoming a girl, daydreaming with delight. But she was at a point in her life where the possibility of gender transition "just seemed like a farfetched dream."

As Margie became a young adult, she continued on the predetermined course paved for men growing up in the postwar era: get a job, get married, move to the suburbs, and have kids. After marrying in 1971 and following the birth of her first child in 1972, Margie told her wife she "liked to dress up," and for years continued to secretly cross-dress at home. Yet, the burdens of a restricted self became unbearable. She had to stop hiding. "I struggled with it like everybody else for all those years until I got to the point where I felt like I was going to explode, and either do something about it, or kill myself."

This turning point occurred in 2005, the result of changes in Margie's life circumstances and her media environment. "I started getting truly involved on the Internet . . . Being able to access other people through chat or websites opened up everything. Being able to create an identity that I wanted but that I couldn't quite have and live helped. Knowing there was a possibility that transgender existed. It also was that my children were grown and didn't have to answer to their peers." With her children out of the house, her business stable and profitable, and the Internet at her fingertips, Margie began to consider gender transition. Exploding was no longer necessary.

In 2010, Margie initiated her gender transition. She was ecstatic and immediately changed her name and the gender marker on her driver's license. Nevertheless, transitioning generated new challenges. Margie struggled to maintain the relationships she had long established with family, friends, and business colleagues. Although many were supportive, some did not understand her decision to transition and distanced themselves from her. Moreover, her marriage was at stake. Margie and her wife were best friends and wanted to remain together. But what would this new relationship look like? In answering this question, they turned to media for guidance. Together, Margie and her wife watched as many transgender-themed films and documentaries as they could find. "The movies," Margie explained, "make it easier to talk about this stuff, which is very hard sometimes." Their media journey took them from movies to transgender novels, works of nonfiction, and advocacy websites. All the while, they talked openly about what they read. They took notes and shared insights. Sometimes they fought. Laboring to live as the couple they were before while managing new challenges was difficult, but they ultimately stayed married.

* * *

I first met Margie at "Trans Chat"—a transgender discussion and support group in the Midwest—while I was conducting fieldwork for this book between 2008 and 2012. She was one of the group's more senior and vocal participants, and playfully referred to herself as its "yenta." When I told her I was writing a book and asked her for an interview, she accepted without hesitation.

During our first sit-down together, we discussed Margie's thoughts on media and transgender representation. She emphatically reiterated the following conviction. "The general public needs to see we're just ordinary people." Knowing I was going to be writing about the transgender community for a larger audience, Margie wanted to ensure that I comprehended the everyday ordinariness of transgender life—a perspective she felt was largely absent from media and popular discourse. Transgender ordinariness was paramount for her because since transitioning, Margie has strived to create her own version of an ordinary life, and even more, a seemingly conservative and traditional one. She has been married since she was in her twenties, has raised two children, and spends much of her free time spoiling her several grandchildren. She resides in a suburban middle-class neighborhood of manicured lawns and minivans. She voted for Mitt Romney in the 2012 presidential election and identifies as a political conservative. Her favorite TV channel is Fox News, although she admittedly takes issue with some of its commentators' political views.

At the same time, Margie is by no means June Cleaver. As a transgender person, *her* ordinary is far more elastic and queer. In many ways, Margie's gender transition ruptured her conventional worldview. It enriched her life and gave her a more nuanced perspective. "Ever since coming out as trans, and living it, my view of the world has certainly broadened." As a queer person, she loves spending nights out dancing at gay bars, partying in Key West, and making friends in the LGBT community—something she never did before her transition. She considers sexuality and gender to be fluid concepts and laments how they are too often narrowly defined. Margie's gender transition also queered her marriage. Recently, Margie and her wife made the decision to open up and redefine their relationship. Both have started to date men. Although they are often mistaken for a lesbian couple when they go out, they routinely check out potential male lovers together. Revealing a playful grin, Margie explained, "The funny thing is when we go shopping and she dotes on me, people perceive us as a lesbian couple. That bothers her a little bit. I love her and I grab her and give her a big kiss, but she doesn't want to be perceived as a lesbian. That's fine. I'd rather have the guys hitting on me anyways."

* * *

Margie's story speaks to the central themes and concerns of this book, namely, the many influences of media and technologies of communication on the everyday lives of transgender individuals. In her life narrative, media were leading protagonists. They both structured the norms that limited her life possibilities and offered avenues of agency and self-authorship. From reading the Christine Jorgensen paperback to experimenting with transgender identity in Internet chat rooms, Margie's media use influenced and interacted with the dynamics and contexts of her life situation to transform how she performed gender, understood sexual subjectivity, and lived her everyday life. Media were used as resources for information and self-exploration, and helped her facilitate difficult interpersonal conversations. They were also ambassadors to the outside world, as she looked to and relied on them to explain transgender experience to broader audiences. Media were also affective engines, as they stirred and moved her. They generated powerful resonances, provoking a spectrum of emotions ranging from disappointment and discomfort to excitement and hope. They reinforced feelings of loneliness, while simultaneously introducing horizons of possibility. Finally, throughout her gender transition, media made a sense of ordinary life more or less within reach.

In chronicling the experiences of people like Margie, this book offers a portrait of how transgender individuals lived with media toward the latter part of the twentieth and the beginning of the twenty-first century. This was a time before the recent wave of transgender visibility in our culture, before what *Time* magazine called the "Transgender Tipping Point" (Steinmetz 2014). It was before Caitlyn Jenner and her reality TV show, before Netflix's *Orange Is the New Black*, Amazon's *Transparent*, and the current transgender reality television boom. It was before the celebrity of Laverne Cox and Janet Mock, and before transgender male models graced the cover of *Men's Health* magazine. Situated during this historic moment, during a time of growing but uneven and scattered access to transgender representation and communication networks, this book offers a snapshot of how transgender audiences made their way toward identity and ordinary life. It explores how they integrated the available media discourses into their emotional, cognitive, and everyday experiences. It investigates the media practices transgender individuals employed to achieve and preserve what Butler (2004) calls a "liveable life" (225), that is to say, a life that consists of "what humans require in order to maintain and reproduce the conditions of their own livability" (226).

Preliminary research into these issues has furnished important insights confirming, for example, that media help transgender communities politically organize, find information and resources, share life stories, perform identity work, and feel less alone.[1] These studies are important first steps, but have only begun to scratch the surface. As Margie's life situation illustrates, the story is far more layered, complicated, mundane, and entrenched in the everyday than this work reveals. This book's objective then is to offer an empirically grounded and deeply contextualized analysis of the intersection between media, transgender experience, and everyday life.

Media Audiences and Everyday Life

This book foregrounds transgender individuals as media audiences and users of technology. It spotlights their thoughts and experiences, allowing them to speak on their own behalf. Aligning itself with their point of view, it privileges an "emic" (Fetterman 1989) or insider's perspective, seeking to understand transgender individuals and communities on their own terms. This approach emerges from a rich tradition in the qualitative, ethnographic study of media reception and use.[2] Broadly speaking, audience ethnographies focus on the interpretive work of audiences (Livingstone 2003), or the meanings they bring to and take away from encounters with media and technology. Audience ethnographies situate audiences within the complexities of living in the everyday world, trying to "get a grasp of our contemporary 'media culture,' particularly as it can be seen in the role of the media in everyday life" (Alasuutari 1999, 6).

This book's inquiry is anchored in everyday life—that intuitive and familiar yet ultimately nebulous concept. While we all have an everyday life, and harbor a sense of what it is, its exact definition is elusive, multiple, and contested. In this book, I approach everyday life in line with Lefebvre (1991), as a kind of "fertile soil" (87), a generative ground beneath our feet from which all human activity grows. It is our home base, our *domus*, an utterly known place defined by repetition, habit, and order (Bonner 2003; Felski 1999; Highmore 2002). In this way, everyday life is "the essential, taken-for-granted continuum of mundane activities that frames our forays into more esoteric or exotic worlds" (Felski 1999, 15). At the same time, everyday life is elastic and ripe for incursion by the queer and the uncanny. As Creed (2005) suggests, "the supposedly stable nature of the everyday, its regulatory laws, are easily undermined," and its character engenders a "strange alliance of familiar and unfamiliar" (485).

The taken-for-granted continuum of everyday life, one always poised for metamorphosis, is a site of competing power relations and a relentless struggle between structure and agency. For scholars such as Lefebvre (1991, 2002), everyday life was fundamentally exploitative: governed by capitalist elites, colonized by the logic of the commodity, and plagued with unequal power relations.[3] Others such as Michel de Certeau (1984) argued that even as everyday life is constrained by a "grid of discipline" (xiv), human agency and creativity ultimately lie at its core. In the everyday, de Certeau (1984) argued, "users make (*bricolent*) innumerable and infinitesimal transformations of and within the dominant cultural economy in order to adapt it to their own interests and their own rules" (xiii–xiv).

I adopt the point of view that everyday life is not fully constituted by structure or by agency. Rather, it is a dialectical relationship between macro-level forces and micro-level individual practices. Following Kaplan and Ross (2002), the everyday exists

> somewhere in the rift opened up between the subjective, phenomenological, sensory apparatus of the individual and reified institutions . . . Institutions, codes, and paradigms are not abstract constructs confronting us in some official "out there." Nor do we come to institutions alone. We live in them in historically specific ways, and we live them. (79)

Everyday life is exactly this space of *living*: living with, living in, living in-between, and living against power. Yet, the everyday is remarkably more than the calculated workings of power, more than a field upon which market forces or politics play out. Even Lefebvre (1991) conceded that everyday life "has a secret life and a richness of its own" (87).

Following in the ethnographic tradition, this book delves deeply into everyday experience to draw out its secret life. It investigates the large *and* small challenges, triumphs, and contradictions of being transgender and living in a world increasingly organized around communications technologies. As Carey (1992) argues, "modern communications have drastically altered the ordinary terms of experience and consciousness, the ordinary structures of interest and feeling, the normal sense of being alive, of having a social relation" (1–2). This book interrogates the relationship between these media developments and transgender life. In other words, it delineates the "media life" of my participants; a life lived "in" media and one made possible through the "interdependency of humanity and technology" (Deuze 2012, xii). Its inquiry does not limit its focus to one particular media form, genre, or narrative. Rather, it examines the "media environments" of transgender individuals, or the ensemble of communications technologies available to them and utilized in the everyday.[4] Cutting across historic space and time, the book examines the media environments of both older and younger transgender people. It addresses what it was like to be transgender in a world when it was generally unseen and unknowable—before cable TV, Netflix, and the Internet. It highlights the realities of living in a more traditional, less diverse media environment, defined by scarcity and technological differentiation. At the same time, it also reveals the social impact of technological change as media have become increasingly ubiquitous, accessible, interactive, and defined by "convergence" (Jenkins 2006), a process in which "consumers are encouraged to seek out new information and make connections among dispersed media content" (3).

In exploring how transgender individuals use media across time (across historic time and across the span of their individual lifetimes), I draw out the similarities among and differences between "old" and "new" technology, emphasizing what they make (and fail to make) possible for users. In this way, I adopt a "practice theory" of media (Couldry 2012), conceptualizing media and technology within the context of their everyday use. Such a "practice" approach understands media in terms of "actions that are *directly oriented* to media; actions that *involve* media without necessarily having media as their aim or object; and actions whose possibility is *conditioned by* the prior existence, presence, or functioning of media" (Couldry 2012, 35; emphasis in original).[5] I situate transgender individuals' everyday media use alongside other life experiences and practices, and at the juncture of various micro- and macroeconomic, political, and social forces that shape their world. In doing so, I aim to generate a theoretical architecture for considering those quieter, less heroic, and less politically conspicuous forms of media use, which typically go unnoticed by researchers.

"He Knows the Ground Rules"

"This is Andre Cavalcante. He is a scholar researching media and transgender issues. I've allowed him to observe our group," explained Reese to the members of Trans Chat, a transgender support and discussion group that met weekly in a small Midwestern city. Reese was the lead facilitator of the group and one of its founders. A member of the working poor, she had little in terms of material wealth but devoted her life to helping transgender and queer communities. Week after week, as I observed the group, Reese offered me the same introduction, always concluding with, "He will be taking notes, but he knows the ground rules." In order for Trans Chat to be a safe and welcoming space, ground rules were essential: everything discussed during the group meeting was confidential, everyone had a right to talk and share their experience, members would treat each other with respect and kindness, and talking over others or having side conversations was forbidden. As an outsider and observer, I also had my own ground rules. Under no circumstance could I record meetings with my digital voice recorder, and I was restricted from documenting the proper names or identifying information about individual group members in my notes. I was, however, allowed to notate recurring themes, general topics of concern, and the gist of individual conversations that emerged.

For two years, I observed and at times participated in Trans Chat's meetings, which were held at a Midwestern LGBT community center and typically lasted two hours. For those who attended, Trans Chat was a sacred space. It reliably and routinely provided feelings of safety, belonging, and affirmation to its members, who were all along the transgender spectrum. Some identified as transsexual, and had or desired sexual reassignment surgery. Others had just begun experimenting with cross-dressing. A few claimed gender-fluid and non-binary identities. Members gathered to discuss a wide range of topics, from the mechanics of gender transition to political activism and interpersonal relationships. Mainly, they shared stories and explored strategies about managing everyday life as a transgender person. In this way, Trans Chat was a kind of naturally occurring focus group. Observing it allowed me to encounter a plurality of voices, themes, and opinions about transgender life through the medium of everyday talk (Lunt and Livingstone 1996). I was able to observe when, how, and if topics pertaining to media organically arose during conversation.

However, when I first began observing the group, many looked upon me with curiosity, even suspicion. Week after week, I walked into the conference room of the LGBT community center wondering how I was going to be received. As a cisgender, or non–transgender identifying person, I was an outsider. Each time I sat at the table, removed my black legal notebook from my bag, and began taking notes, I communicated my authority as a researcher and my outsider status. Indeed, the transgender community has a tenuous relationship with outsiders like me attempting to write about their lives. This is rooted in a history of writings and reportage that suffer from gross misrepresentation, sensationalism, and reductionism. However, I am not completely an outsider. As a gay man, I am familiar with and sensitive to struggles around gender expression and the pressures of conformity. Moreover, as a result of the political mobilizing of LGBT communities, I consider myself a transgender ally. As I became a more regular figure at the Trans Chat meetings, I began to share my own experiences and challenges. In doing so, I moved from "passive observer" to "participant observer," and members became increasingly trusting of and comfortable with my presence. Nevertheless, my status as an outsider never fully evaporated.

Observing Trans Chat was one of the qualitative methods I employed during my extensive fieldwork with transgender individuals and communities in the American Midwest from 2008 to 2012. In addition to this observational fieldwork, I also conducted 35 in-depth interviews with a diverse group of self-identified transgender people. Interviews were semi-structured and many participants were interviewed several times over the course of a few weeks or months. My data collection was not bound by these formal interview moments. Study participants invited me into their social worlds, connecting me with their friends, lovers, spouses, and families. With some, I went out to eat, visited their workplaces, tagged along on shopping sprees, and attended dinner parties. We often emailed back and forth, trading thoughts and insights, sharing news articles and web links. One participant mailed a handwritten three-page letter to my office expressing her appreciation for having the opportunity to share her experiences. These multi-sited and multimedia research moments created a fuller awareness of participants' daily lives, their local communities, and interpersonal networks.

To perform a more immersive inquiry, I traversed across the Northern Midwest to consult with transgender activists, community leaders, social workers, and therapists specializing in gender identity. I attended transgender social events, film screenings, and "clothes swap" parties. I observed Transgender Pride events, political fund-raisers, and public lectures. I went to transgender friendly nightclubs, restaurants, bars, and church services, and joined transgender social networking sites, mailing lists, and newsgroups.

For purposes of comparison, I supplemented my primary fieldwork in the Midwest with secondary fieldwork and interviews in San Francisco, a city with a sizable and highly visible transgender community.

In addition to one-on-one interviews, I spoke with transgender activists and observed community events, attending, for example, a "Sexual Reassignment Fundraiser Party" for a young transgender woman in the Castro neighborhood of the city.

Originating from the Midwest and San Francisco, the participants in this study highlight the diversity of transgender individuals and communities. They vary across age, economic class, relationship status, race, profession, religion, and education. They are social workers, scientists, teachers, political activists, students, web designers, and cosmetologists. Some enjoy middle-class lifestyles, whereas many were struggling to survive during a severe economic recession in the industrial Midwest, where the once plentiful manufacturing and automotive jobs were rapidly disappearing. Some have crossed from one side of the gender binary to another—from male-to-female or female-to-male. A few were gender-fluid and non-binary. Some chose to live "in stealth," concealing their transgender status through passing as a man or woman to avoid stigma and violence. Others refused to pass, publicly affirming their transgender and gender-nonconforming identities, or simply could not, unable to conform to society's strict standards of appearance for men and women.

Nevertheless, the thread that weaves together the participants in my study is their self-identification as transgender people. In its everyday usage, the word "transgender" functions as an umbrella term that signifies a wide spectrum of gender-variant and gender-marginalized identifications including, but not limited to, transsexuals (who wish to change their sexual morphology), cross-dressers (who wear gender atypical clothing), drag queens and drag kings (who impersonate men and women as entertainment), and gender-queer, gender-fluid, and non-binary persons (whose gender identity fluctuates or rests in between or beyond the gender binary).[6] As Valentine (2006) noted about transgender, "the power of the category is that it is actively seen as a collective term to gather in all non-normative expressions of gender . . . transgender experiences are seen to emanate from the experience of 'gender,' not 'sexuality'" (409). In this book, I employ the word transgender as a way of speaking to a person's actual gender, the gender that holds truth for them, which typically deviates from the one they were assigned at birth and/or falls outside normative social expectations and cultural scripts.

Even as all the participants in this study identified as transgender or "trans" (the shorthand version), they use the category and interpret its meaning in deeply personal ways. For example, one participant explained she is a "trans woman." Continuing, "I am a trans woman. Two words not one word. One word suggests that we're apart from women. Trans separated from it says we're women and we have this qualifier." Another participant identified as a "woman," clarifying, "I'm a very particular kind of woman. I'm the kind that has a penis." Some used transgender as a device to express a multilayered identity, as one participant said, "I would say I'm trans and I am a woman, and I am also a boy, and I'm sometimes gender queer, and I'm definitely queer. That's how I would identify. I like to be called with female pronouns." Other participants ignored the language of gender entirely in defining transgender. "There are so many differences in transgender. For me it is just expressing myself the way I truly am. Living my life in a way that feels comfortable to me."

As these definitions suggest, the category "transgender" is unsettled and variable. It cuts across lines of race, ethnicity, socioeconomic class, nationality, ability, sexuality, religion, and age. Importantly, while this book introduces a broad range of voices and experiences, it is not intended to be representative of all transgender people. My research sites were restricted to the northern Midwest and San Francisco. Although trans people of color are represented in the study, my sample skews white. My sample also consists of those who answered my research call and felt comfortable enough talking about themselves in detail and allowing me to observe their world. Moreover, as anthropologist David Valentine (2007) illuminated in his ethnography, the category "transgender" hails certain kinds of individuals and, like all social categories, includes and excludes. His work showed that the working class, people of color, and those with limited education are less likely to be familiar with the language of transgender and may not identify with the category. Despite these conditions, "transgender" has mobilized an array of gender differences under its umbrella, and the term's gravitational center, its connective tissue, "is the defense of the right of each individual to define themselves" (Feinberg 1996, xi). This act of self-definition, however, first requires the realization that transgender identity is possible.

Possible Self, Possible Life

One of the first themes to emerge as I began my fieldwork, and one that would recur throughout, was the question of possibility. At some point in their life, every participant in my study questioned whether trans life and identity was possible, and if so, how. Although they searched, they typically failed to find transgender people in their local community, in their religious organizations, shopping malls, and social events. In their immediate, everyday world, transgender was largely defined in and through invisibility and erasure.[7]

Moreover, participants were also aware of the structural challenges and systematic disenfranchisement that come with living openly as a trans person. For example, the 2009 "National Transgender Discrimination Survey" concluded that the transgender community experiences twice the rate of unemployment as the general population, endures almost universal harassment on the job, and experiences a homeless rate of about one in five.[8] Violence against transgender people is also alarmingly high. Studies conducted by the National Coalition of Anti-Violence Programs (NCAVP) conclude that violence disproportionately impacts transgender individuals—particularly transgender women and transgender people of color. In 2013, 72% of all LGBTQ homicides were trans women and 67% were trans women of color. Transgender individuals were also seven times more likely to experience physical violence when dealing with law enforcement than the general population.[9]

It is no surprise then that the participants in my study struggled against an ideology of transgender impossibility, an entrenched perception that transgender is essentially abject, undesirable, and untenable. This dilemma of possibility—the question of being "real" and viable— lies at the core of queer experience. According to Judith Butler (2004), "the thought of a possible life is only an indulgence for those who already know themselves to be possible. For those who are still looking to become possible, possibility is a necessity" (219). Possibility must loom on the horizon before individuals can take the first steps toward transgender life and subjectivity. My research reveals that media and communications technologies can both impede and/or support this stride.

Media are arbiters of possibility. As instruments of power/knowledge (Foucault 1980), they franchise what is and is not possible. They borrow from the architecture of daily life and, according to Silverstone (1994), furnish the "metaphors and myths of the stuff of everyday experience and discourse" (167). Media help determine the extent to which identities are legitimate, sanctioned, and "real." They set the parameters of everyday life and suggest who is (and is not) deserving of one.[10] Importantly, media and technology are not the only arbiters of everyday possibilities. Educational institutions, medical authorities, religious organizations, market logics, and the state, for example, are equally important forces. Each mobilizes power and exhibits its own force relations in structuring the normative patterns of the world. However, in this book my focus is on media and the ways their publicity, accessibility, and everydayness set the terms for transgender possibilities.

Throughout contemporary Western history, popular media have overwhelmingly constructed being trans and having an everyday life as a binary opposition. In traditional media such as film and television, transgender figures bear the burden of hyperbole and can only live extraordinary lives punctuated with extreme violence, loneliness, or martyrdom. Even with greater diversification, the same often holds true for newer, emergent media. Consider, for instance, the short-lived 2010 iPhone photo application "Peek-A-Boo Tranny." The Apple Store's description of the product read: "Girlfriend, you may think that picture you're taking is super cute, but wait until one of our fierce tranny gals jumps in and makes it a party!" The application altered digital photos by embedding a clownish picture of a transgender woman—typically holding a lollipop with a frothy expression on her face—into the background. "Peek-A-Boo Tranny" staged a kind of gender minstrelsy, turning transgender identity into a cartoonish caricature. Infantilizing and trivializing, the application was a troubling appropriation of the transgender body for non-transgender audiences. Faced with pressure from LGBT organizations such as GLAAD (Gay and Lesbian Alliance Against Defamation) and the Bilerico Project, Apple eventually removed the application from its iTunes store (Simon 2010). Sprung from the dark underbelly of digital media culture, "Peek-A-Boo Tranny" is exactly the kind of imagery that undergirds the ideology of transgender impossibility.

At the same time and equally as important, media are more than engines of impossibility. They are also precious resources of self and life-affirmation. For the participants in my study, encounters with media

Figure I.1. Image of the "Peek-A-Boo Tranny" app.

culture cultivated deep aspirations and feelings of hope and possibility. In looking to become possible and in imagining transgender futures, they turned toward media, securing comfort, communion, and glimmers of self-recognition. Across "old" and "new" technologies, and even in the most unlikely of places such as *The Jerry Springer Show* or comic books, their media use showed them that trans subjectivity was viable and available.

Indeed, since the early twentieth century, the products of popular media have been the most widely available platforms of queer, transgender, and gender-nonconforming visibility (Doty 1993). Although they have often relied on well-worn clichés and stereotypes, these representations have been accessible features of a commonly shared cultural landscape. Queer audiences have, for example, reveled in Marlene Dietrich's cross-gender performance in the 1930 film *Morocco*; delighted in the gay-male melodrama of the 1970 film *The Boys in the Band*; became captivated by the shocking drag of Divine in John Waters's 1972 film *Pink Flamingos*; heralded Julie Andrews playing a woman disguised as a man working as a female impersonator in the 1982 film *Victor/Victoria*; and howled at the campy absurdity of TV personality Pee Wee Herman throughout the 1980s. As MTV became a cultural lightning rod, they relished the androgyny of Boy George, Grace Jones, Prince, and Annie Lenox. They cheered when Ellen DeGeneres announced her lesbianism on network television in the 1990s; laughed at the antics of the openly gay character Jack in the sitcom *Will & Grace* (1998–2006); and ached from the pain and suffering depicted in the transgender themed film *Boys Don't Cry* (1999). As cable television became increasingly competitive and boundary pushing in the 1990s, queer audiences watched the gay-casted makeover show *Queer Eye for the Straight Guy* (2003–2007), and tuned into Showtime's queer-themed dramatic series *Queer as Folk* (2000–2005) and *The L Word* (2004–2009). In recent years, they have rooted for their favorite drag queen contestant on *Ru Paul's Drag Race* (2009–present) and took to streaming video to follow lesbian and transgender characters on Netflix's *Orange Is the New Black* (2013–present) and transgender parenting on Amazon's *Transparent* (2014–present).

Even in times of representational drought, audiences have actively queered media texts by recoding the dominant meanings embedded in them to fit their own sensibilities.[11] In their imaginations, they turned straight characters gay and bisexual (Jenkins 1992), and transformed men into women. Despite periods of censorship, for example during the years of the Hollywood Production Code, queer and gender variant images still routinely slipped through the cracks of the film industry's institutional matrix (Lugowski 1999). Indeed, according to Doty (1993), queerness is not peripheral to media and popular culture, but endures as one of its defining elements.

Importantly, for those living on the margins of society, queer media presence offers a knowing wink and a nod of assurance that they are a part of a larger world, that they matter, and that queer life is possible. As with Margie, transgender writer and activist, Leslie Feinberg, recalled the affirmation she felt encountering the Christine Jorgensen story in news media growing up. "In all the years of my childhood, I had only heard of one person who seemed similarly 'different,'" notes Feinberg (1992). "I had no other adult role model who crossed the boundaries of sex or gender. Christine Jorgensen's struggle became a message to me that I wasn't alone" (6–7).

Offering the promise of queer and transgender possibility, media representations can be profoundly transformative as an outlet for self-discovery. As Stuart Hall (1990) maintains, identity is created "within, not outside, representation" (222). It is an ongoing process of suturing the self to historical and cultural discourses (Hall 1990), and media provide the raw materials (the needle and thread) for its construction. For instance, film theorists have long maintained that characters on the "big screen"—as they perform for us and gaze in our direction—invite opportunities for audiences to participate in fantasy, desire, and identity play.[12] Interfacing with figures on screen, queer audiences strategically adopt multiple subject positions, formulate attractions, and engage in various identifications. Beyond film, media such as television, magazines, websites, books, comics, online video, mobile technologies, and social networking platforms all function as nerve centers for "queer identity work" (Gray 2009), for the process of experimenting with, formulating, and extending the limits of queer and transgender identities. Media are ideal tools for queer identity work because they can be consumed secretly and confidentially, in safe spaces, and during times of one's choosing. They can be collected, saved, and archived in personal media libraries. They can be appreciated over and over again and easily shared and circulated within communities.

Media and communications technologies lend themselves to "tactical" practices of self and life-making. According to social theorist Michel de Certeau (1984), in navigating the structures, organizations, and power relations of everyday life, individuals employ an ensemble of tactics. Tactics are those creative, local, and surreptitious "ways of making do" that work with and against an imposed order (29). As "an art of the weak" (37), they are devices and maneuvers intended to circumvent, challenge, and creatively refashion the world, allowing individuals to carve out their own trajectory through the everyday.

The people who shared their stories with me used media and technology in tactical ways.[13] They turned to digital technologies to cultivate an understanding of their identities and to achieve the common inclusions and routine affordances of everyday life from which they were often excluded. They used mobile applications to help locate gender-neutral bathrooms and visited websites to learn how to talk about themselves. They participated in discussion forums to vent and let off steam.

Leveraging the dialectical tensions of everyday life, the participants in my study utilized media to close the distance between transgender and everydayness that same media helped establish.

Struggling for Ordinary

"I'm not transgender and I'm not gay. Those were alternative lifestyles," explained Lisa. "But after coming to the support group and learning about what it means to be queer, and getting involved with the transgender community, I realized I actually *was* those things." Lisa is a white trans woman in her late fifties from the Midwest who volunteers every week at the LGBT community center where Trans Chat meets. Before she began attending the group, Lisa felt lost. She identified as what she called "the typical woman trapped in a man's body," and struggled with social isolation. Yet, in volunteering at the community center, attending the weekly Trans Chat meetings, and exploring transgender and queer identities online, she eventually adopted a new vision of herself and forged a new life trajectory, a queer life trajectory. "I now live how I want to live . . . I'm not trapped in anything. I'm a transgender woman and I'm queer . . . My wife was also trans, she was non-operable and I was post-op. This is my big queer life."

As Lisa's words underscore, one of queer thought's leading contributions has been its ability to help individuals creatively imagine and boldly practice a "different way to be human" (Wilchins 2004, 4). Queer discourse augments our vision and shines light onto previously unseen identity possibilities. It "cranes like an approaching wave of potentiality" (Muñoz 2009, 185). It complicates borders and unsettles divisions between gay and straight, male and female, and masculine and feminine. It endorses an unsettled and fluid model of identity, undermining the notion of a unified and stable self. More broadly, queerness offers an interpretive frame and a strategic posture that stands against what a culture conceives of as "normal" (Epstein 1996; Halperin 1995).[14] According to Michel Foucault (1995), normalization is pernicious in that it creates stringent rules; differentiates individuals according to dominant norms and averages; hierarchizes individual traits, abilities, and bodies; offers a "constraint of a conformity that must be achieved" (183); and marks rigid boundaries of social acceptability and worth.

In the everyday world, normalization works *against* LGBTQ individuals in the form of violence, discrimination, and systematic oppression. But it also works *on* them, absorbing and assimilating them into its value systems. Duggan (2003) refers to this as homonormativity, charging that it generates a "demobilized gay constituency and a privatized, depoliticized gay culture" (50). Echoing this critique, Warner (1999) argues the trouble with normal is that rather than taking up the mantle of cultural difference, political liberation, and social disruption, it compels queer people to "stay at home and make dinner for our boyfriends" (70).

Indeed, queerness is anything *but* the desire to stay at home and make dinner for the boyfriend. This kind of quiet and ordinary domestic scene, it would appear, is its antithesis, perhaps even its nemesis. Queerness is organized around a "politics of provocation" (Epstein 1996, 153). For some, it is the fulfillment of a radical marginality, a defiant refusal to be known or make sense, an absolute negativity. It is thoroughly "oblique or off line" (Ahmed 2006a, 565). It is "anti-social," located "outside and beyond" all forms of collective life and intelligibility (Edelman 2004, 3).[15] For others, queerness is more hopeful, but equally radical, understood as a kind of utopia, a "forward-dawning" (Muñoz 2009, 28) stance toward the future. It is a horizon, a not-yet-here promise of perfect community, wild imagination, and human emancipation. Queerness has also been conceived of as righteous failure. As Halbertsam (2011) suggests, queerness as "failing, losing, forgetting, unmaking, undoing, unbecoming, not knowing may in fact offer more creative, more cooperative, more surprising ways of being in the world" (2).

But gay men, lesbians, bisexuals, and trans individuals all make dinner. Even the "queerest of the queer" go food shopping. At times, they consciously choose to fit in and do "normal stuff." Sometimes—for a variety of reasons—they are unable to refuse the status quo or resist the media they encounter. Sometimes they do not want to unmake or unbecome—especially when making and becoming have been so difficult. For transgender individuals, a group that typically wields less social, political, and economic power, resistance as a political practice or life strategy is not always possible, or even preferable within the context of daily, lived experience.[16] To be honest, I have always been uncomfortable placing the responsibility of "the revolution" on the shoulders of the most marginal and disenfranchised. As trans scholar

Viviane Namaste (2000) insists, transgender people and experiences are "more than a theory that justifies our existence" and "more than the interesting remark that we expose how gender works" (1). Rather, transgender life is "much less glamorous, than all that . . . forged in the details of everyday life, marked by matters not discussed by academics or clinical researchers . . . constituted in the mundane and uneventful" (ibid.).

Sympathetic to Namaste's critique, this book turns toward transgender experiences in the everyday world and the ways queerness is *lived*. It considers what is unique about transgender life, but also underscores how transgender people live *in* common (*as* common) with others. It attempts to answer why Margie was so insistent that transgender people are "just ordinary people." Critical, cultural scholarship has yet to come to terms—in any serious or sustained way—with why so many queer and transgender identifying people desire aspects of ordinary, orderly life. What exactly does the ordinary mean to them? What is attractive about it? Why the impulse to stay at home and make dinner for the boyfriend?

In this book, I use the word "ordinary" strategically to move away from the clinical, diagnostic, and deeply moralistic connotations of the word "normal." This is not to say that "the ordinary" does not share some of its meaning with the word "normal," as both imply a sense of order. In its earliest usage, for example, the word "ordinary" referred to an imposed order, "something done by rule or authority" (Williams 1983, 225). However, these meanings represent only half the story. The ordinary is far more capacious, more than an expression of regulatory or disciplinary power. For cultural theorist Raymond Williams (1989), the ordinary is inherently "good." "Culture is ordinary," he writes, "an interest in learning or the arts is simple, pleasant and natural. A desire to know what is best, and to do what is good, is the whole positive nature of man" (7). Likewise, philosopher Stanley Rosen (2002) suggests the ordinary revolves around doing "the right thing," determining between better and worse, and striving to "respond correctly to things, experiences, events, and so on, as they actually are" (263).[17]

Ordinariness is also about being in connection and communication with others, sharing space and time with them. It is about existing on a field of social interaction as an intelligible and recognized person. It hinges on recognition, to be recognized in public space (and virtual space) without issue. Ordinariness is about participating in the communication and cultural rituals that allow us to feel communion with others, to feel part of something greater than ourselves. It is about being "together in fellowship," a fellowship organized around "the celebration of shared even if illusory beliefs" (Carey 1992, 43).

At the most basic level, the ordinary was less about the "normal" (and normative) and more about "the everyday" for the participants in my study. Their desire for the ordinary was essentially an aspiration for the rhythms and affordances typically granted in everyday life. Ease, comfort, and mindlessness. Communication, ritual, and routine. The ability to be both someone—to be recognized and affirmed—and no one—to be left alone and ignored. These are some of the gifts of everyday life.

Indeed, as Felski (1999) maintains, the everyday has no "intrinsic political content," nor is it ideologically "reactionary" (31). Rather, it is a site of potentiality, a "bloom space" (Seigworth and Greg 2010, 9). It is a deeply sensual world where our dreams, fantasies, feelings, and emotions germinate and launch. The everyday is where we experience pleasure and pain, love and loss, silence and boredom. In its spaces, we engage with technology to "extend the reach of our sympathies by bringing the world within" (Turkle 2011, 307). Even the seemingly frustrating and colorless characteristics of everyday life have an alternative side. Although the incessant and predictable routine of the everyday can feel monotonous, it can also provide comfort and pleasure. Everyday life offers simple and basic joys, luxuries, and conveniences. These are not just the purchased pleasures of consumer society, but deeply human moments: spontaneous conversations with strangers at a bar or leisurely walks down Main Street.

Perhaps the greatest gift of everyday life is the way it affords us the ability to move through it without much thought or trouble, to operate in the world in taken-for-granted ways. Indeed, an everyday life defined by constant struggle and laborious thought is essentially unworkable and unlivable. However, the taken-for-grantedness of everyday life is unequally distributed, more easily accessible to some than others. For the individuals who shared their stories with me and who defy the gender binary, battle stigma, and face systematic disenfranchisement, the rhythms and routines of the everyday are not simply granted. They are hard-won, practical accomplishments, the end result of individual and collective labor.[18] This *struggle for the ordinary*, a struggle increasingly being waged in and through media culture, is what this book is about.

In attending to questions of ordinariness, this book redresses some of queer, cultural, and critical theory's greatest liabilities: their general lack of engagement with everyday experiences, the theoretical impasse they create through the queer/normal binary, and the reductive framework of politics-as-resistance that underpin their epistemic and methodological ground. Throughout the book I develop the notion of the ordinary by examining the quotidian side of transgender life. I focus on those lower, mundane, and quieter dimensions often overlooked or dismissed by researchers and theorists. I root my inquiry in the microphysics of participants' everyday lives—while not losing sight of the larger questions. I also investigate what "ordinary representations of transgender people" in media culture look like and mean to the participants in my study. Over and again they expressed a desire to see people not defined by their transgender identity, but rather as people who, as they said, "happen to be" transgender. Rather than dismissing this as a desire for assimilation or normativity, I take this sentiment seriously and theorize it as aspirational, as a hunger for everyday life possibilities. I consider participants' wish to "be" ordinary and their struggle to accomplish ordinary status.

In line with Scannell (2014), I conceive of "being ordinary" as the ability to "matter-of-factly *be* in a world that allows me to be about my everyday concerns, whatever that may be, in ways that are essentially unproblematic" (22; emphasis in original). Accordingly, I explore how media encounters can make a sense of the ordinary more or less out of reach for participants, and the ways they use technology in struggling for and achieving a sense of everydayness. Finally, I complicate the queer/normal binary and discuss the ways participants think about and merge the forces of queerness and normality in their everyday lives and in their interactions with media culture. I argue that they envision themselves and navigate the world in "queerly ordinary" ways.

In the chapters that follow, I explore how participants have engaged with media culture to construct identity, preserve self, and try to achieve everydayness. Underlying these practices was an essential tension, one characterized by the pull of queerness and ordinariness, sameness and difference, closeness and distance, stability and instability, and outsiderness and insiderness. The question about how to come to terms with these seemingly contradictory forces manifested throughout my field-work. Indeed, this question is so central to transgender life that it has emerged in other ethnographic work. In his study on female-to-male (FTM) transgender people living in San Francisco, Boston, and New York, Rubin (2003) found that "the tension between the ordinary and the unconventional structures every element of their lives" (3). This tension was equally a concern for me as I tried to make sense of and write about it. I wrestled with how to analyze participant data in new ways, ways that were nuanced and that refused to reduce their thoughts and experiences to false consciousness or mindless assimilation. In this way, this book highlights *two* struggles for the ordinary. The first concerns the work that participants in my study performed, using media to access the taken-for-granted rhythms and affordances of everyday life and to thrive in a world created without them in mind. The second struggle for the ordinary was my own as I tried to find a vocabulary suitable for talking about ordinariness and queerness in the same breath. My goal is to do justice to both.

Overview

Chaz Bono. *Orange Is the New Black*. Caitlyn Jenner. More than 50 gender identity options on Facebook. *Transparent*. "Bathroom bill" controversy. In recent years, a new trans visibility has emerged in media culture. But since the mid-twentieth century, transgender visibility proliferated across various cultural sites, albeit slowly and unevenly. This visibility was made possible through the unfolding of specific historical developments: the construction of gender as a non-binary category, the expansion of transgender discourse, and the sociopolitical mobilization of the transgender community throughout the twentieth century; the rise of gay-themed media content during the 1990s, which set the stage for transgender representations; and the growth of interactive communications technologies that provided space for transgender voices to flourish. The first chapter examines transgender visibility amid these historical developments. In doing so, it provides the macroscopic context for the book, the larger picture against which the stories of the participants in my study play out.

After establishing this context, the second chapter turns to media and the ideology of transgender impossibility they generate. It examines how participants interpreted popular media representations in terms of transgender violence, dehumanization, and delegitimization. I argue that these themes emerge in participant interviews not only because they frequently appear in media, but also because they are fundamentally at risk in the everyday lives of trans people. Remaining safe, maintaining personhood, and being taken seriously are all at stake in living a trans life. They inform the interpretive frameworks and evaluative criteria participants employ in media encounters and transform the notion of transgender everydayness into an object of desire. I analyze transgender ordinariness and everydayness as a site of hope and possibility, and maintain it is exactly the everyday that participants felt was woefully missing from media representations of transgender and what they wanted to see.

Chapter 3 moves from impossibility to possibility, exploring the active construction of self in the face of media power. It delineates how the ability to acknowledge and articulate a possible transgender self emerges through meaningful interactions with media discourses and communication technologies. According to participants, media generate the ability to imagine a trans life and to author plausible stories of self-transformation. Paying close attention to the role of images and language, the chapter reveals how the Internet provides resources that help participants think and talk about their identities and everyday experiences in new and pragmatic ways.

Chapter 4 explores the strength required to achieve trans subjectivity and the affective toll media reception can take on trans audiences. It highlights what I term "resilient reception" or the strategies of adaptation, methodologies of survival, and tactics of preserving self that study participants employ in coping with the affective disruptions and disempowering messages they encounter from media and society. This focus moves us beyond studies of audiences that singularly take into account their ideological and political interactions with media.

Chapter 5 renders visible transgender individuals' *struggle for the ordinary,* or the constant and deliberate work devoted to achieving the uneventful and common inclusions and affordances of everyday, associative life. For study participants, routine daily tasks such as running errands or using a public restroom were often complicated and potentially risky endeavors. To manage, navigate, and overcome these challenges, participants turned to media. However, while the affordances of media were helpful for participants, this chapter also explores their limitations.

The conclusion of the book advances the idea of the "queerly ordinary," a theoretical attempt to move beyond the "normal/queer" binary. The queerly ordinary is a hybrid form of self and life-making that exists as a little bit queer and a little bit ordinary. I argue that this is how study participants think about themselves and their gender identities. The queerly ordinary is what they want to see represented in media, what they use technologies to achieve, and in the end, it is how they live their everyday lives.

1

We Can No Longer Hide in Plain Sight

From the Cultural Margins to the Tipping Point

"The days of that brown wrapper are definitely over," explained Allyson, a white trans woman in her late fifties from the Midwestern United States. Throughout the 1980s, Allyson received a monthly newsletter published by the local cross-dressing organization. It was mailed to her home wrapped in brown paper to conceal its contents. Each time she saw the newsletter sitting in her mailbox, she shuddered with excitement. Flipping through its pages made her feel part of something bigger than herself, and made her look forward to the organization's next meeting. To ensure the safety and anonymity of its members, the cross-dressing organization operated under a veil of secrecy. Mailed correspondence was camouflaged, meeting times and locations circulated by word of mouth, and there were rules about how members should and should not communicate outside the walls of group meetings. Given the group's covert nature, Allyson felt fortunate to have found it. She remembered, "At the time, finding support groups was a major issue for everyone. It took so much effort and many whispers. I found out about the group I went to through word of mouth. It was all very secretive." She continued to explain her experiences with the group. "It met once a month at a hotel. The manager there was understanding and gave us a room to change in . . . I was married at the time and had to hide it from my wife. But I think she might have known. When we would have dinner parties and such, I would end up in the kitchen talking to the women. That's where I fit in the best."

For Allyson, as well as for many trans people living through the 1960s, '70s, and '80s, transgender organizations and their newsletters were some of the only connections they had to a sense of community and their sole source of trans visibility. "There was nothing out there," Allyson insisted, "an occasional something on TV, but that's it." This was, as many of my participants called it, the "pre-Internet age," the mid- to late twentieth century, the era of the mass media dominated by print, radio, film, and television. This media environment was structured around a broadcasting model, where media texts were produced by a small group of elite creators and imparted to a mass audience. Space was finite. There was only so much radio-frequency spectrum available, only so many books that could stock bookstore shelves. Production costs and barriers to entry were high. Audiences were conceptualized as a "mass" (Nightingale and Ross 2003) and overwhelmingly imagined by the media industries as white, heterosexual, and middle class. Audiences themselves had limited capacity to communicate with producers of media and with each other.

Time and again, the participants in my study explained that the media environment within which they grew up was largely a desert of transgender representation, information, and discourse. In trying to locate resources for exploring their identities, they searched libraries, walked the aisles of bookstores, visited video rental stores, and scanned magazine racks. These hunts were conducted in public spaces, so they had to be careful. Showing too much interest in a taboo topic such as cross-dressing or transsexuality was risky to one's reputation and safety. For the most part, their searches were fruitless. Yet every now and then, they would come across a jewel, something that resonated with them. This discovery justified the risk.

In this chapter, I provide a brief overview of transgender visibility in the twentieth and twenty-first centuries, focusing on key moments and decisive historical junctures. I try to show what might have been available to the participants in my study as they perused their media environment. But first, I explore various historical processes that stirred alongside this visibility. These include the construction of gender as a non-binary category, the expansion of transgender discourse and communication networks, and the growing collective consciousness and political mobilization of transgender people throughout the twentieth century.[1] These historical developments help account for the nature of transgender visibility in media culture and offer context to the experiences of those who shared their stories with me.

Gender Expansion, Political Mobilization, and Self-Definition

The word "transgender" brings together—sometimes neatly, sometimes not—a diverse set of gender variant practices, expressions, sensibilities, experiences, and modes of embodiment under one umbrella (Davidson 2007; Stryker 1998). On an individual level, it facilitates the construction of identity and feelings of belonging. Socially and politically, it allows those who experience similar oppressions to organize around a shared identity and speak with a collective voice. But the work that the category accomplishes is contingent on it being recognizable and meaningful, on having epistemic legitimacy. This legitimacy has been achieved over time and is the result of converging discourses: elite discourses developed by scientists, medical authorities, social service providers, and academics as well as the everyday discourses that have emerged on the ground from trans subcultures and ordinary people living their lives.

With respect to scientific discourse, the history of the category "transgender" stretches back to the end of the nineteenth century, a time when sex and sexuality entered the purview of European sexologists, a group of psychiatrists and medical professionals interested in non-normative sex and gender. As they investigated what they called "sexual perversion" and "sexual inversion," their writings increasingly transformed alternative modes of gender and human sexuality into discourse (Foucault 1990). Pioneers in the field of sexology such as Karl Heinrich Ulrichs, Richard von Krafft-Ebing, Havelock Ellis, and Magnus Hirschfeld were interested in non-procreative, non-heterosexual sex and forms of gender "deviance." Starting from a place that considered gender variance to be largely pathological and immoral, the field advanced and its practitioners eventually developed a more sophisticated understanding of gender. Some sexologists became advocates for the trans community. In 1919, Magnus Hirschfeld created the Institute for Sexual Science in Berlin, a social and intellectual nerve center for queer and gender-nonconforming people that developed some of the earliest surgical procedures for altering the body's sex characteristics. Through the institute, Hirschfeld created a support system for queer and transgender people and arranged surgeries for individuals who wanted sex transformation. His work, as Stryker (2008) notes, "set the stage for the post–World War II transgender movement" (39).

One of the legacies of the early sexological tradition was the complex taxonomy of sex and gender it produced. The field multiplied the categories available to individuals who fell outside the gender binary. For example, Hirschfeld coined the word "transvestite" to describe those who cross-dressed and had cross-gender desires. By the middle of the twentieth century, Harry Benjamin, one of Hirschfeld's contemporaries and a trailblazing advocate for transgender people, began promoting use of the word "transsexual" to describe individuals who did not just wish to cross-dress but also wanted to change their sexual morphology via surgical procedures. Yet in the 1950s, the word "transsexual" left the medical world and became "a household term" in America (Meyerowitz 2002, 51). This historic turning point was the result of a highly publicized sex change that sparked intrigue and headlines in the popular press across the United States and the globe.

Figure 1.1. Christine Jorgensen, February 1953. The press swarms around Jorgensen as she returns from Denmark. Credit: Photofest.

Christine Jorgensen, a Danish American from the Bronx, was born George Jorgensen and served in World War II as a private. After her service, Jorgensen traveled to Denmark in the early 1950s to privately undergo a series of sexual reassignment surgeries and hormone treatments only available in Europe at the time. When the *New York Daily News* learned about her procedures, they published the story of her transformation on the cover of the December 1, 1952 issue. The story catapulted Jorgensen into the global limelight and she became an instant celebrity. This attention made her the public face of transsexuality.

Following the global news storm around Christine Jorgensen, transsexuality became part of the American imagination and psychotherapists increasingly saw it as a legitimate object of inquiry (Meyerowitz 2002). As a result, the 1950s witnessed one of the first major professional symposiums on transsexuality led by Harry Benjamin, which was covered in the *American Journal of Psychotherapy*. Also in the late 1950s, psychologist John Money (a colleague of Benjamin) coined the word "gender identity" to differentiate between genital "sex" and one's belonging to a social group that expresses masculine or feminine expressions and behaviors.[2] Money's conceptualizations of "gender identity" and also "gender roles," or what a society expects from its men and women, articulated gender as multiple and unsettled.

By the 1960s, amid the growing social movements of the time—such as the women's, civil rights, and anti-war movements—and within the burgeoning hippie counterculture, gender itself became a site of political and social contestation. Younger Americans began experimenting with sexuality and challenging gender norms, embracing more unisex, androgynous styles (Meyerowitz 2002). On the ground, as Hill (2013) reminds us, there was a large, loosely connected social formation of gender and sexual misfits including transvestites, transsexuals, drag queens, street queens, radical fairies, butch lesbians, sissy gay men, female impersonators, and clothing fetishists. Representative of the political zeitgeist, the spirit of defiance was in the air in the '60s as "a wave of increasingly militant resistance on the part of transgender street people" emerged in the cities (Stryker cited in Currah 2008b, 96). For example, during the summer of 1966, an organization of queer, disenfranchised San Francisco youth called "Vanguard" began organizing to improve the social climate of their local community. Vanguard staged public protests, held social functions, and published a magazine featuring poems, essays, and political writing meant to mobilize queer individuals and reach out to young sexual and gender minorities. Members of the group often met at Gene Compton's Cafeteria—a local hotspot for gays, drag queens, street queens, and transgender sex workers. In August 1966, law enforcement raided Compton's, yet its patrons banded together and fought back, collectively resisting the recurring pattern of police brutality and oppression that haunted their lives. The incident has since been named the "Compton's Cafeteria Riot," an early touchstone of transgender political history.[3]

Three years later a similar act of resistance occurred in downtown New York City's Greenwich Village. The now famous 1969 Stonewall riots also brought together disenfranchised queer people in an act of political rebellion, and street queens were again on the vanguard of this uprising.[4] Young, poor, trans people of color such as Marsha P. Johnson and Sylvia Rivera were leading protagonists at Stonewall, and would continue to be throughout the Gay Liberation Movement. Talking about Stonewall and the role transgender individuals played in the gay liberation movement, Sylvia Rivera (2007), a Latina activist, sex worker, and lifelong advocate for trans people, recalled, "We were front liners. We didn't take no shit from nobody. We had nothing to lose" (118). However, members of the gay community did not always return the favor and advocate on behalf of their trans allies. Trans individuals were not always welcome in gay bars and gay rights organizations, specifically those organized around white, middle-class concerns. Following the Stonewall rebellion, Rivera and Johnson decided to provide structures of support and care for their own community, which led to their founding of STAR, the Street Transvestite Action Revolutionaries, in 1970 and creation of STAR House, a refuge for homeless NYC transgender youth.[5]

Meanwhile, alongside the growing political consciousness and mobilization of transgender people, the 1960s saw another historic development: the publication of Harry Benjamin's (1966) book *The Transsexual Phenomenon*. A critical and thoughtful polemic, the book turned conventional wisdom regarding gender on its head. It argued that transsexualism cannot be cured; that transsexuals should seek psychiatric help; that in some cases hormonal therapy and surgery may be necessary; and finally, that medical professionals have a responsibility to help transgender people achieve self-realization. Benjamin (1966) suggested that in a modern, technological, and scientifically advanced society, the male/female gender binary was inadequate. Instead, he argued that what we think of as "sex" actually encompassed numerous entities. He advocated thinking about individuals as exhibiting different kinds of sex, such as "endocrine sex," "anatomical sex," "psychological sex," "social sex," "sex of rearing in childhood," and "legal sex" (3–9).

While transgender individuals were not necessarily the target audience for books like Benjamin's *Transsexual Phenomenon*, many read them and learned about current scientific developments and discourses (Meyerowitz 2002). For Amanda St. Jaymes, a trans woman living in San Francisco's Tenderloin District during the 1960s, Benjamin's *The Transsexual Phenomenon* was "a guidebook for us" (Silverman and Stryker 2005). The book delineated a transsexual identity and taught Amanda and her friends about the language of gender variance. Armed with this discourse, they were able to articulate their wishes for identity and transformation to family, friends, and doctors using the language sanctioned by the medical field.

The 1960s also marked the beginning of the first transgender advocacy organizations with national and international reach, and the start of a print culture that spoke directly to trans communities. In 1960, Virginia Prince, a pharmacologist, medical researcher, and transgender advocate, spearheaded the first trans-themed publication, *Transvestia: The Journal of the American Society for Equality in Dress*. In 1962, she founded the "Society for Second Self" or "Tri-Ess," a support and social organization for cross-dressers still active today (Stryker 2008). Geared toward heterosexual cross-dressers, the magazine started off small with a mailing list of only 25 people, and was eventually sold via subscription and in adult bookstores (Ekins and King 2005). Published bimonthly from 1960 to 1980, *Transvestia* featured articles, photos, life stories, fictional narratives, and letters from readers. Within its pages, Prince, along with her writers and readers, theorized cross-dressing and developed various taxonomies for emerging trans identities. Notably, Prince and her staff sought to distinguish more "respectable," mainly heterosexual "full-time transvestites" from other gender identities. They created distance between themselves and, for example, part-time cross-dressers, transvestites, drag queens, kinky clothing fetishists, and transsexuals who desired sexual reassignment (Hill 2013). To describe herself and her readers, Prince developed the word "femmepersonation" as an alternative and later, in the 1970s, began to use the word "transgenderist," which she defined as "a third way between transvestism and transsexuality" (Hill 2013, 377). Transgenderists, as Prince wrote, were "people who have adopted the exterior manifestations of the opposite sex on a full-time basis but without surgical intervention" (cited in Hill 2013, 377). The term "transgenderist" would be taken up, resignified, and modified to "transgender" by scholars and activists in the 1990s.

Throughout the 1960s, print media expanded its purview, addressing diverse trans communities. Some periodicals such as *Transformation Magazine* (1969) were examples of erotically charged adult entertainment, while others focused on the art and craft of female impersonating. Generally published by commercial entities specializing in fetish culture, they were circulated on the margins of society, sold in adult bookstores and pornography shops. Magazines including *Female Mimics*, which premiered in 1963, *Female Impersonators*, which began in 1969, and *Drag*, which debuted in 1970, depicted the world of professional female impersonators. They reported on drag balls and contests, published photo essays of professional performers, offered "how-to" guides and tips for female impersonation, printed fantasy fiction, and included listings of clubs and venues where performances could be seen. These magazines were visually stirring and brimming with photos. But even more, they operated as nascent public spheres and counterpublics. Their classified sections allowed individuals to post personal ads and reach across time and space to communicate with like-minded others for friendship, companionship, dates, sex, and love. For example, in a 1976 issue of *Drag* magazine, one reader placed a classified ad looking "to hear from tvs [transvestites] and tss [transsexuals]. I like to read tv stories, especially like to hear from those who can pass in public" (44). Other ads expressed desires for "mature men for dates" (43), "new friends, TVs, females, bi-males and gays" (43), and "exotic get-togethers" (44). Letters to the editor sections revealed just how important these magazines were to readers. In a 1969 issue of *Female Impersonators*, Myrtle from London requested that the letters to the editor section "be extended to five or six pages . . . This is my favorite feature." Likewise, another letter asked the magazine to create a "pen pal section" so readers could learn about each other's everyday lives and experiences.

In 1964, Reed Erickson, a wealthy transgender man, started one of the largest and most well-funded organizations for transgender advocacy: the Erickson Educational Foundation (EEF). The group worked on a variety of socially progressive projects, but its mission was centered on the cause of transsexuality. EEF funded medical research, held conferences, arranged public relations events, and published newsletters and educational leaflets to promote greater understanding of transsexuality (Meyerowitz 2002; Devor and Matte 2007). The organization's pamphlets, small booklets on various topics of transsexuality, were an authority on the topic written to be accessible to a general audience. EEF also offered emotional support and referral services, circulated resource lists, and furnished medical and legal information. They sponsored speaker series, conducted public talks at colleges and universities, and consulted with medical professionals. In 1964, they funded Harry Benjamin's research institute, the Harry Benjamin Foundation. Notably, EEF supplied all of the initial funding for the first university Gender Identity Clinic to provide sex change operations in North America at Johns Hopkins University, which opened in 1966 (Devor and Matte 2007). The establishment of the clinic made national news headlines and granted much needed legitimacy to sexual reassignment surgery.

Into the 1970s, trans advocacy and print culture continued to evolve. In 1970, Angela Davis, a transgender woman, activist, and reporter for the underground Los Angeles press, formed TAO, the Transsexual Action Organization, which published the newsletters *Moonshadow* and *Mirage*. Her organization became one of the first national transsexual advocacy groups. Davis, a former member of the Gay Liberation Front in LA, brought an ethics of transsexual liberation and countercultural philosophy to both her organization and its publications. In the late 1970s, Merissa Sherrill Lynn founded the New England support group the Tiffany Club, which published its own newsletter in 1978 called the *Tapestry*. The magazine addressed issues across the gender spectrum. In fact, the word "tapestry" was chosen for the newsletter because it meant a "'weaving' of all orientations into one."[6] The *Tapestry* was circulated to other transgender organizations and sold in adult bookstores. Over time the *Tapestry* would be renamed *Transgender Tapestry*, and the Tiffany Club would become the International Foundation for Gender Education. *Transgender Tapestry* covered politics, health, and well-being; featured film and book reviews; and published one of the most comprehensive resource lists spanning everything from doctors to support groups. Leaving the confines of the adult world, the magazine was eventually sold in major bookstores such as Barnes & Noble.

Alongside these developments in transgender advocacy and print culture, "a new generation" (Meyerowitz 2002) of trans individuals emerged in the 1960s and '70s. For one, gay communities in the West began to distance themselves from gender nonconformity and "forced transsexuals to find their own point of reference outside gay lifestyles" (Perkins 1996, 55). Moreover, with greater knowledge of and access to information and medical treatment, different subcultures under the transgender umbrella began to take shape. Ekins and King (1996) identify two different communities emerging at this moment. The first were "full-time 'outsiders,'" which included female impersonators, cross-dressers, transgender strippers, showgirls, and sex workers. These were marginal figures on the economic fringe and generally communicated face-to-face. The second community inhabited "'respectable' worlds" and were "more concerned with individual being or identity" (Ekins and King 1996, 50). Similar to Virginia Prince and her organization, this community was highly literate, engaged with the medical literature on gender variation, and rather than shared space, connected with each other through print culture. Esther Newton's *Mother Camp*, one of the first major ethnographic studies of female impersonators, made similar distinctions between "street" and "stage" performers. Living lives of "confrontation, prostitution, and drug 'highs'" (Newton 1979, 8), "street" impersonators were generally younger people who worked as impersonators part-time and lived their everyday lives as trans, fighting stigmatization and struggling to make a living. "Stage" impersonators were older and better-paid performers who identified as gay men and cross-dressed primarily as a job (akin to professional "drag queens" today).

While many of the performers in Newton's study self-identified as gay men, her work bears witness to the emergence of what she calls "hormone queens," those who used hormone shots to modify the shape of their body to achieve conventional female physicality. In the 1970s, legal and underground access to hormones became more widely available.

Importantly, those individuals who took them were often exiled from gay subcultures and condemned by stage performers who no longer viewed them as authentic female impersonators (Newton 1972). Anne Bolin's (1988) work focused on this emerging community, one that sought out surgical intervention and sexual reassignment surgery. Bolin explored the process of gender transition as a rite of passage, a highly stylized practice "with all the facets of a ritualistic and symbolic transformation of status" (8). One of the more compelling insights that emerged from Bolin's (1988) work is that by the late 1970s many transsexuals had developed both formal and informal communication networks and communities of support. They had a collective consciousness, cultivating and circulating knowledge about effective practices for securing hormones, receiving sex change operations, and maintaining a transsexual identity. Indeed, at this time, medical professionals were creating best practices to serve this community. In 1979, the Harry Benjamin International Gender Dysphoria Association (HBIGDA) approved "the standards of care," a set of principles that guides the medical treatment and care of transgender people.

As the 1980s approached, the tensions between transgender and gay communities grew.[7] The solidarity that had once bound them together—albeit a historically uneven and conditional one—became even more tenuous. For example, while gay activists sought to distance homosexuality from medical and psychiatric definitions, transsexuals were unable to divorce themselves from the medical field. They needed psychological services, hormone therapies, and surgical procedures to transition. At the same time, some in the feminist movement viewed transgender women as inauthentic intruders of female space. Further, the same kinds of white, middle-class, respectability politics that shunned individuals like Sylvia Rivera during Gay Liberation placed transgender issues low on the agenda of state and national gay rights groups.

Within this context, the trans community began to more actively organize on its own behalf. Their concerns involved, but were not limited to workplace and housing discrimination, homelessness, dress-code policies, access to healthcare and medical treatment, anti-transgender violence, de-pathologizing gender variance, and police brutality. They advocated for self-authorship in the determination of legal sex and for the ability to change gender markers on official documents such as drivers' licenses, birth certificates, and passports. Taking on these challenges, the number of transgender-oriented political and advocacy organizations proliferated beginning in the mid-1980s: FTM International in 1986, International Foundation for Gender Education in 1987, American Educational Gender Information Service (AEGIS) in 1990, Gender Public Advocacy Coalition in 1995 (GPAC), National Transgender Advocacy Coalition in 1999, Transgender Law Center in 2002, National Center for Transgender Equality (NCTE) in 2003, and Trans Youth Family Allies in 2006. Particularly notable among this group is FTM International. Historically, transgender organizations and the print cultures they spawned were geared toward transgender women. In 1986, when Lou Sullivan, a transgender activist, created FTM International, he filled the void of information and politics that existed for transgender men. Along with offering education and referral and support services, the organization published the *FTM Newsletter*, which would become one of the most widely known and read publications on the FTM experience.

Decidedly, the 1990s was a game-changing moment for transgender mobilization and identity as new possibilities were forged. For one, the AIDS crisis that decimated gay male communities throughout the 1980s drew transgender individuals back into the fold with their gay counterparts. In order to combat the disease, new social and political alliances across sexual orientation, gender identity, age, race, class, among others, were needed (Stryker 2008). Using the word "queer" as a marker of collective identity, groups such as Act Up, Queer Nation, and Outrage brought together gay men, lesbians, trans people, and allies to engage in direct-action political protests to combat homophobic violence, police brutality, and institutional apathy during the outbreak of AIDS. Groups such as Transgender Nation and Transsexual Menace who advocated for transgender liberation enacted similar direct-action politics. Meanwhile, the tragic deaths of young trans people such as Brandon Teena in 1993 (who was murdered for being trans) and Tyra Hunter in 1995 (who was refused medical care following a car accident because she was trans) sparked national outrage and mobilized transgender and gender variant communities.

As with the word queer, the word "transgender" in the 1990s became widely used as a center of identification.[8] Many refer to a 1991 article written by Holly Boswell, a transgender writer, advocate, and spiritualist, called "The Transgender Alternative" as a launching pad for the word's popularity (Denny 2006). Originally published in *Chrysalis Quarterly* and *Tapestry*, both transgender magazines, the essay was a sort of spiritual manifesto for self-actualization that validated a middle path between cross-dressing and transsexualism. It advocated for androgyny, and urged readers to explore gender identities that felt honest and authentic—even if culturally unintelligible.

As it was conceptualized from the ground up, the category "transgender" was intended to rescue ideas about gender diversity from the medical and mental health communities. The aim of transgender discourse in the '90s was to "replace an assumption of individual pathology with a series of claims about citizenship, self-determination, and freedom from violence and discrimination" (Valentine 2007, 33). Capturing the structure of feeling at this moment, Wilchins remembers:

> Surrounded by scores of transsexuals and hundreds of cross-dressers at conventions, it was impossible for differently gendered people to feel the same shame . . . Transsexuals and cross-dressers began to see themselves less as social problems and more as the next oppressed minority. (2004, 23)

Transgender activists urged LGBT coalition groups to more actively recognize them. As a result, the 1990s saw the Human Rights Campaign (HRC), the National Gay and Lesbian Task Force (NGLTF), and the Gay and Lesbian Alliance Against Defamation (GLAAD) begin to advocate more vociferously on behalf of transgender Americans, including them in their mission statements. The "T" was added to the LGBT acronym, which symbolized the alliance between sexual and gendered minorities. Activists also set their sights on media. Realizing the importance of transgender visibility, organizations such as GLAAD began holding the media accountable for their treatment of transgender people and lobbied them for socially responsible representations.

During the 1990s, transgender discourse also escalated with the development and institutionalization of queer theory in the academy, which problematized and politicized gender and sexuality and legitimated non-normative modes of desire and embodiment. The growth of queer theory also helped bring a readership to a rising cohort of transgender writers and intellectuals. Authors including Sandy Stone (1991),

Kate Bornstein (1995), Leslie Feinberg (1996), Loren Cameron (1996), Pat Califia (1994), Riki Anne Wilchins (1997), and Susan Stryker (1998) all contributed to queer intellectual thought. Their work combined auto-ethnography, life history, photo essay, gender theory, historical analysis, and critical, cultural critique to comment on trans issues and politics.

However, even with its political and personal utility, transgender, like all categories, is problematic. It was created in a Western context by mainly white educated people living in urban areas (Stryker 2008; Stryker and Currah 2014). As Valentine (2007) has shown, the category transgender can fail to include and make sense to those it was intended to capture under its purview. In his research on transgender communities in New York City, Valentine (2007) discovered that many individuals who were identified as transgender by medical professionals, social service providers, and academics did not claim that category for themselves. Crucially, these were often the young, the poor, people of color, and the undereducated; those who would benefit most from the services and support provided by these organizations.

Despite these limitations and the classed and racial politics that undergird them, the term "transgender" emerged as a discursive powerhouse in the 1990s. It operated as a sociopolitical adhesive, bringing together individuals who experienced similar modes of oppression and marginalization in order to speak with a collective voice. By the start of the twenty-first century, transgender, like its predecessor transsexuality, was well on its way to becoming a household term.

A *Very* Brief History of Trans Visibility

Throughout twentieth-century America, glimmers of gender variance hid out in the nooks and crannies of media culture, and at times even shined at its center. Stories and imagery that articulated gender as unstable and malleable appeared on the television screen, on the pages of comic books and novels, and in the self-performances of musicians, celebrities, and public figures. From its early days, film was populated with scenes of cross-dressing men and women. In fact, according to Horak (2016), cross-dressing was a routine and fairly unexceptional phenomenon in early twentieth-century American film, something associated with "wholesome entertainment" (2). When set on the frontier or battlefield, for example, images of cross-dressed women represented American strength, individualism, and vitality. Over time, however, transgender imagery took on new meanings. By the 1930s, cross-dressing women represented not American wholesomeness, but rather European *savoir-faire*. Hollywood's leading ladies such as Marlene Dietrich, Josephine Baker, and Greta Garbo employed cross-dressing in their films and in their celebrity personas. Their looks were daring, communicating a sense of cosmopolitanism and bold sexuality. Marlena Dietrich's cross-gendered performance in *Morocco* (1930) is perhaps most iconic. Donning a tuxedo with top hat and tails, she performs at a Moroccan nightclub, tempting men and women alike. Dietrich had always been fond of tailored men's suits, wearing them to the transvestite cabarets she frequented in 1920s Berlin as a young person (Riva 1993).

Early films such as *Queen Christina* (1933) and *Sylvia Scarlett* (1935) also featured some of Hollywood's most famous female actresses—Greta Garbo and Katherine Hepburn respectively—cross-dressing as men. Yet within these films, the act was performed to secure access to masculine power, privilege, and authority. As Garber (1992) has detailed, characters engaging in gender masquerade to achieve things outside their reach has long been employed as a plot device in art, literature, and popular film. These "temporary transvestite films" (Straayer 1996, 42) such as *Some Like It Hot* (1959), *Victor/Victoria* (1982), *Yentl* (1983), *La Cage Aux Folles* (1978), *Tootsie* (1982), and *Mrs. Doubtfire* (1993) feature characters who temporarily cross-dress to accomplish something and then stop after getting what they want.

By the 1950s, transgender representation experienced a paradigmatic shift, moving beyond the temporary transvestite film trope. In addition to portraying transgender subjectivity as something that one *did*, film, news, and other forms of popular media presented it as something one *was*. Gender variance moved from an act to an identity—a shift largely precipitated by the story of Christine Jorgensen and other real people who publicly transitioned gender. Throughout the early twentieth century, newspapers would occasionally print stories of gender transformation and sex change. For example, in 1931 the European press created a public stir with their coverage of Lili Elbe, a Danish painter who underwent one of the first recorded male-to-female sex changes (as dramatized in the 2015 film *The Danish Girl*). Sex change stories were also present in the journalism of the American West, as local newspapers were fascinated with gender benders (mainly women presenting as men) surviving and thriving along the country's wild frontier (Boag 2011).

Yet it was the 1951 front page of the *New York Daily News* announcing the sexual transformation of Christine Jorgensen that captivated the global cultural imagination and instantiated transgender identity as something one can *be* and inhabit full time. Headlining with "Ex-GI Becomes Blonde Beauty: Operations Transform Bronx Youth," the story created a massive sensation. In her autobiography, Jorgensen remembers feeling bewildered at the level of publicity she received, recalling that for a time her story overshadowed news coverage of the historic hydrogen bomb tests at Eniwetok Atoll. On the one hand, her journey stoked anxieties about what it meant to be male and female, and the press presented her as a bizarre curiosity. On the other, amid the social and political anxieties of the Cold War era, Jorgensen's transgender identity was framed as a success story, a triumph of modern science, a daring tale of self-actualization, and a win for Western individuality (Meyerowitz 2002).

Thrust into the spotlight, Jorgensen carefully crafted her image for a 1950s viewing public, styling herself as a classic Hollywood "blonde bombshell." She also identified as heterosexual and articulated dreams of domestic life. Her gender performance was conventional and she was celebrated for it. Those who followed suit also garnered press attention in 1950s America. As with Jorgensen, Charlotte McLeod and Tamara Rees became public figures and models of the "good transsexual" (Skidmore 2011, 272), embodying whiteness, heterosexuality, domesticity, and conventional femininity. In choosing to highlight these women's stories—to the exclusion of women of color and women who were less conventionally feminine—media presented a narrow conception of transgender subjectivity (ibid.). Nevertheless, Jorgensen and others gave sex and gender transgression a human face, and for those who felt similarly to them, they served as role models.

Seeking to capitalize from the new public interest in transgender topicality that Jorgensen's story spurred, film production companies increasingly began to green-light projects with transgender themes. For example, Ed Wood's *Glen or Glenda*, released in 1953, was marketed with the tagline "I Changed My Sex!" Financed on a shoestring budget, the movie told the story of a man who agonizes over the consequences of telling his fiancé he is a transvestite. Wood, himself a transvestite, used the film as an attempt to humanize and explain transvestism. In the film, the character Dr. Alton, a psychiatrist, underscores that transvestism is a harmless and sincere condition of healthy heterosexual men with "normal" sex lives. Into the 1960s, film continued to articulate transgender identity as a medical concern but pushed further, framing it as a dangerous and pathological condition. This was most clearly evidenced in *Psycho* (1960) and *Homicidal* (1961). *Psycho* was Alfred Hitchcock's horror story about a psychopathic cross-dressing murderer. The film became a pop-cultural sensation: "*Psycho* upstaged the presidential campaign . . . teenagers turned the showings into rituals—returning with their friends again and again" (Hoberman 2010). Inspired by the success of *Psycho*, William Castle, another iconic horror director of mid-century America, produced and directed *Homicidal* one year later, which offered another shocking tale of a transgender killer. Both films captured the American popular imagination and offered up images that associated gender transgression with madness, violence, and emotional instability.

In the counterculture of the 1960s, however, underground and cult films offered alternative and more transgressive imaginings. Reflecting the zeitgeist of the space age and a daringness to push boundaries, these films ventured into new, previously unexplored territories. Jack Smith, an early pioneer of queer cinema, screened gender chaos and queer sexual performance in his art piece *Flaming Creatures* (1963). Andy Warhol's taboo-saturated experimental films featured the transgender "Warhol Superstars": Holly Woodlawn, Jackie Curtis, and Candy Darling, all of whom became legends of avant-garde culture and cinema. Holly Woodlawn, for instance, became the inspiration for Lou Reed's 1972 hit song "Walk on the Wild Side." John Waters introduced the world to the fearless and unforgettable drag queen Divine in his early films *Roman Candles* (1966), *Eat Your Makeup* (1968), and *Mondo Trasho* (1969). Divine would later star in Waters's better known works, including *Pink Flamingos* (1972), *Female Trouble* (1974), and *Hairspray* (1988), a film that was by far his most popular. Collectively, these more fringe films depicted gender variance within a queer subcultural celebration of sexual nonconformity, "dramatic artifice," and "a theatrical sense of the absurd" (Bell-Metereau 1993, 119). Made by and for queer people, they created a sense of community among moviegoers who marveled in the self-confident and norm-smashing performances of the trans figures.

The 1960s also produced one of the first serious, non-fiction cinematic investigations of gender variance in the documentary *The Queen* (1968). The independently produced and unusually poignant film revolves around the 1967 Miss All-American Camp Beauty Pageant held in New York City. The film takes audiences behind the scenes, offering a cinema vérité glimpse at Manhattan's drag balls, which have a long and rich history dating back to late nineteenth-century Harlem (Garber 1989). We witness the artistry of drag as the queens apply their makeup and wigs, perfect their costumes, perform in dress rehearsals, and compete in the pageant. During offstage moments, we hear about their everyday lives and learn about their relationships. We view the gritty and unglamorous side of drag, and watch the fierce conflict that arises among contestants. As a matter of fact, imagery from *The Queen* has been recycled for contemporary usage, appearing in the opening credits of Amazon's hit transgender-themed series *Transparent*.

Moving into the 1970s, two films about transsexuality, *Myra Breckenridge* (1970) and *The Christine Jorgensen Story* (1970), inaugurated the decade. In popular culture, it "was a period of liberalization in the industry," Diffrient (2013) argues, "when new previously verboten subject matter, such as sex-reassignment surgery, penis transplants, sodomy, and transvestitism, could be presented to an inquisitive public" (55). Inspired by Gore Vidal's best-selling novel, *Myra Breckenridge* (1970) was an X-rated, trashy, sexually explicit romp that featured Raquel Welch as a transsexual woman, Myra. In the film, Myron Breckenridge visits Europe to have a sex change operation, becoming Myra. Upon returning to the United States, he visits his wealthy Uncle Buck, who runs an acting school. Pretending to be Myron's widow, Myra asks Uncle Buck for money, and he puts her to work at his school. The film is a nonlinear and at times nonsensical farce that was well received among queer audiences who appreciated its camp value, but lampooned by critics and the mainstream press (Diffrient 2013). The second transgender-themed film, *The Christine Jorgensen Story* (1970), was a fictionalized melodrama loosely based on Jorgensen's life. Whereas the film portrays Jorgensen as a sympathetic and sincere individual, to a contemporary audience it feels campy and melodramatic, exuding emotional excess and garish sentimentality. Nevertheless, at the time some acclaimed the film for its portrait of Jorgensen. The *New York Times* review maintained, "Here is a quiet, even dignified little picture, handled professionally and tastefully, minus a touch of sensationalism. Compared to a glittery garbage pail like "Myra Breckinridge," the film is downright disarming" (Greenspun 1970).

Into the late 1970s and 1980s, a corpus of films continued to treat gender variance in more serious and humane terms, albeit within the ideological and imaginative limitations of the time period. *Outrageous* (1977), an independent Canadian film about a gay hairdresser who becomes a drag queen and his friend Liza who suffers from schizophrenia, offered an unexpected story of friendship and compassion. As film critic Roger Ebert (1977) wrote at the time, "Almost any description of 'Outrageous!' makes it sound like a sensational exploitation film but that's exactly what it isn't. It's a bittersweet, endearing, sometimes funny little slice of life." In *Dog Day Afternoon* (1975), Al Pacino plays a gay man who robs a bank in order to pay for his lover's sexual reassignment surgery. Both characters were fully realized with compelling backstories, and were depicted as vulnerable and humanly raw. *The World According to Garp* (1982) featured the character Roberta Muldoon, played by John Lithgow, a white trans woman and former professional football player who works at a center for troubled women. She is an altruistic and grounded caregiver, although her character has little depth. Perhaps the most serious, even devastating, treatment of transgender subjectivity was *In a Year of 13 Moons* (1978), a German melodrama. Produced, written, and directed by Rainer Werner Fassbinder, the film follows the final days in the life of the character Elvira (formerly Erwin), who changes sex for a love that never materializes and becomes a lost-soul.

One of the most notable, and widely seen, transgender-themed films of the 1970s was not a serious drama but rather a wildly campy sci-fi musical. *The Rocky Horror Picture Show* (1975) introduced the world to the character of Dr. Frank-N-Furter, an eccentric, transgender scientist and self-proclaimed "sweet transvestite from transsexual Transylvania." In the film, a straight-laced heterosexual couple's car breaks down and they find themselves stranded at Frank-N-Furter's mansion—an alternative universe of misfits and mischief. Delighted by his new guests, he performs for them dressed in a black corset, stockings, and high heels, effectively staging the erotics of gender transgression. As with *Myra Breckenridge*, *Rocky Horror* created a brazen queer world, an alternative reality that up-ended conventional norms and embraced freaks of all kinds. But unlike *Breckenridge*, *Rocky Horror* appreciated high-quality production values, a compelling and linear storyline, and fabulous music. It appealed to both queer and non-queer audiences alike and has become one of the most celebrated and widely known cult classics of all time.

Whereas popular film offered visually striking displays of gender variance throughout the twentieth century, literature provided textual counterparts. Science fiction in particular offered some of the earliest and most imaginative visions of gender crossing. In Gregory Casparian's *An Anglo-American Alliance: A Serio-Comic Romance and Forecast of the Future* (1908), a woman in a lesbian relationship undergoes a sexual reassignment surgery to escape discrimination and lives out her life happily with her partner. In Isidore Schneider's *Doctor Transit* (1925), a struggling couple switches sex to find happiness by drinking a potion handed to them by the mysterious Dr. Transit. Indeed, body switching, identity exchange, forced gender transformations, magical gender reversals, and gender fluidity populated the world of science fiction throughout the twentieth century. Novels such as Robert Heinlein's *I Will Fear No Evil* (1970), Fred Pohl's *Day Million* (1966), and Ursula Le Guin's *Left Hand of Darkness* (1969), along with fantasy pulp magazines such as *Weird Tales* (1923–1954) and *Science Wonder Stories* (1929–1930), trafficked in these themes.

Like the science fiction genre, comics have also been cultural sites where transgender possibilities have abounded. As Fawaz (2016) argues, postwar American comics had a distinctly queer sensibility that celebrated difference, outsider status, the supernatural, and self-transformation. Expanding the terms of what it meant to be human, popular texts such as *The Fantastic Four*, starting in 1961, and *X-Men*, in 1963, affirmed the biological outlaw and presented the body as a site of transition and mutation. Although these texts did not specifically engage with transgender identity, "bodily vulnerability and gender instability constituted the postwar superhero as a figure in continual flux, visualized on the comic book page as constantly moving among different identities, embodiments, social allegiances, and psychic states" (Fawaz 2016, 10).

In early twentieth-century print culture, two novels in particular offered intimate portraits of gender transgression, albeit with different affective structures and tones. The first was Virginia Woolf's *Orlando: A Biography* (1928), a fictionalized biography about an English nobleman, Orlando, who wakes up one morning as a woman. Beginning during the reign of Queen Elizabeth I and ending in 1928, Orlando lives more than four hundred years with a subjectivity that is in constant change and a body in constant transition. Woolf uses the character's escapade through historic time to comment on Victorian-era norms, gender roles, and sexism. The novel, which became a best seller, was highly poetic and struck a spirited and comical tone. By contrast, Radclyffe Hall's novel *The Well of Loneliness* (1928), released the same year as *Orlando*, was a deeply controversial and somber novel about lesbianism and gender liminality. The book chronicled the life of Stephen Gordon, a sexual "invert" born into the British upper class. When compared to *Orlando*, *The Well* is far more overcast, tortured, and forlorn. Steeped with insights from the growing field of sexology, it constructs a portrait of Gordon's uphill search for identity, love, and happiness. Whereas most critics and scholars have focused attention on the character's sexuality, others have highlighted Gordon's transgender aspects. Taylor (1998) argues Stephen Gordon "irresistibly solicit[s] a transgender reading" because the character occupies a complex gendered domain, assigned female but is masculine-identified (288). Other noteworthy popular novels that centered trans figures in Western literature were Gore Vidal's *Myra Breckinridge* (1968) and *The World According to Garp* (1978) by John Irving, both of which were turned into films (discussed above).

Perhaps the most treasured texts of the twentieth century for trans people were memoirs and autobiographies of gender transition. These books were highly coveted by virtue of being some of the only cultural sites to reflect the lived realities of trans people. As such, they were precious resources for self-making and belonging, and were shared between individuals (Hausman 2006; Stone 1991). Some early examples include Earl Lind's 1918 *Autobiography of an Androgyne* and *The Female Impersonators* (1922). However, the most widely known trans autobiography of the early twentieth century was *Man Into Woman* (1933), documenting the life of Danish artist Lili Elbe (born Einar Magnus Andreas Wegener).

The book was a compilation of her personal writings and recollections, an attempt by Elbe who, after being sensationalized in the press, wanted to reflect her life as she experienced it. The next major autobiography was Christine Jorgensen's *A Personal Autobiography* (1967), which sold 450,000 copies and was later turned into a film (Schilt 2009). On the heels of public interest in Jorgensen's book, several other transgender autobiographies were published. Notable were Jan Morris's *Conundrum: From James to Jan, An Extraordinary Personal Narrative of Transsexualism* (1974), written by the famous travel writer, and Mario Martino's *Emergence: A Transsexual Autobiography* (1977), the only autobiography to be penned by a trans man before the 1990s.

The next autobiography to receive the kind of mass attention that Jorgensen's attracted was Renée Richards's 1983 *Second Serve*. In 1976, when Renée Richards, a successful New York ophthalmologist, competed in a California women's tennis competition, a journalist revealed that she was born a man and had previously played in men's competitions. Although Richards planned to compete in the US Open, the United States Tennis Association prevented her from doing so by instituting a chromosomal test for female competitors. In 1977, Richards won a much-publicized court battle that allowed her to compete in the women's event at the US Open. Her story and the court case that ensued became a global controversy, as she recalled, "much of the population of the world had my name on their lips. It was as if someone had dropped an atom bomb" (Richards and Ames 2007, 48). In 1983, Richards released her autobiography titled *Second Serve*, and three years later a made-for-television film of the same name premiered on network television. As with Christine Jorgensen, Richards's story brought the concept of sex change into the national conversation and captivated the world. One transgender activist remembered reading her book in high school:

> I found her autobiography, and I bought it immediately. I'd never read a book about a transsexual before. Back then, each of us was left to our own devices. I kept it in my locker. I read it surreptitiously. I'd only had experiences with media depictions and other unflattering portrayals. But here was someone healthy, someone multidimensional, and all she wanted to do was compete. (Weinreb 2011, 4)

For both writer and reader, the transgender autobiography is a tool of self-knowledge and discovery. The genre's narrative structure—with a beginning (undesirable or wrong gender identity), middle (transition), and end (arrival at desired or authentic gender identity)—offers a sense of plausibility and coherence to transgender life (Prosser 1998). "To learn of transsexuality," Prosser writes, "is to uncover transsexuality as a story and to refigure one's own life within the frame of that story" (124).[9]

Beyond print culture, gender transgression has long been a feature of popular music; from the cross-dressing of early jazz and blue singers such as Gladys Bentley and Frankie Jaxon to the gender play of glam rockers. Indeed, in the 1970s, outrageous gender performance became a defining feature of mainstream music. The New York Dolls, Queen, and T. Rex playfully blurred gender lines. While pop singer David Bowie introduced the world to Ziggy Stardust, his androgynous space alien alter ego. As Stryker (2008) argues, throughout the decade a "transgender aesthetic" flourished, forging "a new relationship between gendered appearance and biological sex" (91–92). Beyond glam rock, the world of disco also ushered glittering queerness and gender play into the 1970s global mainstream. Defined by "strangeness, gayness, mixing, dress-up, drugs, androgyny, and excess" (Gamson 2005, 141), disco revolved around fantasy, dance floor pageantry, and the thrill of living in the moment. Artists such as Sylvester, the gender- bending disco diva, and Grace Jones, the severely masculine and angular supermodel and singer, were queer countercultural heroes, representative of disco's turn toward gender experimentation.

In the early 1980s, gender transgression also became a mainstay of one of the decade's most iconic brands: MTV. As Zoonen (1995) surmises, "MTV seems to be the only part of mainstream culture in which subversions of gender are no exception or a sign of marginality" (314). The advent and rise of MTV brought gender-bending representations to a national and eventually global audience. Subverting the norms of dress and embodiment allowed artists to produce the kinds of fantastic spectacles warranted by the new medium. As a technological form with particular biases and affordances, the music video made "direct address and personal display necessary for a star persona" (Straayer 1996, 87). The performance of a heightened and visually compelling self was paramount in branding and marketing one's music. Some of the most successful names of the MTV era boldly traversed gender norms. The romantic femininity of Prince, the colorful costuming of Boy George, and the seductive gender play of Annie Lennox, for example, rebelled against an established gendered order. In their music videos and performances, notions of sex and gender were turned upside down and gender signifiers were appropriated across bodies without concern for physical sex. Performances of drag were also included into the mix. In 1985, Divine released the music video "Walk Like a Man," a queer and irreverent take on the classic by Frankie Valli and the Four Seasons.

But it was not until 1993 that drag made its biggest splash with Ru-Paul, a professional drag queen living in New York City. RuPaul's massive hit song "Supermodel (You Better Work)" turned her into a cultural sensation. The infectious, upbeat lyric topped US dance charts and its MTV music video brimmed with drag subcultural references. After the success of "Supermodel," RuPaul's fame surged in the 1990s. She published the memoir *Lettin' It All Hang Out* (1995), earned a seven-year contract for M.A.C. cosmetics to be the "Face of M.A.C. Cosmetics" (the first drag queen to ever do so), covered the song "Don't Go Breaking My Heart" with Elton John, and became a radio personality on New York City's WKTU morning show. On cable television, RuPaul also hosted her own talk show, *The RuPaul Show*, on VH1 from 1996 to 1998, a flashy throwback to 1970s variety programming.

Indeed, cross-dressing has been a fixture of American television from the beginning. In *Texaco Star Theater* (1948–1956), an early and popular television comedy-variety series, Milton Burle frequently cross-dressed in his skits.[10] These gender masquerades became a trademark of his comedy throughout the 1950s. Not surprisingly, his inspiration to cross-dress came from observing New York City's gay drag queens (Nesteroff 2015). Burle's cross-dressing was only the start of a practice that would soon become a reliable comedic device on television. Cross-dressing continued to appear in variety and sketch comedies across the televised landscape including *The Flip Wilson Show* (1970–1974), *Monty Python's Flying Circus* (1969–1974), *Saturday Night Live* (1975–present), *In Living Color* (1990–1994), and *MADtv* (1995–2009).

Paralleling film, it was during the 1970s that television turned toward more sober, everyday transgender narratives. Norman Lear's *All in the Family* (1971–1979) and *The Jeffersons* (1975–1985), sitcoms known for addressing contemporary social issues, were two series that handled transgender topicality with a sense of earnestness—as well as a touch of comedy. In "Archie the Hero" (1975), *All in the Family*'s notorious conservative curmudgeon, Archie Bunker, saves the life of a self-described transvestite and female impersonator named Beverly LaSalle. The episode is filled with the typical sitcom pratfalls and antics involving her gender identity, and in a later episode she is set up with Archie's friend on a date as a joke. Still, the couple befriends Beverly and their relationship crosses episodes and moves beyond the superficial.

In the episode titled "Edith's Crisis of Faith" (1977), Beverly is murdered during a mugging at Christmastime. The murder, which occurred in part as a result of Beverly's transgender identity, devastates Edith and causes her to question her faith. Fighting back tears, she exclaims, "I'm mad at God . . . All I know is Beverly was killed because of what he was and we're all supposed to be God's children. It don't make sense."

Figure 1.2. *All in the Family* (CBS) Season 6, 1975–1976. Episode: "Archie the Hero." Air date: September 29, 1975. Archie and Beverly chat in his living room. Credit: CBS/ Photofest.

In a 1977 episode titled "Once a Friend," *The Jeffersons* also engage the issue of transsexuality. During the storyline, George Jefferson's pal from the navy, Eddie, reconnects with him. Only now Eddie is a trans woman who uses the name Edie. During their first encounter, George asks his old friend why he dresses as a woman, questioning, "If you ain't gay and you're not a weirdo, then what are you?" With coolness and confidence, Edie responds, "I had the operation. I had a sex change. George, I'm a woman now . . . I feel good about myself." Given the time period, the conversation is surprisingly tame and sincere. By the end of the episode, and in quintessential sitcom fashion, George overcomes his initial shock and confusion regarding his friend's transition. He addresses her by her correct name, Edie, and warmly reaffirms their friendship.

Another surprisingly measured and heartfelt treatment of transsexuality for the time appeared in the hospital drama *Medical Center* (1969–1976). In a special two-part episode "The Fourth Sex" (1975), a renowned surgeon named Dr. Pat Caddison, played by Robert Reed who starred as Mike Brady in *The Brady Bunch*, receives a sexual reassignment surgery. Caddison is a well-respected physician and her desire for sexual reassignment is treated as unusual but also genuine and legitimate. The narrative focuses on the difficulty of Caddison's decision and its impact on her relationships with friends, colleagues, wife, and son. Reed plays the part with sensitivity and nuance, which earned him an Emmy nomination for his performance.

While *All in the Family*, *The Jeffersons*, and *Medical Center* broke ground by offering more humanized and sincere depictions of transgender subjectivity, throughout the 1970s and '80s transgender characters were also segregated to limited representational silos. In cop and detective shows such as *Magnum, PI* (1980–1988), *Vega$* (1978–1981), and *The Streets of San Francisco* (1972–1977), transgender characters were murderers and psychopathic killers. On the other hand, comedies such as *Too Close for Comfort* (1980–1987), *Dear John* (1988–1992), and *Gimme a Break* (1981–1987) employed the "transgender surprise" tactic where characters in the show fall for, date, or get set up with transgender individuals, unaware of their identity. By the end of the episode, there is the archetypical moment of revelation scene that generates shock and surprise.

Throughout the 1980s and 1990s, transgender shock and surprise were also mainstays on the television talk show circuit. In his study of the genre, *Freaks Talk Back*, Gamson (1999) argues that daytime talk shows of this era were carnivalesque freak shows that furnished a theater of sexual and gender variance. As highly formulaic texts that rely on the routine production of Otherness, spectacle, confession, and emotional excess, talk shows exploited and further marginalized transgender guests. Perhaps the most egregious and well-known examples were seen on *The Jerry Springer Show*, which broadcast episodes bearing titles "I'm Pregnant by a Giant Transsexual," "Jerry's Tranny Special," and "Transsexuals Attack."

Yet, as Gamson argues, the talk show is a "monster with two heads" (29–65) in which a raucous circus is joined with a respectable public forum, a site where gender variance can be given a human face. In this way, talk shows offered transgender people a platform from which to speak and perform their identities. They were given the chance to "talk back" to the in-studio and at-home audiences, to society, and to authority figures, an opportunity not afforded in other areas of popular culture. Whereas *The Jerry Springer Show* leaned toward a contentious freak show, others such as *The Oprah Winfrey Show* offered more insightful conversation, notwithstanding the draw of the sensational. "Issue-oriented shows" such as *Oprah* presented public and personal matters in socially relevant terms that typically "mix[ed] sensationalism with a liberal political agenda that champions the rights of the disenfranchised" (Shattuc 1997, 9). Within this format, gender-nonconforming people were offered the "Oprah sit-down," an ability to narrate their stories, advocate for understanding, and position themselves as "like everybody else." Yet talk shows were not the only site of transgender visibility in the 1990s. Across the media landscape, cracks in the representational ceiling began to spread and multiply.

The Gay '90s

Throughout the 1990s, the popular media landscape transformed as gay and lesbian visibility proliferated, leading some to coin the decade "the gay nineties" (Walters 2001). Popular culture became increasingly infused with a gay sensibility and politicality, setting the stage for transgender visibility. During this time, marketers began to recognize and exploit the economic potential of the gay consumer market. In gay media outlets, local and national advertisers bought ad space in record numbers (Sender 2004). This commercial interest fueled an explosion of glossy gay magazines and funded some of the first gay websites populating the Internet with a national and global reach. Early gay websites such as Planet Out and Gay.com reached more consumers in the United States than all gay magazines combined (ibid.). As Sender maintains, this rapid development of the gay market had two origins: "The AIDS crisis and associated activism had brought gay people to the attention of marketers, and the economic recession at the beginning of the decade sent marketers in search of new groups of apparently affluent consumers" (21). Politically, queer activist groups such as Act Up and Queer Nation were demanding government and private-sector intervention in the AIDS crisis and making the culture account for anti-LGBT violence and discrimination. Employing street theater as protest, these groups attracted national attention and brought the plight of queer Americans into the public sphere. State-level gay marriage fights were also under way across the United States, placing homosexuality on the national political agenda.

As a result, the media landscape of the 1990s witnessed an unprecedented rise in gay- and lesbian-themed content in television programming, popular film, and advertising, along with a readiness to embrace upscale gay audiences and eventually certain kinds of LGBT imagery (Walters 2001; Becker 2006). As Becker (2006) notes, the landscape of 1990s television in particular revealed a culture coming to terms with the question of homosexuality. Gay characters and storylines appeared in some of the decade's most popular and celebrated shows such as *Seinfeld (1989–1998)*, *Roseanne (1988–1997)*, *Picket Fences (1992–1996)*, *Melrose Place (1992–1999)*, *thirtysomething (1987–1991)*, and a host of others. Moreover, for the first time in media history, network television shows such as *Ellen* (1994–1998) and *Will & Grace* (1998–2005) revolved around gay-identifying main characters.

Gay visibility in media content also expanded as the entertainment industry began to court a lucrative and burgeoning consumer market comprised of younger, socially liberal, upwardly mobile, urban professionals, a group Becker (2006) refers to as the SLUMPY demographic. In order to appeal to SLUMPY audiences, network television incorporated gay characters and gay-themed material. This inclusion added social relevancy and edginess to programming, making it more attractive to the coveted younger demographic. For SLUMPY audiences, claiming an appreciation for LGBT-themed programming was a marker of self-identity, communicating one's liberal values, hipness, and forward thinking (ibid.). Importantly, the gay characters within these shows often looked like the liberal-minded, educated, urban, younger, upwardly mobile and mainly white demographic networks and marketers wished to attract (ibid.).

While the popular culture of "the gay nineties" was largely focused on homosexuality, and in particular gay white men, the decade offered glimpses of gender variance. In literature, Leslie Feinberg's *Stone Butch Blues* (1993), a pioneering and wildly popular queer novel, introduced the world to the gender-nonconforming character Jess Goldberg, a working-class transgender person who exists beyond conventional gender categories. In the novel, Jess struggles to escape the institutionalized violence and homophobia that surround her and find love, intimacy, and a sense of place. Shifting to the world of fashion and advertising, androgyny was an emerging trend. The retail powerhouse Calvin Klein marketed the fragrance "CK One" for both men and women. Shot in black and white to minimize gender differences, its ads featured androgynous individuals scantily dressed in jeans and t-shirts. On Broadway, the musical *Rent*, chronicling the lives of young, queer New Yorkers during the AIDS crisis, debuted in 1994 and became a national sensation.[11] One of the show's leading characters, Angel, a trans woman of color, was an energetic and hopeful ray of light.

Meanwhile in television and popular film, representations of gender variance reached the mainstream's center. One of the defining television sitcoms of the era, *Friends* (1994–2004), introduced a storyline in which the main character, Chandler, reveals to his friends that his father is gay and performs as a drag queen in Las Vegas. Unfortunately, the show relied on well-worn myths conflating gay men, drag queens, and transgender women, and treated Chandler's father in disappointing ways, making him the target of routine mockery. Television dramas also featured transgender storylines, often within the context of victimhood and distress. In a 1997 *Ally McBeal* episode, "Boy to the World," trial lawyer Ally McBeal defends Stephanie, a young trans woman arrested for soliciting sex on the streets. Espousing a sort of liberal paternalism, Ally feels compelled to care for her troubled friend, noting, "I see a kid who needs help." The program airs many hackneyed representational tropes as Stephanie is depicted as a confused kid and sex worker who is tragically murdered by the end of the episode. At the same time, Stephanie is a kind, witty, creative, and lovable character who passionately defends her identity to Ally, asserting, "This doesn't make me sick. This doesn't make me a freak." Stephanie succeeds in winning Ally's affection, as she wonders, "Is it possible to love somebody only two days?"

With varying degrees of sophistication and depth, drag culture also made appearances in some of the decade's popular films such as *To Wong Foo, Thanks for Everything! Julie Newmar* (1995) and *Midnight in the Garden of Good and Evil* (1997). Notable was *The Adventures of Priscilla, Queen of the Desert* (1994), an Australian road-trip film, for the ways it depicted friendship and camaraderie among a group of individuals along the transgender spectrum. As it always had, cross-dressing showed up in hit comedies such as *Mrs. Doubtfire* (1993) and *The Birdcage* (1996). However, dramas such as *The Crying Game* (1992), *Ma Vie En Rose* (1997), *All About My Mother* (1999), and *Boys Don't Cry* (1999) offered multidimensional and thoughtful portraits of transgender individuals experiencing the severe hardships and simple joys of living everyday life as a transgender person. While some such as *The Crying Game* recycled themes of transgender shock and sensationalism, all presented characters that were emotionally developed with full backstories. Likeable and flawed, their transgender protagonists had richly complicated psychological and social lives.

Notably, gender variance was not only a mainstream phenomenon during the gay nineties. The decade witnessed the birth of what cultural critic B. Ruby Rich (2013) calls the "New Queer Cinema," a movement that flourished across the American independent film festival circuit. These films were generally low-budget projects facilitated by the growing availability and affordability of camcorder technology and editing equipment. Emerging during the AIDS crisis and the flowering of a critical queer consciousness, New Queer Cinema was also politically urgent and ideologically radical. Its aesthetics were stylistically daring and its ethos was emotionally raw. It represented the diversity of queer and transgender experience. It celebrated defiance, rebellion, danger, and life on the margins, eschewing the impulse to create "positive imagery" (Aaron 2004).

New Queer Cinema was also defined by the queering of gender norms and privileged non-normative performances of masculinity and femininity. It periodically displayed cross-dressing, transsexuality, transgender imagery, and other forms of gender variance. As Aaron (2004) argues, within this cinematic moment, "the queer figure par excellence was the transsexual" (6). One of New Queer Cinema's canonical films, *Paris Is Burning* (1990), brought to the fore the lived experiences of black and Latino gay, gender-nonconforming, and trans individuals involved in New York City's drag scene and vogue culture. Comprised of personal interviews and documentary footage, the film spotlighted their dreams, resiliency, creativity, and love. Yet its protagonists were disenfranchised and struggled with poverty, displacement, and everyday survival. Ultimately, it offered an optic onto the ways queer and transgender people, out of necessity, create alternative family structures and alliances that work for them within the specific contexts of their lives.

This was the legacy of the Gay '90s: the recognition of a queer market, the great migration of gay and gender-nonconforming imagery into mainstream film and television, and a New Queer Cinema that allowed small glimpses into previously unseen territories of queer and transgender life. These developments helped lay the groundwork for the new transgender visibility.

The Tipping Point

While mass-mediated gay and lesbian portrayals in particular were "all the rage" (Walters 2001) in the 1990s, the start of the twenty-first century has revealed a turn toward transgender. When I conducted my interviews and observations between 2008 and 2012, nearly all the people I spoke with commented on the evolving media and information environment. "It's been changing dramatically in the last 10 years," Allyson contended. "TV shows come out with trans members of families. I think now the general public is aware that the T [transgender] community is a part of the diversity of the planet. It used to be that we were completely invisible to most people. Now we are becoming very visible to people. Where we kind of had the ability to hide in plain sight 15–20 years ago.

We can no longer hide in plain sight." Particularly for the older participants who grew up during a period of "nonrecognition" (Clark 1969), when transgender visibility was virtually absent from the cultural landscape, the change was astonishing.

Some, like Don, were struck by the amount of transgender content online. "When I was growing up we didn't have the Internet and things like that, and I'm 42. Once I decided I was going to transition I immediately got on the national FTM listserv and I've been on that ever since. I think the Internet has been critical to the advancement of the trans community as far as politics, social agendas and things like outreach and resource networking." Others, like Rayanne, mentioned television. "Right now there's more of it [transgender representation on television]. I'm not sure about the quality, but there seems to be more media exposure . . . It seems to me to be kind of a hot topic. You see trans characters going up in scripted television, reality television." The representational transformations that Don, Rayanne, and others were noticing indeed mark the beginning stages of a new transgender visibility. As Rayanne indicated, the quality of this new transgender visibility—its ethos, sophistication, and point of view—is variable and questionable. However, not in question is the rising popular recognition of transgender subjectivity in media culture.

Gender variance has moved from the margins of society to enter the American national conversation. Recognizing this shift, in 2014 *Time* magazine announced that we had reached a "Transgender Tipping Point." Featuring Laverne Cox on the cover, the magazine argued that transgender citizens were "America's next civil rights frontier." In addition to the efforts of a politically active transgender movement, *Time*'s tipping point declaration was the result of the increasing presence of transgender visibility in popular culture at the beginning of the twenty-first century. In the timeline below, I try to capture the high moments and critical flashpoints of this visibility.

- In 2001, the campy rock opera *Hedwig and the Angry Inch* is released. In the film, a botched sexual reassignment surgery leaves Hedwig with ambiguous genitalia, an "angry inch," causing her to suffer from the social and emotional consequences of unwelcomed gender ambiguity. Hedwig searches for authentic human connection and for people to "love the front of me," as she exclaims in the film. CBS aired the short-lived television drama *The Education of Max Bickford* (2001–2002), the first major network show to include a regularly appearing trans character. The show follows Max, a college professor struggling with a midlife crisis, whose best friend Steve becomes Erica. The show's narrative raised the social and political issues the transgender community commonly faces, such as coming out to loved ones, negotiating relationships with family and friends, changing a driver's license, and dating.

- In 2003, Style Network debuted *The Brini Maxwell Show*, starring a drag queen as its host. Originally a cult classic on New York City's Manhattan Neighborhood Network, the show was a campy and colorful take on the home improvement genre.
- In 2005, the film *TransAmerica* is released starring Felicity Huffman as a transgender woman who reunites with her son and embarks on a cross-country road trip. Huffman's performance earns her a Golden Globe for best actress. The film *Breakfast on Pluto* is also released presenting the tale of gender-bending Patrick, nicknamed "Kitten," who commits to searching for his biological mother, a decision that launches a journey filled with eclectic urban characters and chance encounters.
- In 2006, the telenovela *Ugly Betty* premiered on ABC featuring Rebecca Romijn Stamos as Alexis Meade, previously Alex Meade, a fashion magazine editor for the fictional publication *Mode*. As an ambitious businesswoman and strategist, she conspires with the creative director to take over the magazine from her brother.
- In 2007, Candis Cayne became the first transgender actress to play a transgender character on primetime television in ABC's short-lived *Dirty Sexy Money*. MSNBC began airing the *Born in the Wrong Body* documentary series following individuals' gender transitions. News media also spotlighted the gender transition of two public figures: Christine Daniels, *Los Angeles Times* sports journalist, as well as Susan Stanton, Largo, Florida city manager. Daniels chronicled her transformation in a blog she wrote for the *LA Times* titled "Woman in Progress." Stanton, who was fired from her government job after announcing plans to transition from male to female, had her story turned into a two-hour teledocumentary produced by CNN titled *Her Name Was Steven*. A May 21 issue of *Newsweek* devoted its cover story to exploring "The Mystery of Gender," an exploration of how "the new visibility of transgender America is shedding

light on the ancient riddle of identity." The issue's feature article "(Re-thinking) Gender" discussed the changing cultural assumptions regarding gender in the United States as "a growing number of Americans are taking their private struggles with their identities into the public realm" (Rosenberg 2007).

- In 2009, Chaz Bono, the son of Sonny Bono and Cher, publicly announced his decision to transition from female to male. Bono's story was turned into a documentary titled *Becoming Chaz*, a favorite at the Sundance Film festival, which also aired on the Oprah Winfrey Television Network (OWN), inaugurating the network's "Documentary Club." Bono later released the book *Transition: The Story of How I Became a Man*, an autobiographical account of the public figure's life in the spotlight. The cable television network Logo premiered *RuPaul's Drag Race*, a colorful reality drag competition that is still incredibly popular today.

- In 2010, the teen soap opera *Degrassi* introduced the character Adam, a female-to-male transgender high school student, a first for the long-running and popular show. The first transgender political appointees in the country's history were chosen by the Obama administration to serve the executive branch. Dylan Orr was appointed as special assistant to the Assistant Secretary of Labor Kathleen Martinez at the Department of Labor, and Amanda Simpson was selected as senior technical advisor in the Bureau of Industry and Security. Kye Allums became NCAA's first division 1 female-to-male transgender basketball player for George Washington University. According to one sports journalist, the player's participation in women's college basketball was responsible for "starting conversations never before held in the sport" (Zeigler 2010). Microsoft's Xbox 360 video game console changed its "Terms of Use and Code of Conduct," allowing players to identify as transgender in user profiles and gamertags (Robinson 2010). VH1 aired the short-lived reality makeover TV series *Transform Me* featuring a trio of transgender women who give female "fashion victims" makeovers.

- In 2011, ABC's hit reality dance show *Dancing with the Stars* invited Chaz Bono, Cher's transgender son, to compete. Chaz's treatment on the show was mixed, with one judge referring to his dance style as a "cute little penguin trying to be a big menacing bird of prey."

- In 2012, Fox's television hit *Glee* introduced its first trans character, Unique, to the high school–themed show. Famed Hollywood film director Lana Wachowski, whose work includes *The Matrix* trilogy and *Cloud Atlas*, came out as a trans woman.

- In 2013, Laverne Cox, a black trans actress, made her appearance in Netflix's original jailhouse series *Orange Is the New Black*, playing a transgender inmate. Chelsea Manning (formerly Bradley), a US army intelligence analyst, was sentenced to 35 years in prison for leaking classified military documents to WikiLeaks. Soon after her conviction, Manning came out as a trans woman and began transitioning while incarcerated. Kristin Beck (born Chris), former US Navy Seal, published her memoir *Warrior Princess: A U.S. Navy Seal's Journey to Coming Out Transgender*. In 2014, a documentary produced by CNN Films titled *Lady Valor* told Beck's story.

- In 2014, Facebook expanded its gender identity options for user profiles beyond male/female to more than 50 identities, including "transgender," "gender fluid," and "non-binary." Janet Mock, a black transgender woman and former People.com editor, published a politically charged and deeply personal *New York Times* best-selling memoir *Redefining Realness*, which earned international acclaim. Amazon Instant Video branded its original programming catalogue with *Transparent*, a Golden Globe– and Emmy Award–winning series chronicling a Los Angeles family's journey as the father transitions to a woman.

- Also in 2014, AOL launched an original series following the life of transgender punk rocker, Laura Jane Grace, titled *True Trans. Laverne Cox Presents: The T Word*, a documentary about seven transgender youth from across the country, was broadcasted simultaneously on MTV and Logo. VH1 ordered a transgender documentary series titled *Transamerica*, produced by Tyra Banks about transgender women living in Chicago. Sterling Brands, a top brand consultancy firm, released its first annual "trends report" titled *On the Future: A Forecast of Near Future Trends*. Among the 15 trends the report listed for 2015 was "Gender Untethered," defined as "how gender identity is being bent, blurred, reversed and mashed-up" (Sterling Brands 2014, 12). The report advocated for more choices in gender-neutral shopping that would adapt to the growing gender fluidity in society. It offered the example of a "S(h)e Doll," a gender-neutral toy that would allow kids to "experiment with identity via a selection of clothing, hair and accessories without any gender bias" (13).

- In 2015, Barack Obama became the first president to mention transgender Americans in an official capacity during his State of the Union speech. Caitlyn Jenner (formerly Bruce Jenner) publicly announced her trans identity to Diane Sawyer on ABC's *20/20* in a much-anticipated televised interview. The interview attracted 17 million viewers and earned the program's highest ratings in prized demographics in more than 15 years (Kissell 2015). In July, Jenner appeared on the cover of *Vanity Fair* magazine along with the headline "Call Me Caitlyn." Also in July, E! Entertainment launched its much-anticipated show *I Am Cait*, offering an inside look into Caitlyn Jenner's life and transition. The film *About Ray* is released, starring Naomi Watts, Susan Sarandon, and Elle Fanning, about a teenager transitioning from female to male. Netflix premiered an original sci-fi series called *Sense 8* that features a transgender woman as part of its ensemble cast.[12] ABC Family network premiered *Becoming Us*, a reality program following the experience of a teenager whose father transitions into a woman. Discovery Life aired its original reality series *New Girls on the Block*, chronicling the lives of six transgender women. TLC introduced its series *I Am Jazz*, about transgender teenager Jazz Jennings and her family. One media critic noted that at this point in time, content producers were jumping on "The Transgender Series Bandwagon" (Moraes 2015).

These moments, which have led some to suggest we have reached a transgender tipping point, are in part propelled by the growth of a transgender collective consciousness and the political mobilization of gender variant communities. But they are also the result of transformations in media and technologies of communication such as television, the Internet, and social media platforms.

In the 1990s, television moved from a period of "multi-channel transition," with its VCRs, remote controls, and basic cable services, to a "post-network era" defined by an explosion of diversity, choice, and interconnectivity (Lotz 2007, 245). Cable television packages began offering hundreds of channels, video-on-demand services, and web streaming. Content providers looked to new markets and further carved out new audience niches. In 2002, the here! Network was launched as a subscription cable service offering original LGBT-themed television aimed at the larger LGBT community. It was followed in 2005 by Viacom's LGBT cable channel Logo. Rather than being available as a subscription service, Logo was offered in upper-tier cable packages.

As Aslinger (2009) notes, the creation and continued viability of Logo "illustrates the television industry's increasing willingness to target GLBT viewers directly . . . to produce texts that offer up gay protagonists as more than 'textual selling points'" (109). Although a majority of its marketing and programming is geared toward middle-class, gay, white men—and increasingly heterosexual women (Ng 2013)—since its inception Logo has nevertheless apportioned space for screening transgender-themed content. Its teledocumentary series *Real Momentum* devoted several episodes to transgender issues and aired the trans reality dating show *TransAmerican Love Story*. Logo also featured *TransGeneration*, a documentary series following the lives of four transgender college students. Finally, its signature and most successful show, *RuPaul's Drag Race*, is a reality drag contest that spotlights drag queens, transgender performers, butch lesbians, and queeny gay men.

If gay characters were used to hail hip, younger viewers in 1990s television, transgender figures were deployed to do the same at the start of the twenty-first century. This trend was most notable in the reality TV genre, as transgender people were regulars on *The Surreal Life* (VH1, 2006), *America's Next Top Model* (CW, 2008), *TransAmerican Love Story* (Logo, 2008), *I Wanna Work for Diddy* (VH1, 2008), *America's Best Dance Crew* (MTV, 2009), *The Real World: Brooklyn* (MTV, 2009), and *Making the Band* (MTV, 2009). The transgender community made a particularly strong showing in MTV's 2009–2010 television season: *Making the Band* (2000–2009), a reality singing competition, featured a transgender contestant; the documentary series *True Life* (1998–present) featured two individuals undergoing gender transition; and *Randy Jackson Presents: America's Best Dance Crew* (2008–2015), a dance competition, featured a dance troupe with a transgender performer. And in its twenty-first season, MTV's signature reality hit *The Real World* (1992–present) introduced its first transgender housemate Katelynn, a twenty-four-year-old computer whiz from Florida. In the context of cable television, gender variance met the industry's need to push the representational envelope in order to stay relevant, and more, to keep up with the Internet's more cutting-edge content.

In fact, it is the growth of the Internet and the evolution of digital, networked, and convergent technologies that have created the most profound impact on the availability and visibility of transgender representations, discourses, and narratives. As Jenkins argues, in the digital media environment individuals are increasingly "active" instead of passive, "migratory" instead of stationary and predictable, "socially connected" instead of isolated, and "noisy and public" instead of quiet and private (Jenkins 2006, 18–19). Going further, Nightingale and Ross (2003) suggest that beyond being "active," the new media environment provides the opportunity for audiences to be "*activist*" (9).

In light of this emergent media environment, the people I spoke with routinely narrated their life stories in terms of "pre" and "post" Internet. Profoundly expanding the media space and offering up new pathways for content and communication, the Internet offered the promise of change for them. It created a transgender "long tail" (Anderson 2006), a vast catalogue of options and media offerings that extend outward like the long tail of a distribution curve.[13] Whereas transgender content was previously only available in specialty "brick and mortar" shops, the proliferation of websites and online platforms such as Netflix and Amazon made it easy to find and consume.

More than changing the relative visibility and accessibility of transgender imagery, the Internet also helped solve one of the greatest challenges for transgender people: finding reliable and credible information about gender variance. Its long tail furnished space for transgender-themed websites and blogs to convey news and information ignored by most mainstream media outlets. Online websites and blogs aggregated resources and acted as hubs for information. They addressed a vast spectrum of issues and concerns regarding hormones and surgery, healthcare and wellness, news and entertainment, politics and activism, language and identity, style and fashion.

The Internet also supplied unprecedented connectivity to transgender people, who have often been isolated and widely dispersed across space. This facilitated political mobilization and the cultivation of a trans critical collective consciousness (Shapiro 2004). In addition to larger websites such as Facebook and Tumblr, transgender social networking sites such as Pink Essence and TransQueer Nation have allowed the transgender community to connect and develop active and sophisticated online subcultures. The design and architecture of these sites cultivate feelings of group identity, citizenship, and belonging perhaps unavailable in everyday life. The social networking site TransQueer Nation, for example, accomplishes this not only by providing a platform for individuals to connect, but also through its mode of address. Employing overtly nationalistic rhetoric, it identifies its users as "citizens," calls personal profiles "passports," and encourages members to connect with "allies" via the site's communication tools. Through its digital citizenship, the site creates a kind of "imagined community" (Anderson 2006) for its users, a feeling of civic communion and commitment to a nation.

The technological and social affordances of the Internet also helped transgender individuals create personal "communities of choice," carefully managed social groups "that supply the essentials of community separately to each individual: support, sociability, information, social identities, and a sense of belonging" (Wellman et al. 2003, 10). Various studies have shown the ways virtual tools allow gender variant people to tell their stories, find assistance, and redefine meanings of self and community.[14] Transgender youth are especially active in online spaces. In general, LGBT youth spend more time online and have more online friends than their non-LGBT peers (Palmer et al. 2013). One study found that 70% of queer and transgender youth believe online interactions reduced their feelings of isolation and loneliness, while 52% found a community in online spaces (Hillier, Kurdas, and Horsley 2001).

The Tipping Point . . . Reconsidered

While the notion of a transgender tipping point may seem apt to describe our current historical moment, the language seems to imply progress and movement forward. Even as the new transgender visibility clearly generates recognition and awareness, the question remains: To what extent has transgender life on the ground really changed as a result of this new visibility? Moreover, the representational purview of the cultural tipping point remains limited. There are noticeable absences, including transgender men, transgender people of color, working-class individuals, and gender ambiguous or non-binary people. The depictions overwhelmingly focus on the trope of gender transition, the process of moving from one gender identity to another. As Julie asserted, "All we see in the media is the transition. Transition is not everything. We never see before it or after it." Even as transition is an important and defining experience for trans people, it is so frequently recycled in popular culture that it edges out alternative articulations. Transition narratives are also overwhelmingly focused on transsexuals who medically and surgically transition and pass with ease. As Steve, a white middle-aged, married cross-dresser, emphasized: "It is the post ops who get the attention in the media. And so transgender gets equated with transsexual. The vast majority of what you see is them, and yet, they're not speaking for us. We don't all want surgery."

Many participants expressed concern that a specific kind of "transnormative" subjectivity, one with particular race, class, gender, age, and embodiment norms, was becoming a representational convention. The question of transnormativity worried Remi: "They [media professionals] consciously reject transwomen who don't fit traditionally feminine stereotypes. So, you don't see butch transwomen, tomboyish transwomen. You don't see many 20-year-old transwomen. You see straight, White, middle class femininity." Josh expressed similar frustrations. "It would be nice to show someone who is not a middle-class white trans person. Show diversity of transness, like a trans person with disability or a different ethnicity, or like older and younger." Consequently, while the new transgender visibility evidences silver linings and opens up new possibilities, its blind spots can foreclose others.

As Walters (2001) cautioned about the rise of gay representation in the 1990s, media visibility does not necessarily indicate wider cultural understanding or progress on the ground. As she notes, being *seen* is not the same as being *known*, and "visibility can lull us into believing that change has really occurred when it is, too often, purely cosmetic and superficial" (24). In other words, visibility is not equality; representation is not care; and acknowledgment is not understanding. Visibility can also generate regressive backlashes. One only has to look at North Carolina's recent HB2 bill, which sanctions open transgender discrimination, as an example of the dark underbelly of visibility.

Finally, the online world is not a social utopia. It often replicates and even amplifies the kinds of cruelty and injustice that exist in the "real world." Online bullying and violence against transgender people is rampant in online spaces. Anonymous users can easily target queer and transgender people. A 2013 study conducted by the Gay, Lesbian, and Straight Education Network (GLSEN) found that LGBT youth were about three times more likely to be bullied and harassed and four times as likely to be sexually harassed online than their non-LGBT counter-parts (Palmer et al. 2013). In addition to bullying, transgender individuals in online spaces must take care to be extra vigilant about managing their identities. For individuals looking to keep their transgender status con-fidential, the Internet's blurring of privacy and publicity causes unique challenges (Cavalcante 2016).

Conclusion

When I began my research and fieldwork for this book in 2008, the participants in my study noticed a slow but discernable rise in trans-gender representation in media. They felt something was changing, that they were on the verge of a new transgender visibility. Some in the news media referred to this as a "tipping point." But this historical moment did not simply emerge out of nowhere, as it rests on sociopolitical, cultural, and technological transformations: the expansion of the gender binary and of transgender communication networks; the political mobilization of gender variant people; the legitimacy of the category transgender; the legacy of the gay '90s; and the evolution of a digital, convergent, and interactive media environment.

This book is largely about what it was like to live as these historic processes churned, to grow up and come of age before the tipping point, before the new transgender visibility fully emerged. This was a moment of change where transgender discourses were bubbling beneath the sur-face and at times took center stage. The next chapter examines life under conditions where transgender imagery and discourse were widely scat-tered and scant. It explores the experience of living in a media environ-ment steeped in an ideology of transgender impossibility.

2

I Sort of Refused to Take Myself Seriously

Transgender Impossibilities and the Desire for Everydayness

"I started cross-dressing when I was 12 or 13 and I always pictured myself as a woman. Then later on I went to high school, went to college, fought the draft back during Vietnam, and met my wife, got married, had two kids, and was still cross-dressing the whole time behind my ex-wife's back." For most of her life, Lisa, a white, trans woman in her mid-60s from a working-class town in the American Midwest, hid her cross-dressing. She told me she delayed her gender transition until her early fifties because a transgender identity seemed completely out of reach. She recalled, "Being transgender? Impossible. You know it just seemed impossible."

As we sit together chatting in the conference room of a Midwestern LGBT community center, she pauses, gathers her thoughts, and then recalls how her family prevented her from considering the reality of a transgender identity. "In my teenage years, my cousin and I were brought up together like brothers, and my father would take us out downtown sometimes. We would go down to I think second or third street [of a Midwestern city] and there were a couple of bars down there, and he would talk about 'that's where the fairies go,' which were the drag queens of course. But back then, what did I know about drag queens and the transgender community? They were gay and they were fairies." Lisa hesitated for a moment, as if wondering whether to continue, and then confessed, "And I made fun of them. I'll admit it."

Accompanying these experiences was a media environment that taught Lisa that gender variance was a frivolous masquerade, anything but a viable expression of human subjectivity. "I can go all the way back to my childhood, Milton Berle . . . I grew up watching Milton Berle. You know about him and his drag queen character. Everyone used to joke around, a man in a dress type of thing, the ruby lipstick. You know there was nothing back in the '50s and early '60s other than that and the Tony Curtis and Jack Lemon movie *Some Like It Hot*. Other than that kind of stuff there was nothing in the media." Amid this information environment, Lisa kept her cross-gendered thoughts, feelings, and behaviors hidden.

However, when she was in her fifties, Lisa and her wife divorced. In part this was because of problems already present in their marriage, and in part because of Lisa's desire for gender transformation. Soon after the divorce, Lisa started attending meetings of a local cross-dressing organization and began seeing a therapist on a weekly basis. With these support structures in place, she experimented living full-time as a woman. Today, Lisa is a social worker who specializes in LGBTQ issues and has created her own transgender support group in her hometown. She is a tireless activist, who wants transgender youth to be exposed to better imagery than she was as a young person. Lisa has a message for those who wish to represent transgender people: "Show us as anybody else. Show us some respect!"

Throughout my fieldwork, the participants in my study echoed Lisa's sentiments and asserted that media representations made gender variance appear impossible and nonsensical. Kate, a trans college student in the Midwest, distinctly remembered the images she grew up watching and noted how they "all left a horrible memory and made me feel confused and weird about who I was. I sort of refused to take myself seriously. Then I spent a lot of time trying to actively repress these memories." Even though she tries to suppress it, the specter of these representations still lingers, for the ideology of impossibility they transmit is difficult to dismiss.

"Freakish," "sensational," "silly," "crazy," "tragic," and "monstrous." These were the words participants uttered to describe the images of transgender representation they encountered most of their lives. Research supports their critique. While there are some notable exceptions, transgender figures in media have historically been represented in terms of supreme Others: as outrageous freaks (Gamson 1999), duplicitous deceivers (Serano 2007), villainous monsters (Phillips 2006; Sullivan 2000), subservient mammy figures (Ryan 2009), fateful martyrs and victims (Halberstam 2005), and selfless, superhuman deities (Brookey and Westerfelhaus 2001).

This chapter explores the experience of encountering these kinds of representations and how participants make sense of the ideologies of transgender impossibility they convey. Although these ideologies express themselves in many ways, this chapter examines four of particular concern to those who shared their stories with me: (1) the delegitimization of transgender identity, (2) the dehumanization of transgender people, (3) the articulation of transgender experience within violence and a "tragic structure of feeling" (Ang 1985), and (4) the disregard for transgender everydayness.

Delegitimization: "They Don't Really Exist in the Realm of Non-jokes"

"Most of the portrayals up until about 5 or maybe 10 years ago, the trans person was comic relief," explained Anaya, a middle-aged trans woman. "We were the clown on stage." During our interview, the figure of the clown loomed large for Anaya. She referred to it several times as she discussed her encounters with media. In talking about clownish representations, she offered the example *To Wong Foo, Thanks for Everything! Julie Newmar* (1995), noting, "*To Wong Foo*, oh god, give me a break! Nice comedy, but has nothing to do with who we are." *To Wong Foo* is an upbeat, family-friendly comedy that stars three masculine actors—Patrick Swayze, John Leguizamo, and Wesley Snipes. In the film, they play professional drag queens (rather unconvincingly) who embark on a road trip. During the adventure, their car breaks down, leaving them stranded in the small, socially repressed rural town of Snydersville. As the film progresses, the trio eventually befriend the townspeople, spicing up the sleepy little town. They impart folk wisdom about female empowerment and stage an impromptu fashion show, changing lives, opening minds, and liberalizing attitudes along the way.

To Wong Foo is emblematic of a representational trope in which queer characters with "special powers" swoop into an isolated community in order to transform and save it from itself—what Brookey and Westerfelhaus (2001) call a "queer monomyth" (144). With little depth or ambition apart from helping others, the queer characters leave the town as quickly as they entered after completing their service.[1] For Anaya, the portrait of flamboyant, one-dimensional queens whose purpose was to help,

Figure 2.1. *To Wong Foo, Thanks for Everything! Julie Newmar* (1995). Patrick Swayze, John Leguizamo, and Wesley Snipes dressed in character in *To Wong Foo.* Credit: Universal/Photofest.

amuse, and perform for others drove the logic of the film's plot, and subsequently drove her crazy. Even more, she felt the actors' performance of drag was sloppy, for they seemed to be engaging in a frivolous aping of identity. Also picking up on this theme, Ethan, a trans man in his twenties, remarked, "My first instinct when I think about trans people, especially in film, is that they're often confused with drag queens. I see a lot of comic relief and a lot of parody. It's like trans folk and drag queens are synonymous sometimes. Basically, they are there to entertain you and dance around." Importantly, Ethan did not take issue with being associated with drag queens, as he is a big fan of drag. Rather, he objected to the ways in which media culture systematically reduces all varieties of trans subjectivity to staged performance, rendering it a sort of gendered minstrelsy.

At stake in these kinds of representations for participants like Maggie and Ethan is transgender legitimacy, or the ability to be taken seriously as a gender variant person. Legitimacy, broadly speaking, refers to having a "right to" something, to being justified in one's claims over power, authority, self-determination, even existence (Hurd 2015; Bensman 2014). Images of transgender delegitimization undercut these claims. Recalling the transgender media figures she witnessed growing up, Remi, a trans woman in her twenties, asserted, "They were a source of fun, to laugh at. A figure of fun to laugh at. And sort of improbable as well. I mean like they don't really exist, really! And if they do exist you just laugh at them. They don't really exist in the realm of non-jokes. So they only exist to be laughed at."

For Remi, transgender delegitimization was most evident in the daytime television talk shows she grew up watching in the late 1980s and early 1990s. These programs presented trans guests "as weirdos, sort of as carnival freaks." Singling out *The Jerry Springer Show* (1991–present), the epitome of the trash talk genre, Remi wondered, "Why would Jerry Springer, the audience, the TV show do that to trans people? And why would it continue? The fact that it continues and people find it entertaining . . . I would never do that to people. If I was in the audience, I would never do that to somebody." When I asked why she would never do that to someone, Remi explained, "I know how it feels. Well I guess I do have some biting sarcasm sometimes. But it's usually directed to people who are in power. I usually don't direct it at people who don't have power. I have a really clear sense of who's in power and who's not."

The reason Remi was so acutely attuned to transgender delegitimization in media was because she experienced it firsthand in her everyday life. This held true across the participants in my study. On the job market, they struggled to be recognized as serious candidates for employment. In healthcare, they struggled to be understood by medical professionals. In the social world, they struggled to be treated sincerely by their family, friends, and communities. This is why the figure of the transgender clown resonated so powerfully with Anaya as she commented, "I'm tired of being treated like a joke by people . . . I'm not a clown."

At the time I was conducting my fieldwork, one of the most frequently cited examples of trans delegitimization by participants was the coverage of Thomas Beatie—dubbed "the pregnant man" by news and entertainment media. In 2008, Beatie, a trans man, wrote an article for the *Advocate*, a popular LGBT magazine, discussing his decision to become pregnant and raise children with his partner. Titled "Labor of Love," the article was accompanied by an image of a shirtless, masculine-looking Beatie caressing his pregnant stomach. Overnight, the article became a media sensation, what one news organization called "an international furore [sic]" (Leonard 2008). Across the mediascape, news pundits fiercely debated (and often discredited) the ethics of Beatie's male pregnancy. "This story is very disturbing," remarked Wendy Williams on her daytime talk show. *Access Hollywood* began its segment on Beatie with "You gotta see it to believe it." And during a primetime interview with him, Barbara Walters referenced Beatie's picture in the *Advocate*, accusing, "You make a great many people very uneasy . . . Here is a man with facial hair, with a mustache, with scars under his breasts, pregnant! It is a disturbing picture, Thomas." By and large, media outlets framed the case at best as deeply suspect and, at worst, as a freak show.

The participants in my study critiqued the news coverage for abandoning an opportunity to explore trans issues in any serious way. As Jen, a trans woman in her mid-twenties from the Midwest, articulated, "A lot of the spectacle of it wasn't new for me. It couldn't offer me anything new. I was aware of the mechanics of the situation and it didn't surprise me or intrigue me. It seems embarrassing, not that it happened but that it became such a spectacle. It was a big dog and pony show." A few participants, however, noted one exception: Beatie's interview on *The Oprah Winfrey Show* ("The First TV Interview: The Pregnant Man" on April 3, 2008). As one participant commented about Beatie's performance, "He held his own." Although the episode is marked by "freak show" dynamics such as promotional segments that promise shocking revelations about surgeries and sexual practices, the show settled into a structure that foregrounded the ordinariness and legitimacy of Beatie and his wife, Nancy. Both are introduced to the audience in terms of normative class and kinship markers, as a happily married family who run a small business and live in a typical suburban neighborhood. Beatie argued, "Love makes a family . . . And that's all that matters," and explained his decision to get pregnant in humanist terms. "It's not a male or female desire to want to have a child . . . it's a human desire . . . I'm a person, and I have the right to have my own biological child." Nancy's daughter from a previous marriage, Amber, attested "we're just regular, boring people and a regular family." Moreover, the family's obstetrician confirmed the ordinariness of the pregnancy itself. "People say, 'Is this baby going to be abnormal or anything like that?' This baby's totally healthy . . . I consider it an average pregnancy."

Yet even as discourses of normalcy circulated during the show, Beatie made sure to queer his experience. When Oprah asked if he felt "born in the wrong body," he rejected the clichéd terminology and offered a more complicated view of embodiment. Beatie challenged the parameters of male identity, explaining that even though socially, legally, and emotionally he is "male," he also has reproductive organs. And when Oprah questioned it, Beatie confidently affirmed his maleness. "I have a very stable male gender identity. I see pregnancy as a process, and it doesn't define who I am . . . Ironically, being pregnant doesn't make me feel any more female or feminine."

Don, a Latino trans man in his early forties, agreed that the *Oprah* episode offered some nuance to Beatie's story and the issue of male pregnancy. However, as someone invested in politics and social justice, his concern was not with the content of the news coverage. Rather, he worried that media's coverage of "the pregnant man" outshined other, more pressing trans issues.

Right now there are so many big things going on that have to do with the trans community. You had the ENDA (Employment Non-discrimination Act) that was going on with the HRC (Human Rights Campaign), the Senate just held a meeting on employment discrimination, the AMA (American Medical Association) just released resolution 122 which is an extremely pro-trans piece of internal legislation, DSM 4 (Diagnostic and Statistical Manual of Mental Disorders) is in the process of being updated. So there is all this stuff happening now and is any of that showing up on television? NO. But pregnant trans man is in the media.

Punctuating his point, Don continued, "Who cares about transgender people needing employment when all we hear about is pregnant men?" In fact, according to Currah (2008a), during 2007–2008 while the media focused on the controversy surrounding the "pregnant man," the Democratic architects of the Employment Non-Discrimination Act removed gender identity from the bill, which received almost no attention in the mainstream press. Moreover, the American Medical Association's resolution 122, which advocated removing financial barriers to transgender care and argued that public and private health insurance should cover transgender-related treatment, was relatively invisible outside the LGBTQ press. As it often does, popular media overlooked the structural inequalities facing minorities and focused attention on personalized stories of struggle and perseverance (Dow 2001).

As we sat drinking coffee and continued to chat, Don also critiqued the ways media and other forms of institutional power such as government and law intersect to delegitimize transgender life. Of particular concern to him was the fight for transgender access to public restrooms, an issue that undoubtedly rages on today. Labeled "the bathroom bill" by local and statewide media, in 2009 the Massachusetts legislature held hearings on a bill that would amend the State's hate crime and non-discrimination laws to include gender identity and expression, granting legal protections to transgender citizens. Opponents of the bill, spearheaded by the Massachusetts Family Institute (MFI), a conservative Christian advocacy group, were successful in seizing control of public discourse and labeled the legislation "the bathroom bill." A radio ad financed by the group warned it would place children at risk to sexual predators: "Pretty soon, you won't want her to go into a bathroom by herself anymore.

Why? Didn't you know Beacon Hill is about to make it legal for men to use women's bathrooms?" (Keller 2009). In line with the MFI's framing, local media headlines followed suit and referred to the legislation as "the bathroom bill." For example, the *Boston Herald* announced "Critic: Flush Bathroom Bill" (Sweet 2009), and a CBS news Boston affiliate ran a story, "Ad Campaign Fights Transgender 'Bathroom Bill'" (Keller 2009). Even as some news media performed an educative function, discussing the particulars of the bill and its implications for civil rights, the bathroom bill language became the dominant frame for the story and headlines focused on bathroom-themed theatrics.[2] Reacting to this coverage, Don wondered about the implications of this discourse. "How can we get anyone to take our issues seriously when they think we are 'men' using the 'women's' room? . . . If we're not taken seriously in media, then who's gonna take us seriously outside of media? That's where most people's understanding about transgender people comes from."

"There's Even a Drinking Game for It"

While the participants in my study clearly took the issue of transgender delegitimization seriously, many also responded in more lighthearted and irreverent ways. "These things seem to follow a formula," Erin boasted, "there's even a drinking game for it." Erin, a trans woman in her late thirties, was referring to what is colloquially called "the transgender documentary drinking game." The drinking game is a playful critique of the predictable ways nonfiction media represent transgender people. According to the rules, viewers take a drink each time a documentary employs a trans stereotype or representational trope.

I met Erin at a public showing of the transgender-themed documentary *She Was a Boy I Knew* (2007), organized by a community college in the Midwest. Film screenings were helpful research sites because they allowed me to observe conversations about media and technology in organic social settings. They also introduced me to potential interviewees and research participants like Erin, who attended the screening because she heard the film "was not one of those typical transgender documentaries."

She Was a Boy I Knew is an independent documentary that chronicles the gender transition of its filmmaker, Gwen Haworth, over several years.

Weaving together home video footage, interviews with friends and family, phone messages, and original animation, Haworth's auto-ethnography is honest, filled with raw emotion and incisive political critique. Sitting in the audience that night, it was clear the film resonated with viewers. Erin loved the film. "You couldn't really play the drinking game with this one . . . What was really cool about it was that a trans woman made the film. So her voice comes through the film; not just through her voice, but through her editorial choices. You can see what's important to a trans person isn't necessarily important to a news journalist who's trying to create some ratings or buzz. The other really cool thing about that was she had very little screen presence and her story was told through the eyes of her family. There was not a sensational part of it."

Erin's appreciation for the film was fueled by how it departed from a lineage of previous transgender documentaries that employ predictable narrative, editorial, and aesthetic choices—so often repeated that they lend themselves to a drinking game. When I told Erin that I had never heard of the game, she was shocked. "I can't believe you've never heard of the drinking game! So, it's like every time they show a side-by-side picture of someone before and after their transition, take a drink. Every time they show a rear angle, soft focus view of her looking in the mirror, take a drink." Although there is no single author of the game, many point to Gwendolyn Ann Smith's (2015) version as a standard. It reads in part,

> Take one drink: if a trans woman is shown putting on makeup or fixing her hair, or if a trans man is shown shaving or slicking back his hair . . . [or if] a trans woman is shown doing a stereotypically feminine action like shopping in the mall . . .
>
> Take two drinks: if no trans men are shown [or if] the transgender people presented are predominantly Caucasian, and predominantly middle or upper class . . .
>
> Finish the bottle: if the only thing you can find on that has to do with being transgender happens to be *The Jerry Springer Show*. Just don't waste anything expensive in the process.[3]

According to Erin, the game also works well for television specials and news reports that cover transgender people. Created from within the community, the Transgender Drinking Game is a whimsical reaction to and a negotiated reading of media texts that purport to take transgender topics seriously as legitimate subject matter, yet rely on a cliché and narrative formula. The formula fixates on transgender individuals performing their gender, putting it on as they gaze into the mirror and display it like a costume. It also highlights their adherence to gender norms—transgender women performing conventional femininity and transgender men performing conventional masculinity—and privileges those who are white and middle class. Even as these kinds of media attempt to legitimate transgender identity by depicting "real" people in everyday life, they have blind spots that delegitimize transgender subjectivities outside the drinking game's script.

Dehumanization: "Who Will Ever Love You?"

"All norms are not thrown out the window with trans people. We're people. We're not fucking monsters," said Lara, a trans woman in her late twenties from a small Midwestern town. Commenting on the representation of transgender individuals in popular media, she continued, "The character from *Silence of the Lambs* who wears women's skins or even *Psycho* . . . these movies make us seem like we're crazy . . . like we're monsters . . . like we're majorly fucked up . . . I mean they're (the characters in these movies) not *really* trans but the connection is still there." The two films that Lara mentioned, *Silence of the Lambs* (1991) and *Psycho* (1960), are dark, psychological thrillers that feature violent characters who bend gender. While the films are not about transgender people per se, as Lara mentioned, they nevertheless associate gender variance with psychosis. Many participants in my study echoed Lara's critique, arguing that media systematically represent gender-nonconforming characters as dehumanized and deranged figures, as endemically tainted.

This representational paradigm has historic roots.[4] It mirrors the ways transgender identities have been pathologized by medical authorities and psychiatric institutions. As Ekins and King (1996) argue, "medicine has become the culturally major lens through which gender blending is viewed in modern Western societies" (119). Throughout most of the twentieth century, gender variance was understood through a model of mental illness and degeneracy. The mind was not quite sane.

The body was not quite healthy. Those who wanted medical services such as hormones or surgical procedures often had to self-identify as sick or diseased in order to receive treatment. They had to narrate stories of internal anguish and suffering to appear sympathetic and worthy of medical intervention, which would "fix" their condition.

According to Sullivan (2000), the link between gender variance and pathology in popular culture culminated in the late 1950s with the now infamous case of Ed Gein. Gein, a native of rural Wisconsin, murdered two women and, according to those working the case, robbed local grave-yards to collect human body parts. While Gein never laid claim to a trans identity, popular press accounts classified him as a deranged transvestite who wanted to become a woman, and who planned to use the human body parts he stole to construct a female form (ibid.). The case's shadowy mythology served as the inspiration for Bloch's 1958 novel *Psycho*, Hitch-cock's classic film by the same name, and the movie *The Silence of the Lambs* (Sullivan 2000). These texts belong to a corpus of popular films, a "psycho-trans" genre (Phillips 2006), where gender variance is "associ-ated directly with castration, madness, murder, and monstrosity" (85). Following in this tradition, films such as *Homicidal* (1961), *Dressed to Kill* (1980), and *Cherry Falls* (2000) depict cross-dressing and transgender behavior as symptomatic of an underlying pathology. In them, transgen-der characters are less than fully human and stand as symbolic vessels into which our culture's fears and anxieties are filled.

Other minority groups have been cast in a similar light, such as the homosexual predator that lurked in mid-century media (Meeker 2006) or the hypersexualized and violent black buck of the post–Reconstruction Era that appeared in twentieth-century Hollywood film (Bogle 2001). These characters threatened white, heterosexual order and stability. Indeed, transgender figures pose the same danger, but an amplified one by virtue of gender being so intimately connected to the category of human. As gender theorist Judith Butler (1988) reminds us, the acquisition of fully human status requires fidelity to the female/male binary, as "discrete genders are part of what 'humanizes' individuals within contemporary culture" (522).[5] To be a human is to have a clearly legible male or female identity. Allegiance to this binary system grants individuals the rights of personhood. For example, fetuses in the womb become more fully human once a gender is assigned to them. One of the first questions pregnant women get asked is whether their child is a boy or a girl. The pronouncement "It's a boy" or "It's a girl" transforms the baby from abstract idea (an "it") into a distinct person (a "he" or "she"). To transgress this gender binary threatens one's status as ordinary, as human. As Lara said, "Once people find out you're trans, all of a sudden everything changes. You're not a person anymore . . . they either treat you like a crazy person or as some kind of sub-human freak."

It is exactly because trans people face the threat of abjection in their everyday lives that images of dehumanization resonated so strongly with the participants in my study.[6] Over and over again, they discussed how these kinds of representations—coupled with the absolute paucity of humanized transgender imagery—made it harder for them to secure the rights and pleasures of ordinary personhood. One of the pleasures of personhood they most deeply desired was human love and intimacy. In media representation and the visual culture of everyday life, expressions of physical affection, sexuality, and tenderness by or toward transgender people are virtually invisible. Brandon, a trans man in his twenties, explained how this imagistic lack corresponded with his lived experiences.

> When I came out as trans, my brother was like "who will ever love you?" My answer to that is: Your assumption that no one will ever love me or find me attractive reflects your own fear and anxiety about gender variance. That is what I see played out in *Ugly Betty*, and other media as well. There was this one episode where someone was trying to get her [Alexis, the trans character in the show] out of power because of the magazine. They paid somebody to romance her and take her away to Brazil because they didn't want her to interfere. Of course, they had to pay someone! There was another scene where she is shooting hoops in this bar, she is high femme and really gorgeous, with this dude who is clearly coming on to her and flirting with her. Then of course she is like "Oh my god. I think he likes me." The climax of the scene is when he gives her his number and then is like "No way would I ever hang out with you. I know what you are."

Blatantly denied or having to be purchased, love is seemingly inaccessible for the trans character in this scenario. For Brandon, this logic spills from the television screen and colors his brother's understanding. The question of love was also on the mind of Rayanne, a transgender woman in her late thirties from the Midwest. She understood media representation as a crucial variable in legitimizing transgender affection. "What we need is positive reinforcement [in the media] because until it's ok to love trans people we will always have transphobia and violence against trans people. We have to make it okay to love trans people."

Along with love, the participants in my study also discussed the ways transgender sexuality was generally absent from media culture, apart from the narrow confines of prostitution. As sex workers and street-walkers, transgender people are routinely portrayed as fixtures of an urban landscape, unruly representatives of a city's nighttime underground. Commenting on this representational trope, one participant pointed to an episode of *Sex and the City*, a show based in New York City. In the episode "Cock a Doodle Doo" (10/15/2000), the character Samantha feuds with a trio of transgender prostitutes who are keeping her awake at night. In the opening scene, as Samantha attempts to fall asleep, the prostitutes loudly conduct their business in her trendy downtown neighborhood, within earshot of her apartment window. Noticeably frustrated, Samantha throws open her window to catch a look and the show's narrator explains, "There they were: Samantha's friendly neighborhood pre-op transsexual hookers. Half man, half woman, totally annoying."

Although securing above-ground employment is one of the greatest challenges facing transgender people, and some are forced to participate in the underground economy to survive, what bothered participants was the systematic union of transgender identity and sex work in media culture.[7] This coupling has become somewhat of an industry convention according to Calpernia Addams, a transsexual actress and Hollywood insider who runs a video production company. She maintains, "in Hollywood, it's like the two words go together, transsexual and prostitute . . . They don't even question it" (Garvin 2003).

Outside of Hollywood's fictional narratives, news media display similar representational trends. News reports about transgender people resonated powerfully with participants because they were anchored in the real world. Brandon, a trans man in his twenties who lives in San Francisco, noted, "The [news] media says trans women are supposed to be sex workers, and have HIV, and live in SROs (Single Room Occupancies) in a tough part of town. That is the niche trans women are allowed to occupy. You're poor. You're a woman of color. You do sex work. You're on the streets, addicted to drugs. That's what people expect to see, or what they think. It is that image." Jen, a trans woman in her twenties living in the suburbs of a Midwestern city, witnessed the same in her local news: "I recently have been looking at newspapers more. Lately there have been a lot of things going around where there have been sex workers who are transgender getting killed and they totally use their male name and place a big emphasis on the 'sex worker' title. They don't really say anything good about the person except that they're trans, they're a sex worker and they got shot. So, that's the image. If you're trans, you're going to be a sex worker and you're going to get shot." These kinds of stories have compelled Jen to confront her own mortality. "Luckily in my case I have half my family backing me, so if something did happen to me I will be remembered the right way. I made them promise me they would present me as a girl. But imagine if you haven't spoken to your parents in 20 years and you're a female now and at your funeral they dress you up in a suit and put you in a casket."

For a twenty-one-year-old, Jen's thoughts about death are almost too well developed. Even as the threat of violence is real for her, she is never allowed to forget it. When she turns on the television, it stares back at her. To be clear, Jen and Brandon do not oppose media representations of transgender poverty and sex work because they are implausible or fictitious. Rather, they take issue with the repeated stories of transgender dehumanization, economic hardship, and prostitution because these frames quarantine transgender possibilities and prevent alternative narratives from being told.

Tragedy: "You Never Really Hear About Trans People Until They're Dead"

"I think *CSI*, the original *CSI*, has had three or four episodes that featured transsexuals, and almost all of them victims, and in one case, a murderer," explained Rayanne, a trans woman from the Midwest in her thirties and a big fan of television crime procedurals. Her favorite shows are *Law & Order* and *Law & Order: SVU*. But even as she is a fan of the genre, she pushes against the ways it almost exclusively frames transgender characters as victims of violent crime. During our interview, she discussed an episode of *Law & Order: SVU* titled "Transitions" (2/17/ 2010). The episode revolves around a 13-year-old transgender youth named Hailey (born Henry). Hailey's father, Mark, is having a hard time accepting her transgender status. As the episode unfolds, Mark is almost beaten to death by an unknown perpetrator. Hailey becomes a prime suspect, and in a state of crisis, she slits her wrists attempting suicide, but survives. In the episode's concluding trial scene, the audience finally learns that the individual who violently assaulted Mark was Jackie, Hailey's guidance counselor at school. On the stand, Jackie reveals that she took an active interest in the teen's well-being because she too is a trans woman and has been brutally victimized her entire life. To protect Hailey against his intolerance, Jackie attacked Hailey's father, Mark.

The episode epitomizes what Ang (1985) calls a "tragic structure of feeling," an affective atmosphere overwhelmed by tragedy, unavoidable pain, and suffering. Both trans characters in the *Law & Order: SVU* episode exist in such a structure. Hailey is victimized and attempts suicide, and her guidance counselor Jackie was a lifelong victim of violence who ultimately became a perpetrator of it. The omnipresence of violence and tragedy in transgender representation was a flashpoint in my research, one of the greatest concerns for the participants in my study. As one participant described, "All the time I see this. The trans person is trying so hard to fit in, trying so hard to work in society, and society doesn't accept them and they are killed off right before credits roll." For Carrie, a trans woman from the Midwest in her early thirties, tragic structures of feeling saturated the media landscape but were particularly present in the plastic surgery–themed cable drama *Nip/Tuck* (2003–2010). "*Nip/Tuck* really pissed me off. I watched an episode about transgender individuals. It was the episode where the kid of one of the surgeons found out his girlfriend was transgendered [*sic*], and could not handle it. He went and picked up another trans person at a bar and beat the shit out of her, and abused her. The very end of it, when the son was seen by the trans person's friends, she pointed him out to them, and they jumped on him, beat him up, and pissed on him. I think it just portrayed hostility upon hostility and gave the impression that revenge is out there to be had."

Trans identity is so often co-constructed with violence that some participants expressed concern that the two are inevitable. In talking about "the typical transgender plot line," Julie explained, "Very often we are killed at the end. That really irritates me. I think it gets people to al-most expect it, to almost expect if you're trans you will die for it." Like-wise, Wren contended, "There's also a problem in that especially in the news, you never really hear about trans people until they're dead. The trans people you know are the ones who have died. There's always this constant threat of violence and it's somehow dangerous to be this type of person." Some portrayals imply that the violence is deserved, a con-sequence for gender "deception" or for failing to pass completely as man or woman.[8] Citing Julia Serano's (2007) discussion of the trans-gender deceiver trope in her book *Whipping Girl*, Kate commented, "This writer I like talks about the two archetypes of trans people in the media: the 'pathetic' and the 'deceiver,' separated by those who can pass and those who can't pass. I really do see that a lot. If they can't pass they are some horrible freak, but if they can pass they are seen as some awful person who is tricking innocent straight guys into being gay, like they deserve what crap comes their way. There is a lot of victim blaming like 'She shouldn't have pretended to be a woman.'"

Transgender figures are not the only ones historically cast in narra-tives of deception, for deception has been a recurrent theme in films about social identity. The 1986 movie *Soul Man*, dealing with themes of racial crossing, is perhaps one of the most egregious examples. In the film, a white college student, Mark, pretends to be black in order to earn a scholarship at Harvard Law School. His scheme is success-ful. When his real identity is revealed, Mark faces shock and scorn, and gets punched in the stomach. Nevertheless, cushioned by his whiteness, gender normativity, and class privilege, his interpersonal relationships remain intact and he is allowed to continue attending college. At worst, his deception ultimately causes a ripple in his life. Yet what sets trans-gender narratives apart from other stories of social "deception" are the violent and even deadly consequences faced by those who attempt to pass. Indeed, the ripple becomes an earthquake, as violence and cruelty become the only response.

Crucially, I am not arguing—and participants are not suggesting—that transgender lives are not threatened by violence. Just as participants were aware of the socioeconomic difficulties faced by many in the transgender community, but desired representations that moved beyond these dif-ficulties, their aversion to the media's focus on violence perpetrated by and against transgender people is not because such violence fails to exist, but rather because it is frequently the only narrative being told. Many of the people I met in my fieldwork were survivors of assault and aggression. For example, Linda, a middle-aged working-class trans woman from a small farming community in the Midwest, recalled two searing, traumatic experiences. The first involved the day her father caught her cross-dressing as a young teen. "I more or less got thrown against a closet. I was probably thirteen then. He basically told me to straighten up, act like him and my brothers or he was going to take me out of this world." The second violent encounter involved a man she met online as a young adult. "I've actually had one guy try to beat me up and rape me. I wasn't paying attention. I was too complacent with where I was and what I was doing . . . I managed to get my purse and my pepper spray. He took off, and I never heard from him again."

Noticeable is the way Linda implicates herself in the assault, faulting her lack of attention and complacency for its occurrence, rather than the vicious aggression of her attacker. It is as if she has internalized the tragic structure of feeling, accepting it as her own burden to manage. As Meyer (2015) has shown, this is often the case for working-class LGBTQ people, as economic status plays a role in the extent to which people understand violence as severe or ordinary. Living under challenging structural conditions such as poverty, high unemployment, and over-policing, low-income LGBT people are more likely to downplay violence than their upper- and middle-class counterparts, perceiving it as part and parcel of queer everyday life (ibid.).

This is not to say low-income LGBT people accept or embrace violence. Despite the traumatic episodes she lived through, Linda emphatically stressed that her life is absolutely not defined by tragedy and victimhood. She is a survivor who arms herself and is always vigilant of her surroundings. "I've learned to watch my back, especially after dark. When I walk outside at night I always have my pepper spray in my hand ready to use. You never know. You just kind of watch shadows, see if anyone is coming up behind you." At the same time, she is also unwilling to overlook the kindness she has received from strangers. Since coming out as a trans woman five years ago, she explained, "I just experience more openness, more acceptance than I thought. I live everyday like this [as a transgender woman]."

As with Linda, even as participants acknowledged the prevalence of transphobic violence, they too resisted defining the transgender experience through tragedy. Sebastian contended, "I think there is a great amount of violence that happens to trans people either physically or emotionally in our lives, as there is for a lot of people, but I don't know that it is the defining . . . it doesn't define the trans community as some people think it does." Similarly, Don noted, "The one mainstream movie that had a trans guy in it was *Boys Don't Cry*. Of course he's like raped and murdered, which was factual, but maybe one of these days they'll show something else too." According to Don, transgender-themed films based on real events like *Boys Don't Cry* (1999), *Soldier's Girl* (2003), and *The Gwen Araujo Story* (2006) warrant telling, and importantly, depict their transgender protagonists in sympathetic and considerate ways. Nevertheless, these stories are reliant on a tragic structure of feeling and are at risk of becoming wholly representative of the transgender experience, at the expense of others.

It is important to note that some participants embraced associations of transgender with violence in popular culture. Vera, a gender-nonconforming, queer artist and nightclub performer living in San Francisco, admitted, "I really like the idea of queers as dangerous people." Vera is actively involved in the San Francisco drag scene and prefers a style of drag that is intended to "shock and awe" audiences. She finds herself naturally gravitating toward the excessive, flamboyant, and confrontational, what she termed "the outrageous version of queerdom." For Vera, transgender depictions that hinge on violence and danger are exciting. However, she underscored that this is only so when the transgender figure perpetrates the violence. As we sit chatting in a San Francisco café, she referenced John Waters's early work. In particular, she praised the drag queen Divine, delighting in her aggression and colorful repugnance in the film *Pink Flamingos* (1972). As one of her favorite images of all time, the iconic movie poster is framed in her apartment. It depicts Divine in a tight red dress scowling and standing confidently, holding a handgun pointed at a target outside the frame. According to Vera, characters like Divine celebrate power and dominance. They highlight the social defiance and nervy anti-normative sensibilities of queer and trans subcultures. Summarizing her thoughts regarding the "outrageous version of queerdom," she noted, "Do I think politically it was good for us moving forward? No. Culturally, politically and so forth maybe I was more enlightened later when I got to experience firsthand homophobia and transphobia and all of the bad stuff that comes along with those kinds of representations. But artistically, creatively, I think it was fabulous. I am still attracted to a great tranny [sic] killer. I don't think everything should be, at the end of the day, family friendly." Unlike other participants, Vera is less concerned about media as a reflection of daily life. For her, media is about thrill, fantasy, and escapism, different yet equally worthy functions.

"That Stage of Unlearning"

"You have to do a lot of unlearning if you're trans," remarked Andy, a twenty-something trans man currently living in San Francisco. In dealing with media environments that traffic in transgender delegitimization, dehumanization, and tragic structures of feeling, Andy and many other participants in my study engaged in a process of "unlearning." This is an epistemological strategy of shedding the ideologies, schemas, and frames imparted by media and popular culture, which have been adopted in whole or in part. For Andy, surviving and thriving in the world meant unlearning the ideology of transgender impossibility.

Growing up in the late 1980s and early 1990s in rural California, Andy's first encounter with transgender subjectivity was in the media. "My first exposure was definitely media. The movies. It is for a lot of people! I think it is geographical. Depending on where you grew up, media is going to be your outlet. Media is how people start to absorb the world and what the world consists of. It is not always accurate." Recalling the transgender characters that he saw in the media, Andy remembered, "[they] were mentally unstable and villainized. Even if the characters themselves weren't characterized as mentally unstable, somebody else was, and they became the victim of that. And those frames stayed with me for a very long time." These frames conceptualized gender variance as precarious and pathological, associating transgender people with instability, deviance, and victimization. Andy continued, "What it did, is that years later it required me to do much more unlearning. I think it actually had a pretty direct impact in my own journey, in my own realization, in my own willingness to answer myself honestly. And I think that's true for a lot of queer people."

For Andy, unlearning from the media was an essential step in his self-development. But this merely represented "the first door." Andy explained, "Trans people I think sometimes have to go through that stage of unlearning twice because the gay and lesbian community isn't as accepting and doesn't embrace trans people the way the mission statements of the gay community say they do. They don't." In this second stage of unlearning, Andy had to shed the "second-class citizenship" status he felt as a transgender-identifying person in gay and lesbian communities. When he began to identify as transgender in his later teenage years, Andy frequented gay clubs and joined LGBT organizations, expecting open arms. Unfortunately, these spaces regularly perpetuated social hierarchies that placed transgender people at the bottom. Andy remembered, "I just had to forget about the gay scene for a while."

After forgetting about the gay scene, Andy's process of unlearning involved a third and final stage. Whereas the first two stages of unlearning were directed toward the self, the third involved facilitating the process for others. Andy's immediate family and social network also learned about transgender identity from media, adopting a limited understanding of gender variance. In order for them to understand his gender transition, they too had to engage in unlearning and shed their thick shell of misconception. Andy explained, "[Media] also doesn't just affect the individual going through it [gender transition]. It affects their families, it affects their friends, and if you're growing up in a household that's exposed to the same images your parents and siblings are, you all have the same association. So, you've done the work to unlearn that, and now you have to help this group of people unlearn that as well." Summing up, Andy described the ultimate goal of the unlearning he and his family went through. "So it's about being seen as a 'real' human . . . as an ordinary person . . . That's what I find to happen a lot with trans people in the media; the humanization aspect of it isn't the same as it is for other people."

For Andy, achieving "real human" or "ordinary person" status was about changing his own mind, and the minds of those around him, inviting them to practice unlearning with him. This process takes time because unlearning does not happen all at once. It requires persistent intellectual and emotional labor to relax the grip of the ideology of transgender impossibility, which is firm. While removing it completely may not be possible—for ideology does have a way of inhabiting us—over time its hold can be loosened.

"I Want to See People Who Just Happen to Be Trans"

The participants in my study were acutely attuned to the delegitimization of transgender identity, the dehumanization of transgender people, and the articulation of transgender experience within a tragic structure of feeling because these dynamics frequently appeared in media. However, this was not the only reason. They were also sensitized to these representational trends because their lived experiences heightened their awareness of them. Legitimacy, personhood, and safety—fundamental components of everydayness—are all at stake in living a transgender life. Before, during, and after transition, they can become slippery and out of reach.

Everydayness is, according to Lefebvre (1987), the connective tissue that links disparate domains of the lived world. One of the first to deconstruct the concept, he argued that everydayness was "a common denominator of activities, locus and milieu of human functions," as well as a "uniform aspect of the major sectors of social life: work, family, private life, leisure" (Lefebvre 1987, 10). It is a routine of the familiar "known in common with others and with others taken for granted" (Garfinkel 1964, 225). As commonality, taken-for-grantedness, uniformity, and order, everydayness is fundamentally at stake for the participants in my study because they occupy a stigmatized, marginalized, and precarious subject position. As a result, the everyday emerged as a potent object of desire throughout my fieldwork. It conducted a powerful electric charge and carried an almost magnetic attraction.

According to Lauren Berlant (2010), objects of desire present a "cluster of promises we want someone or something to make to us and make possible for us" (93). The closer we come to the object, the closer we feel to its promises. This sense of promise accounts for its magnetism and for our faith in the object. Upon first glance, everydayness may appear to be unworthy of such profound desire. Most work in queer and cultural scholarship examines desire in terms of sexuality, embodiment, and pleasure, paying special attention to those unexpected and non-normative vectors. Yet, desire appreciates what Sedgwick (2003) calls "the freedom of affects" (19), meaning it can openly wander and attach itself (at least potentially) to any object or idea, even something as seemingly mundane as the everyday.

One of the most frequently communicated sentiments in my study was a desire to see transgender ordinariness and everydayness represented in media. As one participant said, "I just want to see, you know, trans people living their everyday lives." This kind of portrayal is both simple and profound. While it appears matter-of-fact, transgender everydayness nevertheless counters the ideologies of impossibility—delegitimization, dehumanization, and violence—so frequently portrayed in media and reveals trans life to be attainable.

Throughout contemporary media history, other minority groups have similarly struggled against ideologies of impossibility. They too have expressed a desire for media portrayals of everydayness. One of the biggest draws of *The Cosby Show* (1984–1992) for African American viewers was exactly its representation of black, domestic everydayness within the context of an affluent nuclear family (the Huxtables)—something that was absent from the media landscape at the time. Although the show was often criticized for being blindly unrealistic, overlooking racial injustice and systemic discrimination, many black viewers appreciated it for being aspirational in its mundaneness. As Inniss and Feagin (2002) note in their study of black audiences' responses to the show, for viewers desiring representations of black life outside negatively codified stereotypes, the Huxtables were role models presented in "a true family setting"; as one participant maintained, "they deal with down to earth issues" (198). Gay audiences have similarly yearned for media to recognize "the existence of normal, unexceptional 'plain gay folks'" (Gross 1998, 92). In his study of Israeli gay men, Kama (2002) noted, "the principal concept that constituted a common denominator among all interviewees was the desire to portray gays as "normal" (200). For the gay men in his study, a "normal" gay man was similar to his heterosexual counterparts, "situated at the heart of consensual society" (200), a part of (but not apart from) the everyday world.

Within my areas of concentration, mainly media and LGBTQ studies, this desire for and attachment to the ordinary and the everyday is overwhelmingly overlooked or dismissed as "normative." Its politics rubs against a radically progressive sensibility that locates sameness and orderliness within a hermeneutics of suspicion . . . and for good reason. Throughout modern Western history, notions of the normal and the ordinary have been used to discipline, shame, and punish LGBTQ people (Foucault 1990). Discourses of normality have been marshaled to justify violence and systemic disenfranchisement. The queer critique of the normal questions its authority, challenges the hierarchies it erects, and exposes the ways it disempowers minorities. But the challenge of studying "real" people in the "real" world is to take their thoughts and experiences seriously, even when they may not seem politically expedient. The reward is a nuanced understanding of how individuals operate in everyday life and the opportunity to square that with academic theorizing.

As I began my fieldwork, I was not expecting to address issues of the everyday and the ordinary. But they were an unavoidable presence, particularly when the participants talked about media culture. Throughout our interview, Margie repeatedly expressed a desire for transgender everydayness. "I want to see professional people who function in everyday life . . . warm and caring people, family people . . . the women who come to this group, one is the lead attorney for the county circuit court . . . the person who works on the [assembly] line at Ford." Similarly, Julie commented, "I want to see normal people who are . . . I don't care if it's factory workers, social workers, lawyers, psychologists, who happen to be trans. That's what I think we need. That's what people need to see. They need to see we are normal people doing normal things."

Margie's and Julie's desires for everydayness are expressed as a wish to see in media the familiar figures that populate their everyday world. Both participants live in Midwestern towns that are largely reliant on the automotive industries. The character types these two participants enumerate (automotive workers, assembly line laborers, factory employees, etc.) reflect their geographic and economic location. Most importantly, the figures they mention exhibit transgender possibility. They harbor the capacity for self-authorship and freedom. They have good jobs. They are leaders in the community and have families. They have positive personality attributes. They defy the ideology of impossibility and, as Margie declared, "function in everyday life."

In articulating everydayness, Julie also employed the word "normal" to describe the transgender individuals she wants to see represented in media. Although it was not too common, the word (a loaded word indeed) did show up in my fieldwork. Importantly, the true meaning of "normal" can only be fully understood within the context of its usage. Consider Julie's remarks. In employing the word, she adopted both inward- and outward-looking perspectives. Toward the beginning of our conversation, Julie is inward looking, employing the first person ("I want to see"). But as she continues, there is a shift in voice to the second person ("we need"), and she concludes her remarks by looking outward, employing the third person ("They need to see").

Within the context of its usage here, "normal" is deeply polysemic and malleable. As Julie's voice and perspective change, so do the implications of the word. When she first employs the word, she expresses a personal preference. *She* wants to see people who are normal *to her*, familiar to her, who exist in her world, and who align with her sense of everydayness. The second time she uses "normal" is during an outward-looking moment, when she reflects on what *others* need to see. This is not necessarily *her* normal. Her normal is far more capacious and expansive. In this way, normal has moved from a context of "I want" to one of "they need." In media studies, this concern regarding other people's encounters with media, people who are seen as less discriminating and knowledgeable than one's self, is called the "third person effect" (Perloff 1993). In the context of the third person, "normal" takes on a slightly different meaning. It reflects a normative impulse to accommodate and assuage an outsider's gaze. The outsider is assumed to be unfamiliar with transgender life and therefore needs to be exposed to a certain more palatable kind of normal—one that is different from the kind that Julie, by virtue of being transgender, can appreciate. Julie underscores this idea later in our conversation. "I know transgender people. They don't. What I want to see is probably not the same thing as what they need to see. They need to be broken in." What unfamiliar audiences need to see, according to Julie, are trans individuals situated in conventional, safe contexts. These portrayals "break in" audiences and soften their potential resistance to trans people.

Julie's comments also reveal another common device that participants used when expressing their desire for everydayness: the phrase "happens to be transgender." This phrase surfaced over and again in interviews and during my observational work. Like the word "normal," the phrase "happens to be *X*" is contentious and politically fraught. Steeped in normative connotations, the phrase has emerged before, for example, with respect to race (someone who "happens to be black") and sexuality (someone who "happens to be gay"). Typically, the phrase operates to downplay difference, to soften its edges, and mitigate its potential threats. With respect to sexuality, for example, scholars argue that the spirit of the refrain reflects a neoliberal politics, one that renders "gays harmless and innocuous, similar to straights and denuded of politics, sexuality, difference" (Walters 2001, 296; see also Warner 1999; Halperin 2012; Duggan 2003). Indeed, I too have argued that media representations of characters who "happen to be gay" reflect an impulse to universalize a text, to create distance from queerness, to declaw it, and to make it agreeable to heterosexual audiences (Cavalcante 2015).

But the question remains: How do we make sense of participants who themselves desired characters who "happen to be" transgender? Are they merely expressing a longing for assimilation or trans normativity? On the one hand, these sentiments may be at play. However, on the other, they fail to fully account for the spectrum of participants' meaning making. I want to resist conceptualizing their thoughts as false consciousness, to move beyond this well-theorized domain and open up new conceptual territory. Consider Andy's thoughts about what he wants to see depicted in media. During our interview, he happily posed the following scenario: "Get a head doctor on one of these emergency room shows who happens to be transgendered [*sic*]. And maybe every fifteenth episode you hear about it. When you do hear about it, it's in a way that's comical. Like if there is an ER doctor and they're helping some adolescent patient who is complaining about her period, you can say something like 'Good thing I don't have that anymore.' In some way, it can be a running joke that everyone laughs at. So, it's funny, but the character is also supported."

Crucially, the ideal character that Andy describes who "happens to be transgender" directly counters the three themes of transgender impossibility discussed in this chapter. Bypassing the tragic structure of feeling, Andy's trans representation is articulated with levity, in a "comical" tone. Rather than work to delegitimize the character's transgender identity, the portrayal affirms it. The character is open about his transgender identity and "supported" by his colleagues. Instead of perpetrating or being victimized by violence, Andy's transgender character, as a medical doctor or surgeon, represents life and hope. He works to rectify the tragic outcomes of violence. Given the risk of violence that transgender people face, "happening to be" is an aspirational state of being that reduces the potential for being marked and targeted for assault. Finally, in Andy's vision, the doctor's transgender identity, his difference, is not erased. It is apparent and commented on by other characters in the show. In fact, transgender identity is boldly asserted through Andy's joke regarding the doctor's absent period.

As with Andy, when I asked Alex and Ethan, trans men in their twenties, about transgender representation in media, they too used the phrase "happens to be trans." Alex offered, "I want to see people who are not professionally trans," remarking, "I want to see people who just happen to be trans and do a million other things with their life. It obviously is a big thing, but it would be nice if the focus of the storyline or interview isn't transness. I think that would be huge!" In the same way, Ethan maintained, "I don't really see representations of 'here's somebody who happens to be trans and is going through life.' It's held at the forefront and you're never really given an opportunity to forget about it. At all, and to be able to be like, 'oh yeah, that's right. There is this other part that exists.' All of these things exist through the lens of transgender."

In their comments, the phrase "happens to be trans" is contrasted with the idea of being "professionally trans" and with trans being "held at the forefront." This reduction of a character to their transgender identity is understood as limiting, as a state of being that undermines potentiality. By contrast, "happening to be" is about the promise of opportunity and possibility. It is about widening the lens and adding layers to transgender life. It is highly significant that both Alex and Ethan follow the phrase "happens to be trans" with the conjunction "and." This happened throughout my fieldwork, for when participants uttered the phrase "happens to be trans," it was almost always followed by "and." For example, Alex wants to see characters that happen to be transgender *and* "do a million other things with their life." "And" is the complexity that defines transgender life. In this way, "happening to be" is not a purgatory of mediocrity within which participants are trapped. Rather, in routinely being followed by the word "and," "happening to be" holds the promise (and perhaps also the threat) of something more. Indeed, a world where transgender people are allowed to "happen to be" is far different from and perhaps more queerly expansive than the one we inhabit today. It is a place where transgender and gender-nonconforming people can easily and comfortably travel, living within and pushing against the norms of everyday life without the threat of aggression, harassment, and erasure.

"Happening to be" and the desire for everydayness are launching pads for transcendence. They are meaningful and grand. They are aspirational, signaling the prospects of transgender self-authorship, agency, and possibility. "Happening to be" and everydayness are what cultural theorists Seigworth and Gregg (2010) call a "bloom space," or "the ongoingness of process . . . as threshold or conversion point, as imminence of potential (futurity), as a vibrant incoherence that circulates about zones of cliché and convention, as a gathering place of accumulative dispositions" (9). As a bloom space, everydayness and "happening to be" are points of convergence that hold the promise and possibility to be more, to do more, to achieve more. This promise may be, in the words of Lauren Berlant (2011), a kind of "cruel optimism," a dangerous attachment to an evasive idea of "the good life" that ultimately "wears out the subjects who nonetheless, and at the same time, find their conditions of possibility within it" (27). But it is not naturally, necessarily, or inevitably such. The promise can go many ways. It might disappoint and wear down, but it also might inspire and nourish.

Conclusion

Throughout the lives of my participants, media and popular culture have principally trafficked in transgender delegitimization, dehumanization, and tragic structures of feeling. These representational trends advance an ideology of transgender impossibility, suggesting that everydayness is out of reach for gender-nonconforming people. As a result of this, everydayness was very much an object of desire. Seeing everydayness in media was about feeling it was proximate, that a life of order, routine, and security—along with the "something more" that these things guarantee—might in fact be possible and within reach. In this way, everydayness was a "bloom space" (Seigworth and Gregg 2010, 9), a promise of futurity.

Crucially, a longing for "happening to be" can only be discerned within the context of transgender life and its challenges, risks, and absences, along with its successes, joys, and triumphs. It is then that this desire becomes more than an assimilationist resignation, more than an apolitical stance or neoliberal fantasy. The desire for and attachment to everydayness is a staunch rebuttal of the ideology of impossibility. It is a summoning of possibilities and the pursuit of something more.

In the next chapter, I shift my focus from the ideology of impossibility to possibility, examining the active construction of transgender identities. In doing so, I address the myriad ways media interact with the realities of participants' everyday lives to create various possibilities of self and subjectivity.

3

I Want to Be Like a Really Badass Lady

Media and Transgender Possibilities

As a young person growing up in the suburbs of the American Midwest, Jess kept a secret stash of comic books hidden in her bedroom. She cherished these books, keeping them near her bed and always within reach. This collection was important to her because the stories they contained involved superheroes inhabiting fantastical worlds. The characters in these books had astonishing strengths and superhuman capabilities. Many could fly, some were blessed with great speed, and others could bend metal. All defied the norms and limits of embodiment. Some even bent gender. As Jess explained, "All kinds of weird shit happens in comics. I don't just mean the stuff you see on *Star Trek*, but stuff you can't get away with on television. There are all kinds of gender transformations in comics, and it happens all the time. It's so frequent that it's really meaningful." For Jess, comic book characters who stretched the boundaries of gender were exemplars of trans possibilities and crucial to her development of a trans self. As she began the difficult task of transitioning, she looked to them for courage and inspiration.

As I argued in the previous chapter, transgender identity is often culturally defined through an ideology of impossibility and systematically framed as abject and undesirable. Yet at some point in their lives, the participants in my study combat this ideology, shifting the notion of transgender subjectivity from the conceptual outskirts into the realm of possibility. This movement happens during small, unexpected moments in their everyday lives as they interface with media and technology and engage in interpersonal interactions. For Jess, the movement toward possibility began with reading comic books. For other participants, it started with seeing a film, watching television, or surfing the Internet. In this chapter, I investigate how this shift toward transgender possibility is initiated and cultivated through encounters with media culture and communications technologies. In many ways, all of the participants in my study had their own secret stashes of media texts they leveraged to support their identity work. These texts contained the promise of possibility, and more specifically, the promise of a possible transgender self. For Jess, they contained the blueprints for being what she called a "badass lady."

Becoming a "Badass Lady"

Jess was a smart, creative child who loved gymnastics and playing dress-up. She was raised as a boy and occasionally cross-dressed with the girls who lived next door. After a while, she began doing it at home. "I would steal my sister's old clothes from the basement. I had like a stash . . . I would sneak into the bathroom at night and dress in girls' clothes. And then I'd just take them off because I didn't have anything to do. But, it was important to me. It was very important to me." In addition to playing dress-up, one of Jess's favorite childhood pastimes was reading comic books.

Comic books appeared in Jess's life at a crucial moment in time, during her teenage years when, like many queer kids, she struggled with social isolation and bullying. At school, she tried making friends with like-minded kids, but had difficulty in this pursuit. Middle school and high school were, as she articulated it, "extremely homophobic . . . It was very difficult. It was difficult because I didn't have any friends . . . So I got picked on a lot, thrown into walls, thrown onto concrete, beat up after school." Jess was targeted as a result of what she called her "gender failure." "There was just absolute gender failure going on. And other kids could smell it. It wasn't that they knew you were trans or that you were queer, but they just knew that something was up and they could smell it . . . It was like a dog whistle that only bullies could hear. It is not that they are identifying you as something. They're identifying the failure." Life at home was similarly challenging, as her father imposed masculine expectations onto her: "I was very lonely . . . My dad tried to encourage me to do social things, but they were things that were social as if I was a country kid . . . I felt like a lot of it was him trying to live out and act out his boyhood through me."

Given these life circumstances, Jess turned to comic books, preferring to spend time inhabiting the alternative worlds they created. She encountered her first comic book, *The Flash*, as an adolescent during a visit to a local barbershop. Sitting on a bench, waiting for her haircut, Jess was bored and picked up the comic book lying on the table next to her. She was instantly taken with the idea of the Flash's lightning speed. After that first encounter, she wanted more. She soon became an avid collector of superhero comics, drawn to stories that featured extraordinary bodies, androgynous heroes, and gender-nonconforming protagonists. Jess was especially attracted to the female characters: "There were really awesome women. I found that the 'team books' with more than two or three superhero characters tended to have the best women characters. I was never into 'Wonder Woman.' I thought she was too all-American. Whereas *Justice League* had characters like 'Fire,' who was Brazilian and had been a singer and her power was that she could turn into a living human torch. She was green and she was totally femme . . . She was a supermodel and that was her job. But her superhero thing, she was tough as nails. I liked her because she was very sexual, but not sexual in the way that she was scantily clad for other people's amusement kind of thing. It was more about having a job, having a really great job, and what you're looking at isn't for you. That was a running motif for her character. She was very sexy but inaccessible." Female characters such as Fire offered up new models of feminine subjectivity for Jess, providing a welcomed departure from the passive, male-dependent, and sexually available models of femininity she had been accustomed to seeing in media.

One comic book in particular, *Legionnaires: Number 13*, was especially significant to her. DC Comics released the issue in 1994 just as Jess turned 12 years old. "My very favorite superhero comic of all time, and very important to my life, was this comic called *Legionnaires*. In *Legionnaires Number 13*, the main character 'Matter Eater Lad' gets transformed into a woman and works with a group of female space pirates to defend the universe. On the front cover is this guy called Matter Eater Lad and his power is that he can eat anything. He can bite right through a table, or steel. The front cover is him looking in the mirror as he is about to brush his teeth, and he sees himself transform into a woman." An imaginative enterprise that expands our sense of what is possible, comic books such as *Legionnaires* traffic in fantasy. As Butler (2004) argues, the promise of fantasy "allows us to imagine ourselves and others otherwise;

it establishes the possible in excess of the real; it points elsewhere, and when it is embodied, it brings the elsewhere home" (29). Summoning alternative worlds and visions, postwar superhero comics in particular, according to Fawaz (2016), are texts that express queer affect and possibility. They revolve around bionic individuals with phenomenal and at times unruly bodies. Shifting between human and nonhuman registers, superheroes in these texts are in a constant state of flux. While their unpredictable bodies can be a source of frustration, they are also a source of strength and heroism. In this way, comics cultivate an "orientation toward otherness and difference that made so-called deviant forms of bodily expression, erotic attachment, and affiliation both desirable and ethical" (Fawaz 2016, 22).

For Jess, reading *Legionnaires, Number 13*, with its valuation of difference, deviance, and queerness, was an electrifying experience. As she recalled her favorite character Matter Eater Lad's transformation into a female space pirate, her voice swelled with enthusiasm. "I was just like 'yes!,' this is it . . . I was like, that's the kind of woman I want to be. I want that transformation. I want to be like a really badass lady." *Legionnaires Number 13* helped Jess imagine a possible self that differed from the male gender identity she had at the time. This was a "badass" possible self, one filled with profound promise. According to Markus and Nurius (1986), possible selves are "the ideal selves that we would very much like to become, the selves we could become, and the selves we are afraid of becoming" (954). They represent "the cognitive manifestation of enduring goals, aspirations, motives, fears, and threats," and as such provide "the specific self-relevant form, meaning, organization, and direction to these dynamics" (954). Possible selves are North Stars that guide individuals toward (or away from) certain identity projects. They spark action and incite the work of self-making.[1]

Replete with possible selves, Jess kept *Legionnaires Number 13* within reach. "I kept this issue by my bed and I would read it all the time. I read it so many times that I had to buy a second copy." Through repeated readings, Jess became increasingly absorbed by and emotionally invested in the comic book and others like it. These texts transported her into thrilling fictional worlds, letting her leave behind the one she temporarily inhabited. Media scholars refer to this kind of deep involvement as "transportation" (Green, Brock, and Kaufman 2004). Transportation involves cognitively and emotionally immersing one's self in the constructed universe of a media text. Inhabiting the space of the text, audiences have the opportunity to imagine their self-identity and life potential in new ways. Generally performed from the safe confines of one's living room or bedroom, this kind of identity work comes with little risk or cost to the individual (ibid.). It happens in private, apart from the prejudices of the real world, and without physical threat.

For Jess, these moments of transportation into the world of *Legionnaires Number 13* with its sex-changed heroes and female space pirates were transformative. "That was my favorite! Nothing even really compares now, like 'that's it, that's me . . . I want to be sexy, but I also want to be like a space pirate. Who doesn't want to be a space pirate? The space pirates were really dykey [sic]. They were in various ways femme and butch and andro, but there was a definite dyke-vibe there. Their society was woman dominated, the space pirate race, and the women were in charge." Sexy, feminine, butch, androgynous, and "in charge," this heroic collection of characteristics offered Jess an aspirational self-template. As she explained, "I needed a hero before I could confidently identify with the category of trans."

As Jess left high school and entered college, a new resource of self-exploration became increasingly accessible to her: the Internet. However, new to the virtual space, her experiences searching for transgender-related content online were at first problematic. "It turned me away. I had all these blind alleys and dead ends. I would find things and be like 'that's not me.' That's not what's going on with me." Specifically, Jess's searches often landed her on pornographic websites or surgery-related ones, neither of which related to her concerns. "I remember the first transgender erotica thing I found involved someone being forcibly turned into a woman and kept in a birdcage in heels. There were creepy BDSM things going on . . . In addition to erotica, I found websites like, 'What does it mean to be transgender?' It was more like 'What does it mean to be transsexual?' It was very surgery oriented. You feel that something is wrong with your body. That wasn't really what was going on with me." During her searches, she came upon the phrase "born in the wrong body," a declaration she strongly objected to. "So this phrase being 'born into the wrong body.' It's my body and I care about it. I wouldn't want to switch to somebody else's body. For me it is much more about making my body into what I want it to be. So it's about desire. My body before I started transitioning and now, in both states, is really beautiful. I'm fortunate in that respect. I've never looked at my body and thought this is a disgusting pile of shit . . . whose body should I have been born into?"

Importantly, the Internet only became a resource for identity work after Jess began learning about gender and transgender theories and issues later on in her undergraduate career. "The Internet wasn't really helpful until I knew what I was looking for . . . Women's Studies and Gender Studies was a huge part and really gave me a vocabulary . . . It definitely gave me the sense that there was gender variation in the world." In this way, education was a crucial variable in directing Jess's self-trajectory. Unlike other participants in my study who could not afford or did not attend college, Jess had the opportunity to participate in classes focusing on women, gender, and sexuality. These classes made such an impact on her that she decided to write a senior thesis about trans representation in literature and pornography. This exercise, according to Jess, was "part autobiography and self-analysis, part literary analysis . . . When you start writing something for a year, one starts to think am I actually writing about myself here? Because it sure seemed like it. But I had no access to resources. At that point I think I was like, I probably need to do this, I probably need to transition." The synergistic effect of her gender studies classes, her senior thesis, her experiences with comic books, and her online activities helped Jess craft the identity she claims today. "I'm queer. I'm queer in a big way . . . Sometimes I'm a Tomboy, sometimes I'm really femme . . . Also, I am a woman. I'm not part man, part woman." Currently, Jess is pursuing a graduate degree in the humanities and explained, "It is a good way to make some money, get insurance and medical care." Attending a large Midwestern university, she now has access to the resources she needs to transition. "I came here. And as soon as I was here, I found a therapist, got onto hormones, and started the whole thing."

"That's When It Hit Me"

As Jess's story illuminates, audiences make deeply personal and absorbing investments in the images of media culture. As visual culture scholar,

W.J.T. Mitchell (1996), explains, images "are things that have been marked with all the stigmata of personhood: they exhibit both physical and virtual bodies; they speak to us, sometimes literally, sometimes figuratively" (72). Throughout my fieldwork, participants discussed exactly how media images spoke to them and why they craved certain forms of visibility. In fact, they articulated this desire for imagery in terms of a basic need. The images they needed to see were not always strictly trans in nature, for as Jess's identification with the female space pirates suggests, other kinds of imagery could facilitate the development of possible selves. However, sometimes they were distinctly trans, as was the case with Avery. A white, twenty-something college student, Avery remembered his teenage years being a representational desert with respect to trans imagery. So, when the first transgender-themed film he could see was released in theaters, he was compelled to see it. "I remember *Trans-America* came out and I was really apprehensive about seeing it, but I knew I *needed* to do it. Trans people were in the movies! In America! I *need* to see this."

Released in 2005, *TransAmerica* chronicles the cross-country road trip of a middle-aged white transgender woman. As an independently financed film project, the movie was intended for "art house" audiences but eventually gained widespread popularity and acclaim. Avery found out about the film from a newspaper article in the local press. Never before had he witnessed a trans person on the big screen, and the thought of it was exhilarating. Describing the night he went to see *TransAmerica*, Avery recalled that the actual content and storyline of the film were secondary to the thrill of seeing a trans body on screen. "The film was okay, not that great. Felicity Huffman did an okay job. The character she played was really annoying at times . . . But seeing a transgender person in the movies, in America, that was worth it." For the first time, Avery was able to "kind of see myself on the big screen—I mean I'm a trans guy and Bree was a trans woman but still, it was a 'wow' moment for me."

The intensity of Avery's "wow moment" speaks to the power and primacy of visuality in our culture. Whereas all our senses (sight, smell, taste, etc.) give us purchase over the world around us, our technological environment prioritizes the act of seeing. Consider the cliché "Seeing is believing." The proliferation and ascendance of visually based technologies throughout the twentieth century have privileged sight and visuality as fundamental ways of knowing. As Weibel argues, "The triumph of the visual in the twentieth century is the triumph of a techno-vision" (1996, 339).[2] This techno-vision, as Foucault (1980) reminds us, is a form of power/knowledge that organizes how we understand and value the world. It can be enlisted in managing and controlling bodies (think, for example, of our current surveillance state), or in creating feelings of impossibility (as I explored in chapter 2). At the same time, techno-vision can open up new fields of imagination and possibility.

For the participants in my study, technologies of vision generated powerful experiences of self-recognition and conferred feelings of "realness" and legitimacy—exactly what is at stake in living a transgender life. These experiences were so deeply consequential that almost all of them remembered their first encounters with transgender imagery and the ways they devoted a great deal of creative agency into reading media texts to meet their personal needs. Jen's story reflects this effort.

Jen is a white trans woman in her early twenties from the Midwest. During her teens, she spent her summer vacation at her grandparents' lake home. At that point in her life, she was experimenting with cross-dressing and knew there was something different about her gender identity. When staying at her grandparents' large country house, Jen had more space and greater privacy than at her parents' small bungalow, where surveillance was intense. As a result, the summer was a time of self-experimentation, when she could cross-dress with less fear of being caught. Sitting in her grandparents' living room one day watching television, she saw her first representation of trans people on a daytime talk show: "I was flipping through the TV stations and I saw Jerry Springer. I saw transsexual women on the show. They weren't really treated that great. But I remember thinking, 'Whoah! People can actually kind of do that!' Then I went downstairs and I talked to my grandpa. I asked him, 'Wow. People can really change genders and sexes?' And he said, 'Yeah.' Now I was already dressing before I saw these people on TV, but when I saw them I was like, 'Wow. I want to do that!' They looked so good and I wanted to look like that too. I didn't dare mention anything because as the show was going on my grandpa was making crude and mean comments."

As Jen sat in front of the television set, *Jerry Springer* delivered a mixture of tawdry freak show and public forum.[3] Like her grandfather, members of the studio audience taunted and made fun of the transgender guests. Nevertheless, Jen saw past their poor treatment, extracting images of a possible transgender self from the show. Seeing transgender women who "looked so good" was aspirational and deeply motivating, furthering her desire to experiment with gender. After the episode, Jen appreciated a renewed energy and resourcefulness for cross-dressing. She practiced it more frequently and began experimenting with new looks and styles. Wanting more encounters with possible selves, she started to actively monitor daytime television and recorded every trans-themed talk show episode she could find. She started to assemble her own "secret stash." Through repeated viewings of these media texts, the idea of transgender life and subjectivity gradually moved from the realm of fantasy to reality.

A similar orientation toward transgender possibility happened for Alex, a trans man in his mid-twenties living in San Francisco, through visiting a newly formed website. A film enthusiast with a love for independent, foreign, and military-themed movies, Alex is a prolific reader, a writer, a former sex worker, and an incredibly energetic individual. With his wellspring of energy, he maintains an active lifestyle. "I'm an athlete and a writer and reader. I don't like to sit in front of a computer all day long. I feel like I could be doing so many other things in my life." So, it is ironic that one of his most memorable and life-changing moments occurred while sitting in front of a computer screen.

Raised female, but never fully comfortable with it, when Alex entered his twenties, he started to further explore his identity. Alex was restless: in his job, in his home, and in his own skin. During this time, a friend encouraged him to visit a website called *XX Boys*, a photography project featuring sharp, glossy images of younger trans men. He recalled, "Somebody called me and said you need to go and check out this site right now. It's called *XX Boys*. It's a photo project of all FTM [female-to-male] boys. They were calling me to tell me to check out this site because these guys were hot. They were like, 'You got to check out these hot guys.' And I was like 'alright.'" Visiting the site was transformative for Alex and spurred an exhilirating experience of self-awareness. "I went to the site and there were all these pictures of FTMs [female-to-male transgender individuals] and I was immediately like 'that's me.' That's when it hit me." The almost tactile experience, the feeling of being "hit" with self-recognition, was soon followed by a bewildering surge of turmoil and creative energy. He remembers, "I lost my shit, drank whiskey and wrote a novel."

XX Boys was the creation of Colombian photographer, Kael T. Block, who in 2004 created the online photography project to chronicle his gender transition (Ross 2012). His motivation for starting the project originated from his own experiences and frustrations with media, explaining in an interview with the website *Mediamatic,*

> In 2003 I was really looking for visual documentation about the [gender] transition, and I wished there was a project, or a website, with pictures and testimonies of other trans boys to help me through my questioning, and fears . . . This project, for me, was a question of surviving. Transitioning when you're alienated is so hard. You try to explain yourself, you fight to be recognized as a boy, you fight against people thinking you're crazy, you fight against people's pity, you fight against being trapped in a gender box, the pink one or the blue one. I wanted something positive, sexy, engaged, showing diversity, giving choices and strength, connecting FTMs, and with a bit of a "fuck you" attitude to be out there.

For the time, *XX Boys* was in many ways the first of its kind, filling a much-needed niche in trans male visibility. Many trans men I spoke with commented on the lack of trans male visibility in media culture. They lamented that trans women, and more specifically transsexual women, comprise most transgender visibility in media. Given this representational landscape, *XX Boys* was groundbreaking for highlighting young transgender men, and even more, for portraying them as confident and desirable. The lighting, settings, and aesthetic design of the photos, along with the poses and self-presentation of the models, reflect the conventions of high-fashion photography mixed with a touch of soft-core pornography. Embracing a punk-like street style, the models emanate youthful energy and bold eroticism (as seen in figure 3.1). After its launch, *XX Boys* became well known in online transgender male communities.[4]

One of the reasons *XX Boys* made such a profound and meaningful impact on Alex, why it "hit" him so deeply, was because underpinning the website was a very specific and intentional "care structure" (Scannell 1996, 2014). Drawing from philosopher Martin Heidegger's (1962)

Figure 3.1. Image from the *XX Boys* project.

work *Being and Time*, media and everyday life scholar Paddy Scannell (1996) argues that care represents "the specific mark of all possible and all actual ways of human being in the world" (144). As a vital resource of and for human being, care can be mobilized and strategically deployed through care structures, which are responsible for constructing the media we engage with every day. More than just the "means of production," care structures are the collective thought, energy, and intentionality that make technology purposeful and ready for use. They are rooted in human creativity and careful concern. Care structures are invisible, hidden in the design and functionality of technology. The care and concern that go into the technology are concealed from us "in order to 'let us be'—to let us be ourselves and to be about our ordinary but always particular concerns in ways that are essentially unproblematic" (Scannell 2014, 25). In this way, care structures account for why users can engage with technologies in effortless and meaningful ways, in ways that complement their everyday lives and identity work.

XX Boys is a care structure, and as such it has two vectors of care and concern. The first vector represents what went into the making of the technology. Clearly, Block created his website with an acute concern for young trans men. He designed it with strength, positivity, diversity, and sexuality in mind, injecting, as he said, a "fuck you" attitude into its ethos. *XX Boys*'s second vector of care and concern involves the care that comes out of the technology, the kinds of user engagements the site facilitates. *XX Boys* helps users care for themselves, generating nourishing experiences of identity and everydayness. These affordances had a profound effect on Alex.

Having never seen anything like the website before, he was taken with its imagery: "I looked at that site like ten times a day. I was looking at these pictures being like 'damn, they're hot,' but then I was also looking at them being like 'I am this guy.' I want to look like that." The images of the young trans men generated a powerful and puzzling knot of desire in Alex. Through the process of untangling it, he started to formulate his identity. He clarified the various feelings of desire the site created in him, ultimately realizing that he wanted to *be* an XX Boy. The XX Boy represented both a sexual object choice and a compelling possible self. This distinction was something he had been struggling to work through for years: "I had been looking at men my entire life thinking this is what my body is supposed to look like, but it looks like this. It was hard for me to separate out sexual attraction from this other thing that was going on. I couldn't decide, 'Do I want to suck this guy's dick or do I want to be this guy?' So, looking at those photos is when it split apart. I could find the guys really attractive and also be like 'that's me.' Maybe it made sense to me because I knew all these men had been born female, and I then knew it was possible. I mean I guess I knew it was possible because I had trans friends at that point, but when I saw those photos it hit me immediately." Surprisingly, the mediated presence of the XX Boys felt more "real" and compelling, and made a greater impact on him, than the presence of his actual trans friends. The media encounter altered the course of Alex's life. He remembered, "So I drank whiskey, wrote a really depressing novel, moved back here [San Francisco] and started transitioning about two and a half years ago."

Much like Alex, Kate, a 23-year-old white trans woman, also had an experience with possible selves on the Internet that served as a life-changing turning point. Kate is a bright, energetic, and anxious undergraduate finishing her fifth year at a Midwestern university. She is an active gamer and a diligent student majoring in computer science and engineering. Her schoolwork occupies most of her day. She began to transition gender approximately one year ago. As someone who transitioned relatively recently, Kate was concerned about talking with me in public regarding her experiences as a trans woman. She was worried others would overhear our conversation and "clock" her, or "out" her as trans. At our first interview, we sat in a small, private room at the university she attended and dined on spicy Thai food—her favorite cuisine.

Unlike many of the other participants in my study, Kate had a firm understanding of gender and sexual variance when she was younger. She credits this understanding to being raised in the Unitarian Universalist Church, which provided her with "a much different experience than most kids have growing up. There was the 'OWL Course' that we had. Our Whole Lives. It is basically sexual education, but it is also very broad, as you get from the name 'Our Whole Lives.' That's where I learned about sexuality and transgender. That was the earliest I can remember where I learned about it." So, when Kate encountered images of trans people in the media as a young person, she had tools for understanding it. "I was definitely identifying with them, but I suppose most of the time I was trying to tell myself I wasn't." This strategy of recognition and denial lasted throughout her teenage years until a chance encounter with an online media text in her first year at college changed everything.

During her first few years at college, Kate spent much of her free time online playing massive multiplayer online role-playing games (MMORPGs). As someone who had trouble making friends, she liked MMORPGs for the sociability they afforded. "My main reason for liking it, the main thing I enjoy is talking to the people online. We talk about many topics outside of the game. It is really no different than everyday conversation in real life." Her other favorite online pastime was reading web comics. One night, as she was killing time searching for Internet comics to read, she happened upon *Venus Envy*. Created by Erin Lindsey, a trans woman who was in her twenties when she began the comic, *Venus*

Envy follows the experiences of a trans high school student named Zoe. According to Lindsey:

> Venus Envy is a typical high school romantic comedy, with the welcome addition of lesbians, cross-dressers, and of course transsexuals . . . a segment of the population that you rarely see in entertainment (or at least you didn't when I began the comic in 2001) . . . Ultimately, all you need to remember to enjoy this series is that transsexuals are ordinary people who live extraordinary lives. (cited from the Venus Envy website "about" page)

Like the participants in my study, Lindsey desired representations of transgender ordinariness and everydayness, and, given its absence in media culture, created a web comic to represent them. As a transgender care structure, *Venus Envy* was intended to portray transgender life in terms of "relationships and everyday situations" (Crowder 2009). Its objective was to give readers a good time and to offer a more lighthearted, comedic portrait of transgender life. According to Lindsey, "I like to think of VE [*Venus Envy*] more as a romantic comedy. It has its

Figure 3.2. Description of the main character Zoe from the web comic, *Venus Envy*.

serious moments and horrific scenes, but in the end, I always want to come back around to a joke" (ibid.).

The ordinary everydayness of the comic coupled with the age of its protagonists and their life challenges immediately resonated with Kate. "When I read it I had this feeling that could have been me. This girl Zoe had just transitioned and had moved away. Her whole family moved away from her old high school. She was going to go to a new high school, under her new name and gender. It was about her meeting new people at the high school and dealing with that." The comic paralleled Kate's everyday life in significant ways. At the time, Kate had also moved away from home to attend a new school (college), struggled with meeting new people, and started the beginning stages of her gender transition. Like Zoe, Kate was also managing a contentious relationship with her brother. "She had a lot of little battles with her brother who thinks she's a freak for being trans and is very unhappy with having to have moved to a new high school, leaving his old friends behind. A lot of sibling rivalry, since the parents have to focus on Zoe a lot cause there are a lot of issues that come with being trans."

Similar to Alex and *XX Boys*, Kate read *Venus Envy* over and over, integrating it into her everyday routines. With these repeated readings, she became increasingly invested and transported into the narrative, creating deep parasocial (Horton and Wohl 1956) relationships with its characters. "While I was reading it, I got more into it, got more attached to the characters." As she finished this sentence, tears streamed down her cheeks. For a few moments she was silent, and then explained, "I got into a really bad depression and that was the point at which I was like 'I have to own up to this. I have to confront this and deal with this.' That is when I decided I needed to get help. That is essentially how I came out to myself and eventually got help. It [*Venus Envy*] just really got to me. It finally pushed me over the line."

For Kate, reading the comic was like gazing into an alternative past—one where she was living harmoniously with her own wishes and desires. "It brought up a lot of feeling of what I missed out on. The life I could have had if I dealt with this earlier."

Her facial expression shifted and she again began to cry, as if mourning her childhood. Her affective encounter with the comic was profoundly layered—involving a mixture of sadness, regret, excitement, and, most important, hope. Crucially, the character Zoe operated as a transgender possible self for Kate. She offered her an opportunity for self-recognition and motivated her to change her life. Talking about the identity work she performed after reading *Venus Envy*, Kate noted, "The first thing I did after that was, there is a free therapist available for students, and I went there first. This happened about a year and three months ago during midterms of winter semester. I had an initial interview where they tried to get me someone who was knowledgeable about trans people. Then I was sent to a different guy. He was nice, not that helpful, but nice. He eventually directed me to someone who had experience with this kind of thing. This led me to the Gender Services Program at the hospital. They finally set me up with a therapist. I've been seeing him ever since then. I was finally approved for hormones this past December and started them the end of January. Estrogen in February. That is where I am now, more or less." Like a powerful engine, *Venus Envy* set in motion Kate's trajectory toward a transgender self.

Jess, Kate, Avery, Jen, and Alex all had interactions with media that offered flashes of self-recognition, helping them to imagine a possible transgender self. Yet the exact nature and outcomes of their interactions were contingent upon the nature of the media forms they encountered and the care structures that underpinned them. Interfacing with film and television, Avery and Jen were involved with more traditional media forms geared toward larger, mass audiences, which required active semiotic reworking and negotiation. By contrast, Alex and Kate interfaced with online media texts that were created and sustained by transgender care structures, which better served their needs for identification and recognition and necessitated less compromise.

"Now I Could Hear It!"

Dylan, a white trans man in his twenties, grew up traveling the country, following his parents' Christian missionary work. In his early teens, his family settled in the American Midwest. At this time, he began identifying as a lesbian. "I came out as a dyke [*sic*] and I was like 'Oh, I think I like girls.' And I just went on with my life." Fortunately for him, Dylan found a group of friends who felt similarly and also identified as lesbians. Yet as they grew older, their sense of self expanded, and they began to question the category, for it felt increasingly inadequate. "We were like butches. We were sort of boyishly running around with each other, with girlfriends. Then we started talking and thinking that this was cool, and it feels kind of right, but not exactly right. We had a friend who had a copy of a book called *Body Alchemy* by Loren Cameron. But he goes by Rex now. It's just a book of photography of trans men. Some of it is surgery pictures and some of it is interviews with before and after pictures. Some of it is of Loren. Loren is a bodybuilder so he took lots of pictures of himself. So we saw that and were like 'oh my god,' 'I can't believe that,' 'it's so crazy!,' 'I can't believe people do this.'"

In portraying individuals before and after gender transition, the photographs in *Body Alchemy* were visual testaments of possible transgender selves. Each series of "before and after" photos and each interview in the book captured a journey of embodiment, one previously considered unthinkable to the teens. After this initial encounter, the group of friends wanted more. In addition to seeing the images of transition, they wanted the language. Dylan and his friends wanted the capacity to utter that very ordinary phrase, "I am," to say it out loud for themselves and others.

In order to accomplish this, they mined the media landscape, looking to print culture and the Internet. "We started reading more. We started reading Rikki Anne Wilchens's *Read My Lips* and we read *Stone Butch Blues*. It started being something like 'oh people really do this.' So, we started researching on the Internet 'how do you do this?' We found there were communities and hundreds of people doing it all over the world. We couldn't believe it." This was the mid-1990s, a time when queer and transgender theory flourished in the academy. The group of friends read and shared the work of an emerging group of transgender thinkers and writers. They also immersed themselves in online communities. Synthesizing what they learned from print culture and online discourses, Dylan and his friends achieved fluency in the language of gender variance.

This new language served as a cipher for decoding feelings that had long remained unnamed. Painting a poignant word picture, Dylan explained, "If you've ever been in a room and there's fluorescent lights, and all of a sudden someone is like 'can you hear that buzzing?' And you listen. And all of a sudden you can hear it, but you couldn't hear it before, but now you can. And now it's all you can hear. Now I can't be in this room anymore because all I can hear is this buzzing. There was always that subconscious sort of hum, and you knew there was something, but didn't know what it was. And someone would be like 'Is it this?' and you would be like 'Oh my god!' You could hear it! Now I could hear it!"

Dylan's new vocabulary allowed him to interpret the relentless buzzing occurring inside him. Whereas previously it had escaped language and rested beneath the surface, the subconscious hum now rose to the level of awareness and recognition. He could "hear" it. This moment was a critical shift in consciousness and made a possible transgender self feel within reach. Being able to discursively construct a self and communicate that self to others made everyday life feel more livable. As Butler (2004) maintains, livability and intelligibility are entwined: "to live is to live a life politically, in relation to power, in relation to others, in the act of assuming responsibility for a collective future" (226). Similarly, Lennon (2006) declares that everyday life is rooted in mutual intelligibility, in the ability for "people to 'find their feet' with each other in everyday interactions . . . [a] kind of making sense to ourselves and to others" (Lennon 2006, 28). Drawing from Derrida, she argues that trans individuals' desire for an "originary language," a language of one's own where the truth of identity is contained, is "a desire we all share" (30). While this language of self will always be limited by social and institutional norms, it grants a sense of ownership over the body, provides expressive equipment for sociability, and allows us to feel knowable and "real" as we move through the spaces of the everyday.

Dylan and his friends were not alone in their desire for language, for a vocabulary that would decipher the hums and buzzes occurring inside them. Many participants experienced their identities as an unknowable riddle. As one participant made clear, "How do you identify if you don't have the words for it? The words just weren't there for me. Having the words is so important . . . particularly for FTMs [female-to-male transsexuals]. What helped me come out was having the words and knowing where to hunt for them." Throughout their hunt, the participants in my study overwhelmingly took to the Internet to construct a working vocabulary for their gender variant identities. In fact, the Internet was so significant that many divided their life-worlds into "pre" and "post" Internet eras. Soaring rhetoric about the technology was not uncommon across participant interviews. For Sidney, "the Internet changed everything." A white trans woman in her forties, Sidney grew up in a mid-sized, blue-collar Midwestern town. She remembered, "When I was younger, I wasn't comfortable with the thoughts in my head. I sort of knew I didn't want to be a boy. Didn't know if I wanted to be a girl . . . then I went to a college not too far from home and I sought information out on the sly. I went to video stores, libraries, even an adult bookstore. I went looking for all forms of gender bending. I had a few VHS tapes where I taped documentaries I had found, like Discovery Channel type stuff." But Sidney's secret stash was ultimately small and incomplete.

In the early 1990s, an article in *Playboy* magazine served as a crucial addition to her stash. "It was about the model Tula, who is a transsexual woman, and who actually was a James Bond girl. She did a *Playboy* spread along with a huge interview. Of course it was the interview that was compelling to me. It was one of the first times I truly understood the word for what I was, which was transsexual. Growing up where I did, it immediately seemed out of my grasp. But once I realized there was a word for it, it crystallized certain daydreams I had. I felt like a person with a name." Yet, even as this was a revelation for Sidney, her media environment precluded further self-exploration, "But of course there was no Google to search and learn more about it. I had a term for myself, which was truly a relief, but that was it." Still consumed by the ideology of impossibility, Sidney remembered, "I felt like it was an impossible dream. If I admitted it to myself it meant that I had to do something about it. And that seemed impossible to me. I was not prepared. I didn't know how passing or being in stealth would work. I didn't even know what those words meant." Looking back on that time period, she said, "I'm so glad those days are over."

It was not until she began her activities online, learning the language of gender variance and chatting with like-minded others, that Sidney began thinking about transgender life and subjectivity as possible. Armed with a newly minted vocabulary and awareness, she finally felt prepared, explaining, "It pushed the snowball down the hill for me. It helped me figure out the language. I didn't know the words 'passing;" or 'stealth' before. I sort of knew the concepts and I knew I needed to be those things, but I didn't know the words . . . I started to use the word 'trans woman,' and everyone knew what trans woman meant. It was a lot easier. Before, it was difficult to have a conversation. I didn't know the words and I had no one to talk to. Now I had the words, I had people online to talk to, I had somebody to relate to." Sidney continued her activities online, exploiting the social and technological affordances of the Internet. She began blogging to chronicle her coming out process. In time, she became the administrator of her favorite online transgender blog aggregator. Today, Sidney feels she has a stake in the development of transgender language. "I am a very active blogger. I talk to a lot of people on the Internet. We are helping create the language as we go along. It's all an evolution, and it's all still pretty new."

The evolution of transgender language and the explanatory power it holds allowed participants to, as Sidney put it, feel "like a person with a name." Language conferred personhood status and authorized individuals to join the community of the named. It furnished identity and gave meaning to the indescribable buzzing that they felt inside, helping them to feel less ghost-like and more "real." And even though language can be exclusionary, deceptive, and frustratingly imprecise, and even though it can create new binaries and erect new closets, the vocabulary of self that participants learned was experienced as a gift. It normalized their experiences and allowed them to share in the everyday world as mutually intelligible actors.

Barriers to Becoming "Badass"

"If you are reading this, it means that I have committed suicide and obviously failed to delete this post from my queue," began Leelah's suicide note (Lowder 2014). The teenager's last words were publicly posted to her Tumblr page, timed to appear after she took her own life. The note continues, "When I was 14, I learned what transgender meant and cried of happiness. After 10 years of confusion I finally understood who I was" (ibid.). Despite this realization, however, Leelah was confined by her life situation. Her parents, suffering from religious myopia, refused to acknowledge her queer identity, subjecting her to "conversion therapy" after she told them about her desires for gender transformation. Leelah also endured other punishments, explaining in her letter, "They took me out of public school, took away my laptop and phone, and forbid me of getting on any sort of social media, completely isolating me from my friends" (Lowder 2014). Under these circumstances, on

December 28, 2014, 17-year-old Leelah Alcorn, a white trans high school student and artist from Ohio, committed suicide by jumping in front of a tractor-trailer.

The public nature of Leelah's death sparked international outrage and, particularly on social media, a collective sadness and mourning. Following the tragedy, numerous vigils were held commemorating the teen and celebrating her life, many of which occurred in the place she felt most comfortable being herself: online. Vigils abounded on Facebook and spread across Tumblr, one of her favorite websites.

Lealah led a very active life online. On Tumblr and Reddit, she was able to express the various parts of herself that were so ruthlessly silenced at home. Leelah was an artist, and already had a job drawing caricatures at a local amusement park. Her Tumblr page, titled "Lazer Princess," was her showroom. In one piece titled "Princess Boy" (figure 3.3), Leelah constructed what appeared to be an aspirational self-portrait: an anime inspired figure, very petite with large glassy eyes, earrings, long evening gloves, and a stylish dress. With her arms joyfully stretched out at her sides, Princess Boy smiles, staring outwardly and optimistically against a sparkling backdrop. This was Leelah's own space pirate, her own version of a "badass" comic book hero.

As with so many of the participants in my study, Leelah came to realize and cultivate a possible transgender self online. Its care structures and communities provided her with an outlet for self-expression and artistic experimentation. Nevertheless, Leelah was trapped, plagued by the ideology of impossibility, and unable to be the "Princess Boy" she knew she was outside of the virtual world. Ultimately, her prolific life online—as meaningful and important as it was—could not rival the exigencies of her lived circumstances.

I introduce Leelah's story here because it serves as a powerful and necessary concession, a counterpoint to the stories of media and transgender possibility discussed thus far in this chapter. Leelah reminds us that the possibilities afforded by communication and information technologies are always limited, circumscribed by our life circumstances, and contingent on the sociopolitical, economic, and everyday life structures within which we live. Sandy's story offers a similar lesson.

A black trans woman in her forties from a small Midwestern city, Sandy struggled in the economically disadvantaged "Rust Belt" dur-

Figure 3.3. Original artwork from Leelah Alcorn.

ing the Great Recession. Unable to find consistent employment, she explained, "I'm staying with a friend right now, rent free. I also stay with my sister's family, sometimes the people from church." Of all her family members, Sandy's sister was the only one who stayed in touch with her after her transition. While she sometimes stays with her sister, Sandy does not want to impose on her. She is currently staying with a friend from the transgender support group she attends. Friends from this group are her only connection to transgender community and belonging. "I have a couple of transgender friends now from the group who I talk to every single day. We talk EVERY SINGLE DAY. But I can only really be Sandy on Tuesdays [when the group meets] or when I'm with my friends. But most of the times, I feel alone." Hearing some of her friends talk about their experiences online, Sandy, who does not have a stable home let alone access to the Internet, listens with envy. Desiring human connection, she believes the Internet would help. "I want it for just talking and hanging out. You know, not so much for a dating thing, just like a meeting place to be friends and find out where they are at and meet to be friends." The friend she is staying with, a black trans woman similarly struggling financially, does not have an Internet connection in her apartment. Sandy also cannot afford the service on her cell phone.

As we continue talking, however, Sandy's perspective shifted and she questioned the potential benefit of the Internet given the parameters of her current life situation. She conceded, "Even if I did have it [the Internet], what can I do with it? I still don't have a job." Sandy's story reveals how the politics of race, class, and place shape the experience individuals have with media technologies. As a black woman without work and a steady place to call home living in the Midwest during the Great Recession, the possibilities that technology could afford her are ultimately circumscribed by her life situation and the macro-level conditions that structure her world.

Yet even those who had access to the discursive world of the Internet struggled to capitalize on the possibilities it could afford in terms of identity work. For many, finding a vocabulary of self proved difficult. Transgender terminology is generally not part of our everyday vernacular, and while this is changing, words such as "transgender," "transition," "passing," "stealth," "gender fluid," "MTF," "FTM," "non-binary" and "cis gender,"[5] for example, which are central to articulating transgender experience, are located in more specialized and niche regions of the Internet. They hide out in activist circles, academic literatures, and queer and transgender subcultures. By virtue of their race, class, and level of education, many of the participants in my study lacked road maps to these kinds of spaces and communities. Moreover, when conducting a search online, transgender women in particular often had to sift through a dense pile of pornography before landing on something instructive. Some participants found images of transgender erotica exciting, as it affirmed the attractiveness and sexuality of transgender bodies. However, as I explored in chapter 2, for others, witnessing the routine fetishization of transgender identity distanced them or scared them away. Frustrated with the results, some merely discontinued their online searches. For transgender men, the struggle was different in that they had difficulty finding any information at all that spoke to their experiences. Feeling overlooked and underserved, many lamented that most of the information online covering gender variance related to trans women's experiences. Finally, the language used to talk through transgender issues and subjectivity is complex and in constant flux. As anthropologist Don Kulick (1999) argues, the language of gender variance "exceeds fixed meanings, remains always plural, and continually disrupts the marking of boundaries" (616). The terminology embraces ambiguity, liminality, and fluidity. Achieving fluency takes time and practice.[6]

Aside from language obstacles and the structures of race, class, and place, the technologies themselves—their structural design, organization, and governance—also influenced the kinds of possibilities they afford users. At the time of my fieldwork, YouTube and Facebook were both censoring images of trans men. In 2010, Dominic Scaia, a Canadian trans man, had his Facebook account disabled after posting a shirtless photo of himself. Scaia recently had "top surgery," removing his breasts, and, as he explains, was "proud of my new chest and wanted to show it off" (Blaze 2010a). Yet, Facebook removed the image for violating its "Statement of Rights and Responsibilities," which prohibits "nudity or other graphic or sexually suggestive content" (ibid.). Scaia objected to the censorship and the story soon garnered attention from the queer and progressive press. Under scrutiny, Facebook eventually reinstated his account and encouraged him to repost his photos (Ruddy 2010).

However, later that same year, Scaia had a similar encounter with YouTube after he posted a video of himself showing off his chest two and a half weeks post-surgery. Employing similar language, YouTube argued the video was "sexually provocative" (Blaze 2010b). Again, after Scaia and the queer press focused attention on the decision, YouTube reloaded the video and offered an apology, insisting they will be "doing some additional training around these issues" (Blaze 2010c). For Scaia, and other transgender individuals involved in these disputes, at stake are legitimacy, "realness," and personhood. In censoring his images and disabling his account, Facebook and YouTube undermined his male identity. They became de facto arbiters of gender and subverted his capacity for self-definition.

Even as Facebook has become more gender-inclusive, allowing users to customize their gender identity in 2014 by offering more than 50 options, their enduring and strictly enforced "authentic identity" policy is problematic. The site requires individuals to use what they term "authentic identities" on their profiles, the one's that people "use in real life" (as explained in the website's "Help Center"). To help enforce this policy, anonymous Facebook users can report names they believe to be fake to website administrators. This sets into motion a course of disciplinary actions. Facebook can lock suspected "fake" users out of their profiles, delete their accounts, and mandate they verify their "authentic identity." This verification process involves the choice of handing over either "hard" documents such as driver's licenses, birth certificates, and passports, or "soft" documents such as bank statements and library cards—however, the identification document must include both a birthday and photo. Structured as it is, the policy overlooks names that exist outside of and apart from institutions, and grants authority over one's name to anonymous accusers. Even more, the identities of the accusers are kept from the accused.

This structural norm built into the website's operation forecloses the ability to have self-chosen and fluid identities. It instantiates identity as singular and unitary, disenfranchising those who adopt multiple or non-normative identities for good reason such as transgender people but also, for example, survivors of rape, native people, and political dissidents. As MacAulay and Moldes (2016) argue, real name policies render "consumers and citizens transparent to markets and the state" (7). In this way, just as media and communications technologies allow for transgender possibilities, their design, and governance, the fact that they are oriented toward users *as well as* market and state forces circumscribes the extent to which someone can become a "*badass lady.*"

Conclusion

In looking to media and the kaleidoscope of possible selves and life itineraries they offer up, the participants in my study realized that transgender identity was in fact possible and, as a result, became architects of their self-identities. They mobilized personal media ensembles, collecting and repeatedly engaging with media texts and integrating them into their daily lives and identity narratives. This self-work was a creative and often secret practice of appropriation and composition with the materials they had at their disposal. For some, it was imagery circulated by the Internet's transgender care structures that set into motion self-discovery and allowed them to make claims of transgender selfhood. For others, it was learning a vocabulary of gender variance, a vocabulary that offered a sense of clarity to parts of themselves that were previously out of focus and inexplicable.

In so many ways, media and technology were "partners in crime," engines of hope that facilitated transgender possibilities. It is exactly this question of possibility—whether or not transgender can be conceived of and realized as a legitimate and authentic home—that marked participants' experiences with media and technology. However, the technologies themselves, not necessarily designed with queer and transgender people in mind, permitted a limited range of uses. In order to leverage them for identity work, transgender individuals had to petition the media industries for change or actively "queer" technology, being creative with their use. The affordances of technologies were also governed by life circumstance, by the material and social relations within which individuals operate. Factors such as education (as with Jess), religion (as with Kate), and class (as with Sandy) determined the extent to which media were valuable resources for self- and life-making. One must know what to search for amid the information wilderness of the Internet and have more than a computer in order to make transgender life possible. This active pursuit of a transgender self, however, requires great strength and grit. The next chapter explores this resilience.

4

You Have to Be Really Strong

Practicing Resilient Reception

"I'm tired, tired, tired, of seeing movies that I feel have done violence against me by making me sit there and watch this scene over and over and over again!" As we sat together in a San Francisco hotel, Sebastian discussed the raw experience of watching a film that depicted violence against a trans person. He recalled being in a darkened theater, seated among a crowd of strangers, watching a scene where a young person is raped. This media encounter is seared into his memory. As Sebastian spoke to me, his body communicated the sheer force of the viewing experience. His voice rose, his body became tense, his eyes swelled, and his hands collapsed into tightly clenched fists. He had hoped for a relaxing and enjoyable evening with friends, but instead watching the film was a challenge that tested his emotional strength. Its subject matter clutched him in its grip and refused to let go.

Sebastian saw the movie at the annual Frameline Film Festival, a popular event that screens LGBTQ independent movies from around the world. Almost every summer since he moved to San Francisco, he has attended the film festival. Sebastian is an outgoing twenty-eight-year-old trans man who works as a social worker and counselor. Raised in suburban Wisconsin and spending his teenage years there, Sebastian lived much of his life in places where queer events like the Frameline Film Festival did not—perhaps could not—exist. His parents were Evangelical missionaries and maintained tight control over his information environment. Suspicious of secular entertainments, they monitored and restricted Sebastian's media fare. As a result, he had to watch his favorite TV show, *My So-Called Life*—a high school drama about a group of intelligent, angst-ridden outcasts living in suburbia—secretly in his bedroom via the Internet. Sebastian summarized, "I was raised really super religious so I wasn't allowed access to a lot of television or non-religious media. I was pretty sheltered in my small town and I didn't see anything transgender related until I was like nineteen."

Nineteen was undoubtedly a pivotal year for Sebastian. He moved away from home with his girlfriend and landed in Madison, Wisconsin, a bustling college town he perceived as "the big city." There, he encountered transgender identities for the first time in his young adult life: "I had trans friends where I lived . . . I had some trans male friends who I hung out with. We had like a group! I mean I had a group of queer friends and then someone started a drop-in trans male social support group." Surrounded by like-minded others, it was within this new social and informational environment that Sebastian experimented with his subjectivity and eventually began his gender transition. However, he ultimately wanted to settle in San Francisco, an urban hub of gay, lesbian, transgender, and queer life. So, he picked up and moved, embarking on his own version of what Howe (2001) calls "the queer pilgrimage."

Upon arriving in the city, Sebastian enrolled at the University of California in San Francisco and promptly became familiar with the city's social ecology. He immersed himself in the very active and visible transgender communities there and migrated toward politically conscious circles. He also attended the many queer cultural events San Francisco has to offer. One such event was the Frameline Film Festival. As one of the largest and longest running queer-themed film festivals in the world, Frameline is the most highly attended LGBT arts event in San Francisco. A loyal participant, Sebastian goes every year. Yet he has developed a strong ambivalence toward it. The festival offers him the opportunity to spend time with his friends and learn about cutting-edge developments in queer film. At the same time, Sebastian believes that although Frameline is marketed as a symbol of queer diversity, it nonetheless suffers from a myopic vision and marginalizes trans narratives. He clarified, "Frameline's a big deal. It's a huge moneymaker. They have a history of mostly showing films about gay white men, then doing peripheral programming around people of color, women, trans folks, people who aren't hairless and thin. It can be terrifying, but you still go every year."

Sebastian recalled a particularly terrifying experience he had at Frameline a couple of years ago. He explained,

> I saw a really terrible film . . . It was a story about an intersexed girl.[1] She
> was being raised as female. She is introduced to a guy her same age. She is
> also introduced to younger men in her community. Eventually there's this
> horrifying rape scene. There is almost always this horrifying rape scene in
> every film or movie or storyline or plot that includes transgender people.
> Like *Boys Don't Cry*. [His voice grew louder.] . . . When I got out of this
> movie I was so upset . . . I'm tired of feeling violated! [He punctuated
> the word "tired" by smacking his hand against the surface of the table.]
> I feel like I am getting assaulted every time I have to sit in a room with
> 300 people and watch another trans body be destroyed and violated for
> everyone to watch. I'm tired of it. I had a total meltdown after that movie.

After the film, and noticeably shaken up, Sebastian wanted to talk through his feelings and channel the energy that pulsed through him. He shared his fury and frustration with one of his friends. However, his friend suggested he was being overly sensitive. Sebastian commented, "I'm tired of non-trans people representing me, telling me it's not a big deal, there's nothing really to be upset about, that I should be more reasonable about it and not take it personally. I'm just like 'Shut the fuck up!' I was pissed that I put it out there, that I felt like it was really violating, and that nobody either felt that also, or people wanted to argue with me about how it wasn't violating."

Unfortunately, these kinds of experiences—these electrifying shocks and disturbances to Sebastian's affective and cognitive life—are not uncommon for him. They are part and parcel of living everyday life as a trans person. The very ordinary act of watching a movie with friends generated powerful upheavals in Sebastian's mind and, perhaps even more so, in his body. Certainly, the film stirred his thoughts and prompted him to resist its ideological messages. Similar to the participants I discussed in chapter 2, Sebastian objected to the movie's privileging of violence and victimhood as the defining frame for transgender experience.

This kind of ideological engagement has been well documented in media studies.[2] In his now canonical essay "Encoding/Decoding," Hall

(1980) argued that when interfacing with the products and discourses of media, audiences generally accept, negotiate with, and/or resist their ideological messages. Hall's theorization of ideological resistance has become as a gravitational center in the field, "central to an understanding of popularity in a society where power is unequally distributed" (Fiske 1987, 316). Audience resistance asserts "the power to be different," and the "power to construct meanings, pleasures, and social identities that differ from those proposed by the structures of domination" (ibid., 317). Resistance is important because it confirms that audiences are essentially actively engaged with media and that, in the face of media's ideological power, they are often critical and discerning consumers of information and entertainment (Jenkins 2002). In this way, scholars generally revere resistance to media messages as transgressive and empowering.

However, researchers' acute focus on resistance and on the ideological effect of media suggests that audience experiences are worthy only insofar as they are politically or ideologically charged. This sets up the practice of resisting media as an ethical apex, as the fullest expression of audience agency. Moreover, as Ang (1996) suggests, throughout the 1980s and 1990s, audience research "suffered from an image problem" because it uncritically exaggerated audience agency (8). For example, while pioneering work by Fiske (1987) and Jenkins (1992) focused much needed attention on audiences, it was critiqued for over-celebrating their creativity and industriousness. At times this work also too easily conflated resistance to media messages with democratic participation and social change. Indeed, at stake in studies of resistance is granting audiences an excess of social power—power that they perhaps do not appreciate—and misconceiving them as fully resistant figures—without a clear understanding of what they are opposing. This is not to say that resistance is a useless concept; rather, it is a complicated one and only part of the story of how audiences engage with media.

Clearly, Sebastian's media experience at Frameline was in part a practice of ideological resistance. He challenged the film's placement of the transgender body within a violent framework and a tragic structure of feeling. However, Sebastian's media encounter was more than a rational and cognitive exercise. It was also a profoundly emotional and visceral one. He processed the film in and through his body, as a jolt of symbolic violence that sparked feelings of violation, sadness, and rage. In outwardly suffering "a total meltdown," he broke a fundamental "feeling rule" (Hochschild [1983] 2003, 18) that discourages this kind of vivid emotional display in public settings. He *felt* the film so deeply that his friend suggested he be more "reasonable," encouraging him to sublimate the rush of energy charging through his body into reason and rationality—something he was unable and perhaps unwilling to do at the time.

The film at Frameline was such a powerful trigger that, years later during our interview, Sebastian is still noticeably shaken. As we sit talking about that night, it is clear he harbors a sort of "muscle memory" about his experience: his voice falters, he strikes the table with his hand, and his body alternately tenses up and releases. It is as if talking about the film transported his sensory system back to that moment in the theater watching the rape scene. In the San Francisco hotel room, overlooking the Castro district, I see Sebastian try to manage and contain his feelings—the way his friend told him to.

Echoing Sebastian, many participants recalled similar experiences of agitation and upheaval, articulating words such as "hurt," "angry," "tired," "frustrated," "worn out," "shaken up," "devastated," and "fed up" to describe their encounters with media. As they spoke, their bodies mirrored these sentiments. They squirmed in their chairs, gazed downward, tightened their jaw, and exhaled heavily. They rolled their eyes, puffed their chests, and vigorously shook their hands. A few welled up with tears.

In this chapter, I foreground these kinds of embodied audience encounters investigating media as affective technologies, by which I mean technologies that not only engage our mind but also our bodies, our senses, and emotions. I examine the various affects—or the sensations, feelings, and experiences of "intensity" (Massumi 2002, 27–28)—that media and communications technologies transmit and the practices audiences deploy to manage and come to terms with them. As Gibbs (2002) argues, "what is co-opted by the media is primarily affect . . . the media function as amplifiers and modulators of affect which is transmitted by the human face and voice, and also by music and other forms of sound, and also by the image" (338). Affect is raw and "preconscious" and involves "being attuned to and coping with the world without the input of rational content" (Leys 2011, 442, note 22). It is the quaking of the senses within the body, a turbulence of inner stasis. Affect is similar to emotion, as both refer to "the feeling of bodily change" (Ahmed 2004, 5). However, emotions feel familiar and are less abstract. They typically follow cultural norms and expectations.[3] Emotions are intelligible, both on a cultural and individual level, and we have license to feel them. Emotions are also normatively charged. There are "proper" and "improper" ways, for example, to *feel* about media. Society accepts emotional responses such as sadness, fear, and happiness to provocative media content. However, other responses are less socially acceptable, knowable, and apparent. This is the realm of affect. Affect can be opaque and "emerges out of muddy, unmediated relatedness" (Seigworth and Gregg 2010, 4). Although we feel them and register them in our bodies, sometimes affects cannot be easily named. They can be difficult to explain or control.

Media traffic in both affect *and* emotion. They move us and build intensities that are both within and outside the immediate realm of our understanding. They heighten our emotional capacities and create undulating, embodied experiences. They vex the senses and dig under the skin. On one level, they can reproduce high moments of intense disruption, and on another level, they create more "ordinary affects," or "the varied, surging capacities to affect and be affected that give everyday life the quality of a continual motion of relations, scenes, contingencies, and emergences" (Stewart 2007, 2).[4] Media affects are also incredibly diverse. Audiences can experience a wide spectrum of sensations during a media encounter, and audience members encountering the same media can experience diverse affects and emotions. For example, whereas the film did not *stick* to or affectively disturb his friend, Sebastian's experience was one of shock and disorientation. This is because audiences bring their own affective histories to each and every media encounter, histories that contain both positively and negatively codified experiences. This is why media encounters are so powerfully and electrically charged, for they can be reruns of previously felt trauma.

Given this reality, how do transgender audiences like Sebastian engage, manage, and come to terms with the emotional and affective power of media representation? How do they deal with the shocks, with the negative experiences? One participant offered a hint, "There are a lot of people who I think are the victim of how our media has portrayed and continues to portray trans people . . . you have to be *really strong* to not let these things get to you." In this chapter, I focus on this process of being "really strong" and the various methodologies of adaptation and survival participants deploy in coming to terms with media's disempowering messages and the affective turbulences they generate. I analyze how participants rebound and rebuild their sense of self that popular discourses threaten to erode. I foreground how they construct self-protective armors, guard and protect their integrity, and thicken their skin. I call this audience practice "resilient reception." Resilient reception offers a framework for thinking about audience practices in less heroic and congratulatory terms than resistance, while still affirming the activity of viewers in everyday life.

Resilient Reception as an Affective Audience Practice

I return now to Sebastian in order to further clarify what I mean by resilient reception. Although he experienced feelings of violation and assault after viewing the movie at the Frameline Film Festival, Sebastian employed strategies of rebounding, re-centering, and "making do" (de Certeau 1984, 29). Directly after the film, he stepped away from his friends, removing himself from the situation. He recalled, "I almost had to leave to take a walk by myself. I was so pissed I couldn't even be around anybody." Claiming this physical and emotional distance allowed him to steal a few deep breaths and collect himself, so as to continue with his night out. This strategy of self-distancing represents only one in a cache of strategies that Sebastian has developed.

On a much wider scale, Sebastian told me that his ability to "deal with" and "move on" from the personal disruptions he experiences from media and everyday life is the result of several things. First, he firmly roots himself within local trans and queer communities in the San Francisco Bay area. He actively cultivates a sense of connection and belonging through meaningful interpersonal relationships with trans and queer friends, as well as with non-trans friends and allies. These social networks provide him with multiple layers of interpersonal and emotional support. Sebastian also secures a sense of self and purpose by engaging in service to the LGBT and queer community. For example, he works with homeless queer youth in San Francisco, serving as an advocate for those less fortunate. He also sat on a local governmental committee that assessed the needs of trans men. Finally, Sebastian is a lifelong learner and regularly informs himself about trans identity and politics through reading trans-themed books, websites, blogs, etc. In building his vocabulary and knowledge base regarding queer subjectivity and politics, Sebastian constructs a cognitive and affective self-armor, which helps to fortify him from popular discourses that repudiate his sense of self. Establishing social capital, rooting himself in the local community, and building an affective self-armor through knowledge: these are Sebastian's practices of resilience. And he carries them with him throughout his interactions with media and popular culture.

Experiences like Sebastian's are often overlooked in the study of media audiences, which have disproportionately explored the relationship between media use and the workings of ideology. While this has contributed to our understanding of media reception, the "affective turn" (Clough 2007) offers the opportunity to understand audience interactions with media, such as Sebastian's, in more multidimensional ways. The affective turn denotes an effort by researchers to tap into and render intelligible human experiences of embodiment, feeling, and being that are related to but not necessarily subsumed by ideology. The literature on affect marks a crucial shift "to bodily matter" (206), to embodied phenomena, and the "privileging of movement, emergence, and potentiality in relationship to the body" (219).

Audience research in particular, whose objects of inquiry should include a vast range of audience-media encounters, has inadequately tapped into audiences' affective experiences. As Shouse (2005) argues, "the power of many forms of media lies not so much in their ideological effects, but in their ability to create affective resonances" (3). Importantly, this is not an either-or situation, for ideology and affect are thoroughly entwined within the practice of media reception. My fieldwork and the stories participants tell lay bare the ways ideology and affect, cognition and emotion, the conscious and non-conscious, intermix and work in tandem during the audience experience.

In addition to their minds, participant bodies and sensory systems were all deeply activated as they engaged with media and communications technologies. In fact, participant media encounters were so profoundly visceral, and processed so tangibly in the body, that they required a form of affective resilience. They involved what Hochschild ([1983] 2003) calls "emotional labor," or the act of managing one's feelings "in order to sustain the outward countenance that produces the proper state of mind in others" (7). Emotional labor is the work involved in expressing, regulating, and understanding our emotions and the emotions of others. The word "labor" is key because it signals the expenditure of effort, "a coordination of mind and feeling" that "draws on a source of self that we honor as deep and integral to our individuality" (7).[5]

Although resilience has yet to gain currency within media studies, there is a considerable body of scholarship on the concept across other disciplines. Increasingly, thinkers in global politics, environmental science, and urban planning, for example, are turning toward resilience to help understand how the complex systems we rely on daily—such as economies, environments, public health infrastructures, cities, etc.— function, rebuild, and sustain when faced with disruption and crisis.[6] Within these fields, a resilient structure is "more than simply sustainable," it is fundamentally "regenerative and diverse, relying not only on the capacity to absorb shocks like the popped housing bubble or the rising sea level, but to evolve with them" (Cascio 2009, 92). Perhaps the most useful conceptualization of resilience for the study of media audiences comes from psychology. Reviewing resilience as a psychological construct, Luthar, Cicchetti, and Becker (2000) summarize it as "a dynamic process encompassing positive adaptation within the context of significant adversity" (543), an achievement of "competence despite adversity" (554). However, in deploying resilience as an analytic tool, I break from this definition in one important respect. Rather than understanding resilience as a "positive" or "competent" adaptation in terms of the external criteria used in psychology—such as ethical values, prosocial behaviors, and ideas of mental health—I delineate resilience as a more deeply personal endeavor. My fieldwork unveils that practices of resilient reception are multiple, diverse, and at times morally and politically ambiguous. They have no inherent nature. While they certainly can be, they are not necessarily expressions of progressive politics, "healthy" human adaptation, or moral virtue. Rather, practices of resilient reception are, at base, survival strategies enacted as pragmatic responses to the powerfully affective encounters individuals have with media and society in the everyday.

In this way, resilience is something one does. Even more, it is something one does quite ordinarily. Rather than being remarkable and unique, psychological research confirms that resilience is common, "a phenomenon arising from ordinary human adaptive processes" (Masten 2001, 234). Yet, although it is common and humans generally have the capacity for it, it bears noting that resilience is not equally achievable for everyone. The capacity for resilience relies on multiple personal, contextual, and institutional factors. Often outside of an individual's control, variables such as one's socioeconomic class, social capital, geographic location, formal education, power, and privilege all play a role in determining what resilience looks like and whether it is accessible. For example, participants with greater social and economic capital generally managed life challenges easier than those with less. They also had access to a wider range of coping mechanisms and resources for support.

Similarly, within a media context, audiences practice resilience at the crossroads of media power and personal agency. Certainly, the media industries as global institutions wield tremendous economic, cultural, and political power, and their narratives often rise to the level of cultural myth. However, while resilient reception acknowledges the authority of media and its ability to affect, it also highlights the actions and life choices audiences bring to bear in their media encounters.

Broadly speaking, practices of resilient reception are acts of orientation and re-orientation. They are the positions and movements we adopt toward and away from media. According to Ahmed (2006b), who draws on classic phenomenology, one of the defining features of everyday life is the endless orientation of self to the various objects of perception that inhabit our world. Orientations are strategic and well-intentioned acts of self-positioning, the "directions towards objects that affect what we do, and how we inhabit space" (28). Pragmatically, we engage in orientation to help us "find our way" and "feel at home" in the dynamic conditions and changing environments that characterize our world (1, 7).

In managing media's affective fallout, participants in my research engaged in the kind of positioning and movement that Ahmed theorizes. They adopted various stances of orientation, which secured and reclaimed their sense of self. These acts of re-orientation occur regularly over time and evolve as they are tested and adjusted. Thus, resilient reception conceptualizes audience practices as developing within everyday life's temporal flow and moves us past the "moment of reception"—or that actual, bounded occasion when one consumes media. Audiences are not simply affected by media within the context of a single viewing moment, but continuously and ceaselessly struggle with the messages of media culture, contending with its influence over their self-worth, integrity, and emotional life on a daily basis.[7] For it is only through time, and throughout a lifetime, that cultural symbols acquire their affective power and "stickyness" (Ahmed 2004).

Through repetition and a history of articulation, symbols accrue their capacity to cling to us, boil our blood, cut to the core, and dig under our skin. For example, the reason Sebastian felt so unsettled after watching the film at Frameline was because he had, in many ways, seen this movie before. This particular film was merely one in a long succession of similar cultural representations that have made him feel defiled and caused him to enact strategies of resilient reception. Moreover, media engagements are not the only agents of disruption in Sebastian's life. Living as a transgender person, he has frequently contended with systematic prejudice, restricting social norms, and caustic misunderstanding from others. His media engagements are energized and intensified by the affective residue of these lived experiences. In this way, his media encounters and practices of resilient reception exist within a much wider context and should be understood as constitutive of a larger struggle he experiences in everyday life.

Notably, other minority groups have also shared in the struggle of continually preserving and rebuilding the self in the face of disempowerment and everyday disenfranchisement. In confronting the affective turbulence of living in a media culture not created for them, they too have adapted strategies of orientation and resilience. In her analysis of black female audiences, bell hooks (1992) discovered that the mundane act of seeing a movie was often "less than pleasurable; at times it caused pain" (121). According to one of her participants, "I could always get pleasure from movies as long as I did not look too deep" (121). For those who looked too deep, their viewing experience could be profoundly distressing. In confronting and managing this hurt, hooks (1992) delineated the many strategies black women employed. Some talked about and critiqued the films while they were in progress on the screen. Others were "on guard" (126) and emotionally distanced themselves from what they saw. Many chose to "look the other way" (120) or simply turned off their critical mind and forget the racist elements that blared before them. In a similar study of black spectatorship, Stewart (2003) noted that black audiences often adopt a practice of laughing back at the screen, mockingly and sarcastically chuckling at racist elements they perceive in a text. She argues that this affective strategy exists somewhere between "passive complicity and vocal critique," and at the intersection of "laughter" and "pain" (677). Some of the participants in my study deployed analogous strategies of coping to manage media affects. I now turn to the experiences of Remi, Avery, and Alyssa to examine their practices of resilient reception.

Remi

Coming of age in the 1990s, Remi, a transgender graduate student attending school in the Midwest, occasionally came across *The Jerry Springer Show*, an infamously tawdry daytime television talk program. As it was one of the only sites where she witnessed gender variance, the program confirmed that transgender people existed. Gazing at her through the television screen, the show's transgender guests spoke on their own behalf and claimed identities that were new and exciting for Remi. Even as a young person, she had an intuitive sense that her gender identity was far more complex than the male sex to which she was assigned at birth, and the show in part offered her a comforting sense of self-recognition. At the same time, *Jerry Springer* represented transgender people as problematic human anomalies and freaks.[8] Nonetheless, Remi watched and, as a young person struggling to develop her gender identity, the show stirred many emotions: "I watched *Jerry Springer* . . . I am angry at myself for doing it sometimes. So, I watched it and felt really angry and disturbed, upset, and sad. [Her voice grows louder.] They're like making fun of trans people and everyone laughs."

Remi perceived these talk shows as an assault on transgender life and subjectivity, and in watching them, was overwhelmed with feelings of sadness and humiliation. The shows got under her skin. They profoundly resonated with a sense of "being crazy," a feeling she was struggling with in desiring gender transformation. Remi explained, "All your life you learn that it's sort of a crazy thing if you want to change gender. It's just

crazy. When I talked to people about it they would mostly not understand. They're like 'what?' 'Why would you wanna do that?' And you're
kinda of like, well I'm crazy right? In the midst of all this, I watched
Jerry Springer." In addition to exacerbating feelings of "being crazy," the
show's organizing structure, which pits the studio audience against the
transgender guests, reverberated with her own experiences of living in
fear. "I was growing up as a boy who was feminine, and from the very
beginning from when I was 5, you know you're not acting in the 'right'
ways. So, you have a sense that violence, power, are wielded in an awful
way and I don't want a part of that. *Jerry Springer* definitely brought
back memories of growing up and what boys do to other boys, that kind
of violence happening on a daily basis. Whether it's physical or verbal."
Given this personal history, watching *Jerry Springer* was a reliving of
trauma for Remi, an affective return to a form of everyday violence that
made her feel alienated.

In fact, throughout our first interview, Remi repeated the word "alienation" or "alienated" five times. She explained that throughout much of
her life, expressions of gender nonconformity were virtually invisible in
the world she perceived around her. "You start to see the gender schema
on TV. I mean not just on TV, but in the world in general. The pallet of
genders that are acceptable in everyday life, appearances and so forth,
is extremely limited." Also limited was the kind of racial diversity she
perceived. This was particularly the case with television, for it was the
medium she was most exposed to as a young person. "I'm South Asian.
Chinese Philippine. Yeah, so I never saw anyone on TV who looked
like me . . . [TV shows] are not true to life. I mean to my life. I don't
see myself in them. Or people who are like me in them. Or like people
who are in my life in them." Remi's multiracial identity coupled with
her gender variance caused her to feel "disillusionment with the media"
and "really distant and alienated from media." Even on those chance
occasions when she found television shows she enjoyed, the relationship was typically short-lived and eventually discouraging. "I would get
attached to TV shows and they would get cancelled. It's like the same
thing with relationships. I like to get attached and then not have them
go all of a sudden . . . I liked *Buffy the Vampire Slayer*, which I still like,
but then it would just get annoying how I would never see anyone like
me. So, I just started feeling more and more alienated. So just as far as

race is concerned, and gender wise." Remi equated her connection with television shows to interpersonal relationships, mentioning her fear that both had the potential to end. She revealed a powerful parasocial inter-action (Horton and Wohl 1956), deeply investing in media narratives and bonding with characters as if they were actual people.[9] The highly intense nature of this connection and its affective power explains why her feelings of alienation were so strong, for television was imbued with a sort of personhood.

In attempting to protect herself from feelings of craziness, memories of violence, and bouts of alienation generated by encounters with media, Remi has practiced several strategies of resilient reception. One of the first included was what Ahmed (2006b) calls an "orientation device," or a maneuver that strategically positions oneself toward (or away) from an object. Remi oriented herself toward media with diminished expec-tations. She attested, "I just sorta expected to be disappointed when I watched. I developed that thing where I expected to be disappointed." This strategy was preemptive and furnished a protective emotional buf-fer. Remi also became increasingly purposeful and careful in her media choices. "I became very selective." With fierce intentionality, she oriented herself away from more mainstream media forms, becoming immersed in queer subcultures. She voraciously read lesbian fiction, viewed inde-pendent LGBT films, and attended transgender-themed theater. "I actu-ally had this moment where I stopped consuming any media that wasn't queer. And I think that has persisted, or that it actually persisted for quite a while. It wasn't until a couple of years later that I thought I could handle media that wasn't queer. So, I made a conscious decision that this was just pissing me off, I didn't relate to it." In light of the affective labor demanded by encounters with non-queer media, Remi spun a protec-tive cocoon around herself by creating a personal media ensemble. Dur-ing this time, she strengthened her layers of defensive armor that would eventually allow her to again "handle" non-queer media and culture.

Remi's practices of resilience also included finding a home in certain "communities of choice" (Wellman et al. 2003, 10) that were located both online and in the "real world." Remi sought out online communities to come to terms with two of the larger challenges she faced as a teenager: being transgender and coping with depression. "I realized I was dealing with depression around the same time I realized I was trans. It was when

I was like 15 or 16. I was clinically depressed when I was 15 and searching for why I was so unhappy. So, I found depression support groups on-line. It was random because there was a connection between the depression support groups and the trans support groups. Some people were in both." Remi's interactions in these communities offered her emotional support and pragmatic strategies to help her cope with her depression. They also affirmed her desire to transition gender and furnished feelings of inclusion. "I felt like I belonged to there more so than in other Internet settings that aren't sexual or gender specific."

Remi also secured feelings of place and belonging in "real world" communities of choice. Before moving to the Midwest to pursue graduate school, Remi grew up in California within driving distance of San Francisco, and she eventually attended college there. Within close proximity of the city, she took advantage of its diverse communities. "Even before I lived in San Francisco I would visit there . . . When I was growing up, I would just go up to San Francisco to hang out. There's lots of queer stuff going on and going to those would make me feel like I belong in some way . . . There was this thing where queer writers would come to this coffee house. So, there was this scene, the writer scene that I was really into." As a social resource of resilience, this writing scene encouraged Remi to turn inward for self-knowledge and inspiration—rather than gazing outward toward the specter of media and popular culture. She began to thicken her skin and fortify herself, investigating and embracing her own life through the self-reflexive exercise of writing. "I just started feeling like mainstream media was a waste of time. And I felt like my own life was a lot more interesting. And the things I was writing, I'm a big writer. So, I would write stuff about my life."

Today, Remi's writing skills are helping her pursue a PhD in the humanities. In large part, her doctoral research is directed at studying the politics of representation. As with Sebastian, Remi remains resilient to the affective shocks of everyday life through better understanding the world and by securing a sense of control and ownership over that which rattles and disconfirms her. More than supporting resilience, this academic pursuit also bolstered her capacity for resistance: "I decided to make my life's work, at least for now, resisting and critiquing that [media, politics, and culture]. So I am channeling my anger everyday through my work." Remi explains that her experience on the margins as a multiracial, transgender person fuels her work. It motivates her to speak out against and articulate counternarratives to the dominant cultural scripts she struggled with growing up. In looking at the various orientation devices she adopts, it becomes clear that Remi's experiences with media are fundamentally layered. They include practices of resilience, as she buffers herself from media's affective resonances. However, she simultaneously opposes (Hall 1980) ideological incorporation through her coursework. In this way, resilience and resistance are coexisting and supplementary practices she deploys in her everyday encounters with media.

Avery

"I'm not masculine identified. I'm not feminine identified. I don't believe gender's a spectrum, I believe it's a landscape . . . landscape identity means you are actually in a physical space and that you are not just on a linear plane. You're wandering, you're moving. It's dynamic," Avery explained as he gulped down his café latte. Throughout my fieldwork, most of my interviews began with idle conversation that established communicative rapport. However, from the moment we sat down at the small coffee shop, Avery was ready and eager to talk. Politically conscious, socially aware, and acutely self-reflexive, Avery is an undergraduate who lives in a housing co-op with 29 other people in a Midwestern university town. He is incredibly energetic and has a relentlessly hyperactive and prolific mind.

Although he suggested I use masculine pronouns to describe him, Avery has a complex understanding of his gender, identifying as trans, non-binary, and gender fluid. At times, this subjectivity can cause confusion for some of the people in his life, including his professors. However, most of Avery's friends support and accommodate this complexity. "So right now, the way that it works where I live is that people who know me well in the house will use the pronoun that people don't expect for me. They'll use "he" when certain people are in the house, and make a point out of it especially when I am in a skirt." As with gender, Avery's conception of his sexuality is equally nuanced. Identifying as polyamorous and pansexual, he enjoys practicing kink and BDSM—a range of sexual practices that includes bondage, discipline, dominance—submission, sadism, and masochism. However, Avery currently has a boyfriend who he described as "a heterosexual, monogamous guy. He is very low on the Kinsey scale. So, what does it mean to be dating? Does it mean I am contained to woman? Sometimes. And that's pretty tough." The fixity and bounded limits of heterosexual coupling, and the imposition of the category "woman" that his current relationship at times demands, is difficult for Avery to accept. He explained, "I need an identity that is fluid . . . I can be okay with him being heterosexual and dating me as long as that doesn't make me heterosexual."

In a world that seeks simplicity and aggressively defends binaries, Avery's sophisticated worldview, his gender fluidity, and queerness have often made his everyday life difficult. Throughout his childhood and teenage years, Avery never fit in and regularly struggled with fear and crippling anxiety, with the sense that danger was always looming. In part, this fear was driven by his complicated relationship to his body and the strict social expectations of the sex he was assigned at birth, which was female.

When Avery entered college in the Midwest, he started experimenting with his gender identity. However, he was still gripped with fear, and again, a sense of dissonance. "My friends at college knew I was trans, but I would not say I had sexuality with that because so much was driven by fear. It was very much a scary topic to bring up with me, like 'what does this mean?' I was very defensive and I think they could tell that. I would not go by masculine pronouns even though I said I wanted them. I was afraid it would make me think about what my life could be. It was a really scary thing." Avery soon transferred colleges, in part to achieve a greater sense of safety and place. While his current college environment does a better job of providing these feelings, Avery still battles anxiety.

At school, Avery engages in advocacy work, currently volunteering with the LGBT Speakers Bureau and giving public talks on and off campus about transgender issues. However, his role as a speaker has become increasingly difficult. "I used to do a lot of talks, but I had a really negative experience early this term where I was really trying to convince this freshman class that 'look I really am not a woman,' and they needed adequate convincing. I got really tired of being in that role where I always had to prove myself . . . I find that I get worn out being radical here and I find it is also very necessary, which is what keeps me doing it." Even though Avery feels compelled to speak, the activity is an emotional labor that depletes his spirit.

Avery also experiences an exhausting affective toll in his encounters with media. "So much of what I see in media, mainly films, is enforced gender normativity and a lot of abusive family and partner dynamics. That has really turned me off. That is why it takes a lot of energy to see these things. They can be triggering." Avery's words suggested a deeply visceral relationship with media, an emotionally taxing one.

To cope with these affective states and to work through the feelings of fear, disruption, and exhaustion that media generate, Avery has engaged in several practices of resilient reception. The first is a strategy of withdrawal. In withdrawing, Avery orients himself away from certain media forms to preserve his "energy": "Every time I would hear that 'this is better, this is something that would appeal to you,' I was consistently disappointed. Like *The Crying Game*, where it's like 'Look we're making progress.' And I would be continually disillusioned. And so it grew into an eventual withdraw. It takes a lot of energy to convince myself to go see a movie." For Avery, his energy is like currency, a cache of savings that can be depleted and replenished, and he refused to invest it in mainstream, mass media.

However, his strategy of media withdrawal and divestment provoked an unintended consequence. It created feelings of social isolation. Unable to engage in pop culture small talk with others, Avery lost an important form of communicative exchange: media talk. Media talk, or informal conversation about media, is an essential part of sociability in contemporary everyday life. It establishes interpersonal connections and affinities between individuals (Duits 2010, 249–250). Talk about the latest summer blockbuster or a viral video on YouTube is a relatively low-risk form of communication, an easy entry point into dialogue with others. Yet in withdrawing, Avery lost this asset, explaining, "With some people, I had nothing to talk about." To remedy this, Avery has somewhat cautiously decided to reengage with media, but in doing so, mindfully maintains a critical distance. "I'm really trying to get up the 'umph' (oomf) to sort of engage with popular culture so I have something to talk about with people. Rather than taking on the moral tone of 'I know I am not going to like what I see so why bother.' So right now it's kind of at a distance."

Besides strategically orienting himself toward and away from media, Avery's practices of resilient reception also involve blogging on the website Live Journal. This activity is both a critical and a social exercise. It connects Avery to like-minded others within the queer community and provides the opportunity to articulate counter-discourses to mainstream, dominant ideologies on race, sexuality, and gender. "I keep a live journal blog. I use it to keep in contact with friends since I transferred here from another school. It is very much social critique. I write a lot about social identity. I also belong to this online community that looks at racial politics, a lot of identity politics work. It really makes a commitment to get rid of racism and a lot of other 'isms.' And there is a large trans community actually on that blog." Blogging reinforces Avery's progressive politics, for most in the online community share similar political ideologies. As a practice of self-articulation, blogging also allows Avery to "talk back" to popular media, countering the feelings of disillusionment and disappointment it often generates in an empowering way. "People I blog with *care* about this stuff . . . Largely the people I am connected to are queer in some way through Live Journal, but in varying degrees of visibility." In a very real sense, blogging is an act of resistance for Avery, the kind of resistance media scholars have heralded. At the same time, this activity rests alongside practices of resilience. Blogging helps Avery fortify a transgender sense of self. He finds strength, belonging, and support in a community of bloggers who "care about this stuff."

Notably, this notion of "care" was important to Avery. The sense of belonging to a community of care—one that cares about social and political issues *and* about Avery himself—was something he called "absolutely necessary." The necessity of care, for Avery, lies in its functionality. Whereas resilient reception depletes one's energy, it seems that care replenished his reserves. Like stopping to refuel on a long-distance road trip, Avery's fairly regular virtual interactions on blogs replenished the energy he needed to resist and remain resilient as he journeyed back out into the "real" world.

Alyssa

"Between my family not talking to me, and all that I had to put up with during my transition from people . . . I really don't pay attention to it [transgender-themed media]," Alyssa admitted. "I mean the last thing I want to do right now is go through it all over again." Alyssa is in her mid-twenties and works as a cosmetologist at a mid-sized shopping mall in the suburban Midwest. While she identifies as trans, she prefers to be identified as a woman. Unlike most of the participants in this study, Alyssa expressed that she has never had interest in and has paid little attention to transgender-themed media. In fact, throughout our many interactions with each other, she offered few concrete statements and opinions on media and culture. Alyssa was also hesitant to talk about her own life and experiences. This was unexpected because Alyssa is a very outspoken and talkative individual.

Nonetheless, meaning can reveal itself in absence, and slip through a blanket of silence. In fact, part of Alyssa's strategy of self-protection, that which allows her to persist as a trans woman, is the deployment of silence, a refusal to engage, to not "go through it all over again." The "it" she refers to is the overwhelming pain and affective magnitude of her gender transition. "Transitioning was really hard for me," Alyssa conceded. She suddenly stopped talking, took a deep breath, and remained silent for a few more moments. The air became thick and heavy. She then continued, "My family sucked. I hardly ever see them. My father and I don't even talk now." These statements represent the only concrete insights Alyssa offered into her relationship with her family. Regarding her gender transition, she disclosed one more thought. "Thank God it's over."

I first met Alyssa the one and only night she attended the Trans Chat group I observed during my fieldwork. Throughout the two-hour meeting, she did not speak. She simply sat quietly next to her boyfriend, Derek, a twenty-something bank teller who self-identified as a queer man. As a couple, they were fabulously hip: stylishly covered in tattoos, piercings, and dressed mainly in black and denim. Upon the closing of the meeting, Alyssa and Derek approached me, complemented *my* outfit, and we started a conversation. After I explained my research project to them, we went out to a local lounge, a sort of speakeasy that served craft cocktails, the kind that was becoming trendy at the time. Over drinks, Alyssa and Derek agreed to participate in my study. Over the next several months, I met with the couple almost weekly.

Over dinner at their home one evening, Alyssa, Derek, and I began talking about transgender representation in the media. Somewhat surprisingly, as the conversation progressed, it seemed that Derek was more eager to talk and had more to say about this issue than Alyssa. In fact, Alyssa looked somewhat uncomfortable with the conversation, becoming tense and befuddled. Yet Derek spoke ardently, insisting that the gender-bending character Dr. Frank-N-Furter from *The Rocky Horror Picture Show* was one of the sexiest film characters in recent times. He confessed that he cried during the transgender-themed movie *Boys Don't Cry* (1999), and he encouraged me to visit a local theater that staged campy drag shows. Offsetting Derek's playful enthusiasm and chattiness was Alyssa's intense rawness and noticeable brevity. She offered, "I don't know. I just don't really pay attention to it." She recounted that as a teenager, the trans representations she saw in the media troubled her. "When I would see a [trans] girl, which was not a lot, I would get all upset. I'd get all upset and wonder why they were never attractive." When I pressed Alyssa to further elaborate on these past encounters with trans images, she said nothing more. Silence. Attempting to prevent any conversational lull, Derek would often speak on behalf of Alyssa—something she seemed to merely tolerate.

What soon became apparent was that Alyssa's silences, her intentional economy with words, represented one of her practices of resilient reception, one that was dependable and always accessible. Rather than signs of submission or weakness, her refusals to engage with, to comment on, and to even acknowledge, are survival strategies, ways she protects herself. As Wendy Brown (2005) argues, silence can function as a "shelter," "refuge," or "barrier" (86–87), a "means of preserving certain practices and dimensions of existence from regulatory power, from normative violence, as well as from the scorching rays of public exposure" (85). Brown maintains that within human experience there are "deadening (antilife) things that must be allowed residence in a pond of silence rather than surface into discourse if life is to be lived without being claimed by their weight" (93). In some cases, silence may be the only way to manage those things that wield the power to take us over, to drown us.

In sheltering herself and in refusing to be weighed down, Alyssa has also consciously chosen to remain distant from transgender subcultures and communities, orientating herself away from them. She was never involved with transgender advocacy, and explains, "I'm not into politics. Never have been," and never considered herself part of a trans community. Yet, a few years ago during her transition, she made several trans friends, participated in online transgender discussion forums, and frequented a club that hosted transgender-inclusive parties on Saturday nights. However, this period of engagement was brief, and she has since pulled away. "I mean I can see why some people get all involved, but it's not my thing anymore. It's just too much. It's just too much." This too much-ness represented the affective baggage that, for Alyssa, weighed her down. Being involved means giving of herself, giving pieces of herself. Instead, Alyssa chose to reside in Brown's "pond of silence" (2005, 93).

I want to pause briefly here and suggest that my exchanges with Alyssa, even though they are one-on-one, are also powerfully informed by a collective consciousness. More than just personal memories and associations, participants arrive to media encounters with the weight of cultural memory—aware of what transgender communities have experienced in the past, how they have been treated in popular representation, and their current tenuous place in society. For example, returning to Sebastian, he feels violated not only in the singular, as an individual, but in the plural sense, as part of a community that has experienced routine and often sanctioned violation and abuse. Likewise, when Alyssa claims that, "it's just too much," she draws on a collective experience of suffering and struggle commonly experienced by transgender individuals and communities. Throughout our interviews, she discusses representative examples of other people who struggle living as young transgender women in the industrial Midwest. One of her friends was kicked out of her home. Another fights the nagging pull of depression and terminal unemployment. Even as she tries to orient herself away from them, she inevitably taps into a larger social fabric of collective, affective transgender memory. She experiences the cumulative weight of her own, and others' like her, affective experiences as "too much." So, she strategically avoids trans-themed media, and distances herself from trans communities.

Finally, to combat the overwhelmingly "anti-life things" (Brown 2005), Alyssa orients herself toward the soothing effects of drugs and alcohol. Throughout my time with her and Derek, drugs and alcohol were typically on hand and frequently used. As Alyssa explained to me, during her high school years she began smoking marijuana, made available to her from a neighbor. Smoking pot reliably numbed her sadness and rage regarding the hostility she encountered at home and at school. Now, as a young adult in her twenties, she and Derek generally smoke a joint every evening after dinner. Riding out their high together, they listen to music, watch YouTube videos and horror movies. Derek paints at an easel in their bedroom while Alyssa flips through fashion magazines, commenting on the celebrities' makeup. These moments of leisure, escape, and release punctuate the end of their workday, and help revitalize them for the next.

For Alyssa, strategies of silence, self-distancing, numbing, and escape protect her from being overwhelmed by the gravity of the social stigma and abject rejection she experiences from her family and society. They help her mitigate the demands and pressures of an identity politics that requests she foreground her gender identity, become publicly visible as transgender, and actively participate in the transgender community—things she does not feel comfortable doing. In fact, Alyssa recalled that she only attended the Trans Chat meeting where we met because her boyfriend encouraged her to go. "Derek wanted to go. Honestly, I don't think I would go back to that group again . . . It's just not for me. I don't need to go to a group or watch the documentaries or go to the clubs. It's just too much."

Conclusion

What becomes clear from Alyssa's story, and what connects her to the other participants cited in this chapter, is the way their media encounters and everyday experiences require the emotional labor of resilient reception. Sebastian's quelling of turbulent feelings at Frameline Film Festival, Remi's channeling of anger into his graduate work, Avery "getting up the oomf" to see trans-themed media, and Alyssa's silence in the face of media and everyday moments that are "just too much" speak to a continuous and labor-intensive management of affect.

However, it is important to note that although this chapter has explored resilience in media reception and everyday life, sometimes the burden of emotional labor hits a breaking point or the politics of a certain time period require stark opposition. These are moments when resilience is no longer possible or politically sound. That is to say, I am not arguing that resilience is preferable to resistance. Nor do I believe that just because people can be resilient that there is no need for deep structural change, political resistance, and collective efforts for social justice. Rather, my aim has been to balance the scale, to show how resistance is only one part of minoritarian audience practices. Resistance is and must continue to be an important analytical tool of media and queer studies, and a critical strategy for enacting sociopolitical change. But, we cannot overlook its close relatives, those strategies of resilient reception that minorities perform on an ordinary, everyday level: orientation devices of distancing and withdrawal, building self-armors through education and knowledge, becoming embedded in communities of choice, blogging and life-writing, deploying silence, and engaging in alcohol and drug use. These help individuals cope and make do. Continuing to explore similar kinds of practices, the next chapter shifts from transgender resilience to daily life management. I examine how the participants in my study engage with media and technology in tactical ways to achieve the rhythms and affordances of everyday life.

5

We're Just Living Life

Media and the Struggle for the Ordinary

"My girlfriend has this skit that she never had a trans breakfast cereal. There is no trans anything," Billie said through a smile and a quiet chuckle. Billie is a white trans woman in her early twenties, a student who lives in the Midwest. She and her girlfriend, Jess, also a trans woman, share this running joke involving breakfast cereal. Whenever they find themselves in a situation where transgender absence is glaringly apparent, they turn toward each other and ask, "Where's the trans breakfast cereal?"

During our conversation, the topic of trans breakfast cereal surfaced as Billie discussed the social climate of the Midwestern town where she grew up. Billie's high school was an "extremely homophobic environment," and in her local community, "there were no visible trans people around, and I guess that's true of most places." Nevertheless, as a child, rather than sitting down to a bowl of trans breakfast cereal, Billie appreciated another gender nonconforming morning ritual. Before leaving for school, she would secretly watch the TV show *Jem and the Holograms* (1985–1988), a fabulously flashy animated series about the adventures of a female glam-rock group. Drenched in bright pinks and blues, the female-driven series followed a music executive who employs a holographic computer to live a double life as a rock star. As a young boy, Billie knew this was not the kind of show she should be watching, with its overt displays of femininity and gaudy, glittery aesthetics. But she did anyway. The show brought her tremendous pleasure, and more, she used its characters' fashions and styles as a template for her childhood cross-dressing. She recalled, "It would come on in the mornings when I was getting ready for school and I'd be sitting there watching television and I would watch it. And whenever my parents would come into the room I would change the channel. I would snap up the remote and just switch channels. I was aware they would be upset. But I had to watch. I played dress up with the girls next door. I never really played with Barbies, I thought Barbies were stupid. But I liked *Jem and the Holograms* a lot and I really liked playing dress up and dressing like them." Stealing this gender-nonconforming media moment in the morning, and using it as inspiration for playing dress-up, was Billie's daily alternative to the transgender breakfast cereal she never had.

As a mundane and familiar item that routinely appears at the kitchen table each morning, breakfast cereal is a seemingly insignificant thing. However, it is exactly its ordinariness that makes it enticing and marks it as the target of Billie and Jess's joking. The notion of a "trans breakfast cereal" is inconceivable to them because the pairing of "transgender" and "breakfast cereal" is culturally incongruent. Cereal is a sanctioned part of the everyday world, constitutive of its ordinary material culture, whereas transgender typically is not. However, by calling into being a transgender breakfast cereal, Billie and Jess playfully reconcile and unite the opposed logics. They close the gap between transgender and every-dayness. It is this sense of closeness—the closeness between transgender and the everyday—that is missing from their lived experiences and it is what they long for as they joke with each other.

Indeed, the ordinary and the everyday are fundamentally about closeness. According to the philosopher Stanley Cavell (1984), they convey an orientation toward "the common, the low, the near" (193). Like a breakfast cereal, they are immediate, routine, and we experience them in habitual ways. As one of the first thinkers to take the idea seriously, Lefebvre (1991) imagined the everyday as a kind of common ground within which we are all rooted and from which all human activity grows.[1] It is our first position, our home base.[2] Its contours and patterns are thoroughly familiar, comfortable, safe, and predictable, offering feelings of physical and ontological security (Giddens 1990, 1991).[3] Ultimately the ordinary and the everyday, as Garfinkel (1964) contended, is "the world of daily life known in common with others and with others taken for granted" (225).

However, what struck me as I conducted my research was how the people who spoke with me generally lacked the luxury of taking *anything* for granted. Although they tried anchoring themselves within the rhythms and routines of the everyday world, as Billie and Jess show us, even breakfast cereal served as a jostling reminder of their marginality.

Throughout my fieldwork, these themes of ordinariness and everydayness emerged as critical flashpoints. Sometimes, they surfaced as primary concerns and organizing principles. At other times, these themes materialized more as apparitions, as invisible and unacknowledged presences that imposed a tangible force. Given their presence, this chapter explores why the ordinary and the everyday emerged as organizing concepts in my fieldwork and what they mean to participants in the context of their lives. Like a transgender breakfast cereal, participants encountered the ordinary and the everyday as elusive, as close at hand but often out of reach. As a result, they had to devote constant and deliberate work to achieve their considerable benefits and routine affordances, waging a struggle for the ordinary in and through media and technologies of communication.

"Ordinary Life Means Not Having to Worry"

During our first interview, Cameron, a soft-spoken, white trans man in his late twenties who works for a technology company, stopped midsentence and declared—as if drawing a conclusion—that he just wanted "an ordinary life." I asked him what he meant by this. At first he struggled to supply an explanation, as the question seemed to catch him off guard. Yet after a few moments he offered the following: "Ordinary life means not having to worry every time you're in a gender-restricted area such as a bathroom. It means waking up, going to work, and getting home to go to sleep like every other person. It means not being scared to ask someone on a date."

This vision of ordinary life that Cameron described is noteworthy for a variety of reasons. First, it captures the quotidian and shared nature of the everyday. He describes commonplace moments experienced by "every other person" and wishes to be a part of that collectivity. Second, he speaks to the cyclical nature of the everyday. He mentions waking up, going to work, arriving home, and going to sleep, a set of events repeated over and over again. This kind of predictable structure and orderliness presents itself as an object of desire. Third, Cameron acknowledges how the cyclical and orderly routine of the everyday is contingent on a sense of safety and security. For him, using the bathroom, one of the most mundane acts we all perform, and asking someone on a date, a perfunctory social ritual, generates intense fear and anxiety. Finally, Cameron's words pronounce the ordinary and the everyday as elusive.[4] He talks of familiar and mundane scenes with deep reverence, articulating them as luxuries.

Many participants discussed the quiet affordances and clandestine orders of ordinary life with a similar sense of longing. Ethan, a twenty-something trans man living in San Francisco, articulated a desire for one of the ordinary's most fundamental features: the cloak of anonymity. Drawing from Blanchot's (1962) meditation on "le quotidian," Sheringham (2000) suggests that our default subjectivity in everyday life is a state of being a "nobody," that the underlying "pull of the everyday" is toward a nameless anonymity (189). Yet, according to Ethan, being a nobody is somewhat impossible for many trans individuals. Cast in a perpetual state of visibility, they are constantly marked as "Other" both in media representations and in everyday life. As Ethan put it, "I think there's ways in which trans people don't get to become invisible." Along these lines, another participant, Sandy, mentioned that both her gender and racial identity intersect, making her a marked person. "Being a black trans woman makes you stand out even more . . . I currently don't have a home so when I'm in the black neighborhood people look at you for being trans. When I'm in the white neighborhoods they look at you for not being white *and* for being trans. I can't hide."

Like Ethan and Sandy, Steve, a white cross-dresser in his forties from the Midwest, also felt perpetually visible and desired the capacity to dissolve into the background of everyday life's Gestalt. As Steve (who came cross-dressed as Yvonne), his wife, and I sit eating lunch at a restaurant in a Midwestern suburb on a Saturday afternoon, customers walk by our table, gazing and gawking. Two teenaged boys point in Steve's direction, outwardly laughing. Noticing them and clearly embarrassed, Steve explained to me that he has come to expect this kind of unwanted attention when he cross-dresses in public. But he refuses to go out in what he calls "DRAB" ("dressed as a boy"), especially on the weekends, which are sacred because he is not working and can cross-dress full-time. Trying to ignore the public scrutiny erupting around him, he expressed that he eagerly waits for the day that gender variance becomes "boring . . . that it becomes so ubiquitous that it's ordinary." Steve's wife, who is also clearly bothered by the attention, echoed his thoughts. "The majority just want to be ignored, just part of the landscape." Punctuating her point, she referenced popular television. "I watch *House Hunters* on Home and Garden TV and you will see any number of combinations of couples, like interracial, homosexual, and they are just presented as just another couple. So, I think that's probably what the transgender population want to have happen to them for the most part."

As my participants describe it, the ordinary is not just about complete anonymity, but an optimal balance of invisibility (non-recognition) and visibility (recognition). Even as they want the potential to be invisible in everyday life—seen as ordinary and unworthy of being marked—they recognize that this state is dependent on a certain level of visibility and recognition in other contexts. Yet the balance of visibility is off for them. In those spaces where the parameters of ordinary life are constituted, such as media culture, politics, and the economy, spaces where they want to be visible, trans people are largely unrepresented. If trans was "so ubiquitous that it's ordinary" in media, it would help to create the conditions for transgender anonymity in everyday life. But trans individuals are generally invisible in media, and when they are represented they are made hyper-visible as "others." Similarly, the concerns of trans people are largely absent in business, government, and healthcare—precisely where they want acknowledgment and representation.

Standing over six feet and three inches, Callie, a trans woman in her forties from the Midwest, struggled to secure that optimal balance between visibility and invisibility in her everyday life. She mentioned that her larger size and body type make it difficult for her to pass as a woman. But, the feature of everyday life she discussed the most was something else entirely: sociability. According to the sociologist Georg Simmel (1971), sociability is a "play-form of association" (130; emphasis in original), an equitable and amiable mode of communication that prizes talk as "a legitimate end in itself" (137). It is "talk for talk's sake," and its primary aim is a feeling of connection with others, however fleeting. Good-natured, casual, and frictionless, sociability lies at the heart of daily interpersonal interactions.

However, when she began her gender transition, Callie was struck by the fading presence of sociability in her life. Work colleagues who knew her for years suddenly stopped engaging in small talk with her. They gossiped about her transition and spread rumors that she was "a danger to them." Everyday social interactions with others in her local community also lost their sense of ease and inevitability. She stopped receiving what she called "the Midwestern hi," a friendly greeting complete strangers typically offer each other in public. Considering herself an outgoing and affable person, she registered this loss with deep sadness. Callie also struggled with more formal relationships. For instance, dating was difficult. "I would like to have a nice normal loving relationship with a man, but wow it's really hard . . . Dating! Dating is a horror. Meeting people is a complete nightmare . . . Even the men who might be willing to think about it or consider a trans woman as a viable part of their dating pool really can't afford to because it's so highly stigmatized."

Summarizing her experiences, Callie noted the new level of thoughtfulness demanded by living everyday life as a transgender person and the many "hidden costs" of her gender identity. She remarked, "There are things you don't realize that you have to think about until you're actually living it and going through it. It's like buying a house. There are many hidden costs nobody tells you about." As these comments reveal, beyond sociability and the opportunity to date with ease, Callie lost the basic taken-for-grantedness of everyday life. Rather than moving through its structures and spaces with ease, Callie must devote considerable thought, time, and energy to participate in the everyday scenes she once took for granted.

Although this particular story is unique to Callie, a majority of the participants in my study echoed her struggle for the ordinary. They testified to how quotidian tasks such as using a public restroom, finding clothes that fit, interacting with strangers on the streets, or having a vocabulary to talk about one's self were labor-intensive endeavors. Less of a given, for them, everyday life was "an endless, ongoing, contingent accomplishment" (Garfinkel 1967, 1). As Harvey Sacks (1984) argues, the ordinary is not only something one "is," but perhaps even more, it is also something one "does." It is a "business" to which individuals devote considerable effort: "an initial shift is not to think of 'an ordinary person' as some person, but as somebody having as one's job, as one's constant preoccupation, doing 'being ordinary'" (414).

The idea of everyday life as an accomplishment has its roots in a subfield of sociology called "ethnomethodology." Its aim is to discover how the organization of everyday life and its social interactions are created and carried out in local contexts. In fact, one of ethnomethodology's cornerstone studies, published in 1967 by sociologist Harold Garfinkel, documented the life of a transgender person. Garfinkel was part of a team organized by the Psychiatry Department at the University of California, Los Angeles to determine whether a 19-year-old person named Agnes should be granted a sexual reassignment surgery. Assigned male at birth, Agnes had been struggling to pass as a woman for years. Of particular interest to Garfinkel was how her everyday rituals were highly problematic challenges that required careful planning and strategic execution. He called these her "management devices" (183), observing: "The scrutiny she paid to appearances; her concerns for adequate motivation, relevance, evidence and demonstration; her sensitivity to devices of talk; her skill in detecting and managing 'tests' were attained as part of her mastery of trivial but necessary social tasks, to secure ordinary rights to live" (180). Standing outside the taken-for-granted world gazing inward, Agnes achieved these "ordinary rights to live" through careful attention to how everyday life is generally performed and organized. In Garfinkel's eyes, she was a practical methodologist who developed a repertoire of management devices to help her avoid "detection and ruin" (137).

The participants in my study faced a similar world, one full of "tests" and hurdles. They too had to discern everyday settings as practical methodologists in order to develop successful management devices. They too had to work to accomplish the ordinary, as slippery as it is. However, since Garfinkel's study of Agnes, the world has undergone profound and historic changes with respect to the world economy and developments in media and technology. As a result, participant stories differ from Agnes's in a decisive way: the centrality of media to their struggle for the ordinary. In fact, media and communication technologies are hardly mentioned in Garfinkel's study of Agnes, which today appears almost inconceivable.

In the following sections, I focus on how participants in my study leveraged a diverse range of media and technology to construct their own understandings of the everyday and to accomplish its rhythms, orders, and affordances. Informed by the work of de Certeau (1984), I understand participant media use as "tactical"—as an "art of the weak" deployed within the "space of the other" (37)—and explore the various strategies and methodologies participants used to successfully navigate a world organized without them in mind.[5]

Importantly, this larger world—one not only comprised of technology but also the political, economic, and social institutions within which they exist—greatly determined the extent to which their tactical struggles for the ordinary were feasible and successful. The sense of order Cameron imagined or the level of invisibility that Steve and Ethan desired involve, for instance, city ordinances regarding bathrooms or state policies about changing the gender marker on one's driver's license or birth certificate. Their yearning for employment and physical security are sutured to legal frameworks that sanction violence in the public sphere and discrimination in the workplace. Thus, even as I focus on media and individual life in what follows, it is important not to lose sight of the other, larger structures that circumscribe trans experiences. Even more, technology was no panacea. Its capacity to be an arbiter of possibility was finite, limited by its design and select capabilities. For example, even though she was active on social media, technology was unable to supply Callie with everyday sociability and the "Midwestern hi." Even as technology was able to open up some possibilities, it was ineffective at bringing the entirety of ordinary, everyday life within reach.

Relearning "Doing Being Ordinary" with Media

The introduction of this book opened with Margie's story, her experiences with media, and her emphatic pronouncement that trans people are just "ordinary." I return to her now in order to explore how she and her wife "do" being ordinary. Margie is a 59-year-old white trans woman who lives in a neighborhood 25 minutes outside of a Midwestern metropolis. She was raised as a boy and grew up in what she called "a typical conservative suburban community" in the American Midwest. In 1971, she married her wife and they subsequently had two children together. After working in the corporate world for years, Margie opened a successful small business. Eventually Margie's children went to college, moved out of the house, got married, and had children of their own. Margie had been cross-dressing in private throughout her marriage and as she raised her children. Although she wanted to live full-time as a woman and undergo sexual reassignment surgery, the timing never felt right.

However, as she entered her late fifties, her life circumstances changed. The first change was technological. Margie and her wife purchased a new computer and set up a high-speed Internet connection in their home. The technology brought new possibilities and potential interactions to hand. As I have argued, "As personal computers with Internet access became progressively embedded in the everyday, transgender individuals' phenomenological orientation to media shifted. They moved from media audiences engaged in reception to technology users engaged in practices" (Cavalcante 2016, 113). Margie immediately began searching the Web for resources and information about transgender. She explained, "The Internet did make everything possible: what to call myself, how to do everything. Through the Internet and certain chat rooms I found out there was a pre-op and a post-op. There are support sites and the ability to actually learn about people in your own area. There was initially chatrooms and sub-sub rooms. There were ones for transsexuals, and then cross-dressers, and that's how I started to network with people . . . I discovered resources. I discovered I could take hormones."

The second life change for Margie was professional. Her small business became fully stable and profitable. The years of work she and her wife put into it had finally paid off. Given this was during the Great Recession, she was in a fortunate class position. Finally, the third life change involved her family. Her children were now adults and moved away from home. She worried less about how her gender transition would affect their lives. "Our children were adults so there was no baggage there. It's not difficult for them to explain to their friends. That made it kind of easy for me . . . So, I found a good counselor, a gender therapist, and started going there. I found a medical doctor who treats trans people and it just really snowballed." The timing was finally right for Margie.

Following many candid conversations, Margie and her wife planned her gender transition. While supportive, her wife was profoundly shaken by this turn of events and worried about what the future would bring. Yet the couple decided to remain married. They deeply loved each other and wanted to retain what Margie called an "ordinary life" and a sense of "things as usual." As Margie contended, "We're just ordinary people . . . The general public needs to see we're just ordinary people. I don't think any of us are living a lifestyle. *We're just living life.*" Yet, for Margie, "just living life" as an ordinary person took work, and it also required the participation of her wife. One of the most difficult challenges that Margie and her wife faced was being viewed and treated as "ordinary." As a result, the couple devoted themselves to "making it happen." They re-envisioned and redrew the parameters of their worldview, relationship, and everyday lives. Importantly, in doing so they enlisted the help of media and technology.

The couple began their struggle for the ordinary by watching transgender-themed documentaries and teledocumentaries. Margie recalled, "I guess it started with a lot of documentaries on Learning Channel and Discovery Channel . . . We've watched all the documentaries together and all the movies together. My wife wanted to know what she was getting into and why she was doing this, and sometimes she still wonders." For the couple, watching the films was an active, social process. They used filmic narratives as conversation starters, as communicative platforms from which they leaped into discussing their own thoughts and feelings. "There's a lot of pausing during the movies. We talk about the wife's point of view, which I am trying to understand, and the point of view of the trans person, which she is trying to understand." Notably, through watching the films and her conversations with her wife, Margie realized an "ordinary life" was possible. She learned the importance of communicating openly and honestly in her marriage. From their film-watching experiences, her wife learned "that she has to make herself happy and not answer to anyone else."

One of the most influential media texts for the couple was a 2009 *ABC Primetime* interview with Chloe Prince, a middle-aged married trans woman with two children, and Chloe's wife. According to Margie, the couple's story intimately mirrored her own. Both women were married. Both were white and resided in the suburbs. Both had children and generally lived middle-class lives. Although Margie was significantly older than Chloe, Margie's grandchildren were approximately the same age as Chloe's children. The television show helped Margie and her wife imagine what a relationship with their grandchildren might look like. Margie noted, "My grandchildren are basically the same age as her children. And so we watched to get an idea of what to expect with mine." After watching the show, Margie decided to tell her grandchildren about her gender transition and asked that they call her grandma. Proudly, Margie exclaimed, "My grandchildren just call me grandma now. It's just like the Chloe Prince story."

In addition to documentary, Margie went online to learn how to "do" being ordinary and transgender. One of the greatest hurdles for Margie was how to manage her changing feelings toward her wife as she began living full-time as a woman, taking hormones, and eventually undergoing a sexual reassignment surgery. Indeed, things did change. Margie began losing her sexual attraction toward her wife, which surprised her. She experienced new, unexpected desires to experiment with her sexuality and date men. In addition to talking with her therapist about these feelings, Margie went online to participate in transgender chat rooms and forums, seeking advice from others who had similar experiences. From her online interactions, she became aware that there were a variety of relationship models and arrangements available to trans individuals and couples. She decided to forge a new way of being a "regular old married couple." Margie explained, "I told my wife I was attracted to men. Strangely enough that was easier for her to accept than me going out with another woman. It doesn't bother her as much. She knows our romantic life together has been long gone. She is not attracted to me because I'm female. But we really love being together. We do everything together. There is no sense in getting a divorce because we're best friends forever. That is the way our relationship is now."

As we sat drinking coffee and Margie explained the evolution of her relationship and everyday life, she looked proud of what she and her wife have accomplished. "I have a supportive wife who is now my best friend." With a sense of anticipation, she tells me that after our interview she will immediately do three things. First, she will go on her surgeon's website and read about her upcoming sexual reassignment surgery: "I love learning about her and my treatment through her site. I am always there reinforcing my decision and getting excited about it. I have my pre-surgical consult on Tuesday. My surgery will be in January. I am really excited about that and right now it's like the only thing I can think of." Second, she will visit her grandchildren and drop off gifts she recently bought for them. Finally, she is going to drive to the church she used to attend. "I became the head elder of the Lutheran church while the kids were going to school. But now they would not be accepting at all of me. I think I am going to drive by there and see if anyone I knew is there so I could stop and wave and say 'hey.'" As she articulated these plans, she laughed at herself and took the final sip of her coffee, gratified with the way she does being ordinary.

Safe 2 Pee?

One evening before the transgender discussion group Trans Chat begun, two members were having an animated conversation—the kind that fills the space of a room. They were discussing what Halberstam (1998) identifies as "the bathroom problem" (20), a pressing and pervasive issue for the transgender community. As spaces where gender is actively and aggressively policed, public bathrooms are "zones of intense scrutiny and observation" (21). By dividing the world into male and female domains, their mere existence both reflects *and* reifies the gender binary. Within these zones, gender-ambiguous individuals are perceived as suspect and often interrogated about their presence. Some are physically assaulted. As a result, for many trans and gender-nonconforming people, using a public restroom is an experience defined by intense anxiety and fear.

In discussing this issue, one support group member, Michelle, recalled a troubling experience using the women's restroom at a restaurant. She was at her favorite spot on a Friday night and, as she had always done, she visited the women's restroom. While she was using the facilities, Michelle was suddenly "outed," or as she said "clocked," by a fellow customer, who quickly found the manager and loudly complained about her within earshot of the restaurant's patrons. Impartially, the manager refused to take sides and did not push the incident further, successfully defusing the situation.

However, the experience was so thoroughly embarrassing for Michelle that it motivated her to search for online resources to mitigate the complexity of this perfunctory daily task. She eventually came across the website safe2pee.org. A digital transgender care structure, Safe 2 Pee was an open-source database created by and for the transgender community. The website and its iPhone application, TranSquat, detect gender neutral and single-occupancy restrooms. The digital tool allows users to enter their geographical location, and through the application of Google Maps, locates nearby bathroom options. It includes a street address, the

Figure 5.1. Safe2Pee map showing users where bathrooms are located.

exact location of the bathroom inside the establishment, and whether it is wheelchair accessible.

Safe2pee.org also instructs users on how to do "being ordinary" and act "naturally" to successfully access the bathroom. For example, after I conducted a search for a restroom in a Midwest suburb, Safe2Pee identified a gender-neutral option at a local restaurant. It recommended that I enter from the rear of the building, act like I was shopping, and casually walk to the facility.[6]

The technology was so helpful for Michelle that she began routinely using it before leaving the house for long stretches of time, charting potential bathroom locations along her anticipated route. It became an indispensable tactic in her practice of everyday life. However, at the time of this book's writing, the Safe2Pee website no longer exists and the TranSquat application has been discontinued.

Meanwhile, a new website called Refuge Restrooms has taken their place. According to Refuge Restrooms' "About" page:

> When the Safe2Pee website passed out of functionality it left a hole in our hearts. REFUGE picks up the torch where Safe2Pee left off and makes the valuable resource available to those who find themselves in need of a place to pee safely once again . . . The first 4500 entries are thanks to the old Safe2Pee database. The rest of our database is generated by our users. If you know of a gender neutral or safe restroom, please add it to our database!

The disappearance of Safe2Pee and TranSquat and the new emergence of Refuge Restrooms speaks to the ephemeral and unstable nature of digital technologies within the contemporary media environment. These transgender-created and -operated websites and applications are very much tactical arts of the weak (de Certeau 1984). They emerge in response to gaps within the official structures of everyday life, and struggle to remain viable. In fact, Refuge Restrooms' website notes that the designers and engineers devoted to maintaining it are generally unpaid and underemployed. So, the truth remains that while these kinds of digital technologies are valuable partners in the struggle for the ordinary, they can be elusive and ultimately unreliable—here one day and gone the next.

Indeed, the transgender care structures I discussed in the previous chapter, the website XX Boys and the online comic *Venus Envy*, met similar fates. XX Boys moved from an actively maintained website to a Facebook page that no longer updates. To the dismay of its fans, *Venus Envy* also ceased producing new content. The story of these "orphaned" websites highlights the continuous effort and upkeep that digital care structures require. While much academic and industry discourse celebrates technological creation and innovation, equally as important—albeit less sexy—are practices of maintenance. To be everyday technologies, to be accessible as taken-for-granted resources, digital care structures depend upon maintenance, that invisible and time-consuming form of labor. While larger, commercial websites have the human and financial capital to sustain their digital infrastructure and evolve their offerings over time, smaller, more amateur efforts such as Safe2Pee, XX Boys, and

Venus Envy lack these resources. They often rely on the unpaid commitment of individuals whose passion for the cause motivates their work. Unfortunately for those who rely on them, the exigencies of everyday life, the need to support one's self, and the demands of an increasingly commercialized Internet environment make maintaining these labors of love difficult, and for some impossible.

Having a "Day Out"

What does it mean to have a "day out"? Who is and is not able to have one? Throughout the course of my fieldwork, study participants wrestled with these questions and frequently worried whether their gender variant identities and queer subjectivities were compatible with everyday life, with the ability to have a day or a night out. They struggled with what it meant or what it would look like to be a transgender person operating within the daily round. This was particularly the case for Linda, a trans woman in her forties from a small rural community in the Midwest who works "night freight" at Home Depot, stocking and organizing the retailer's shelves.

Linda grew up on a farm ten miles north of her current residence. In describing her childhood and life trajectory, she claimed they were largely shaped by the domineering influence of her father. "I tried to do what he wanted. I eventually graduated high school, got married, and had two kids. I never did go to college. I worked. I worked in a factory in Lansing. I worked there a couple of years. It just did not work out. I kind of floated around with odd jobs here and there. But like I said, I was married and had two kids. I stayed married for 23 years." Throughout her marriage, Linda discreetly cross-dressed in private, never in public, hiding it from her friends and family. While she had "a lot of curiosities at that time," Linda by and large abandoned the thought of ever adopting a transgender life or subjectivity. Her class and social position made it incredibly difficult. Having never gone to college, she lacked the kind of discursive tools and social capital that would allow her to claim a new gender identity and traverse a new life course.

However, this all changed when Linda turned 40 years old. Her family purchased an Internet connection for their computer. Linda began doing what she called "research," searching for transgender-themed cyber communities and websites. She recalled, "Anything I could find to read, I just read, and read, and read trying to learn because I was curious. Whoever I could find that wanted to chat, I was open to . . . I used to be on 30 different websites. I'm only on five now." Roughly one year after the introduction of the Internet into her home, Linda and her wife decided to end their marriage. The timing was right for the split because, like Margie, their two kids had graduated from high school and began living on their own.

After the divorce, Linda moved in with an old friend, where she continued doing her research. Her favorite website to visit was called "Pink Essence," a social networking site geared primarily toward trans women. "I like Pink Essence because it's not a hook-up site. It's more information and sharing photos and things. It's about having fun. I always have fun when I am on there." More than providing pleasure and enjoyment, Pink Essence mitigated one of the more vexing uncertainties that Linda faced, namely, what it looked like to live a transgender life.

Pink Essence is, as the name suggests, smothered in pink. It is a visually driven website filled with amateur photos and user-generated content. It features member profiles, discussion forums, user blogs, and a seemingly endless supply of selfies. During our first interview, Linda was brimming with excitement to show me around the website. Together, we read blog posts on how to secure a wig and cope with religiously conservative in-laws. We glanced at the many member photos and she showed me her own profile. Yet, most of our time was spent looking at what Linda called "My Day Out" images and stories.

On Pink Essence, My Day Out content depicts members participating in everyday scenes and activities, going about their daily concerns. They are titled with phrases such as "Day Out Shopping With My Cousin," "First Day Out As Myself," "First Day Without a Wig," "Going for a Drive," and "A Great Day Out with my Daughter." For transgender individuals who spend much of their lives hiding their identities and cross-dressing in the secluded sanctuaries of their homes, being "out in the world" is transformative. It marks the movement of a transgender self from what Goffman (1959) calls the "backstage region" to the "front stage region" of everyday life. In this way, being out in the world indicates the transformation of transgender from a private to a public articulation of self. This is clearly illustrated in the following Pink Essence blog post by Rachel:

> Two weeks ago yesterday I traveled from home to a town in TN as Rachel. I have to admit I was on an all day high. Felt so natural and was treated as the woman I am. Did a little shopping, dinner and some wine at Applebee's. The time was so wonderful. Wish I could do it every week. OK who am I kidding, wish I could do it every day. Look forward to doing it again. I wore jeans and a sweater set for the day and a really nice sweater dress from Cache for the evening. Had a wonderful conversation at dinner with a nice lady and her hubby. Made me feel so at home as Rachel. I need to get out more and do this more often.

As Rachel's post makes clear, My Day Out content is powerfully meaningful in its mundaneness. The picture she paints of her day is in all regards utterly unremarkable. Wearing jeans and a sweater, she shops, eats dinner, sips on wine at Applebee's, and chats with a married couple. However, these moments are infused with a deeply felt sense of pleasure and accomplishment. They make her feel "high" and encourage her to "do this more often."

My Day Out posts are also meaningful in that they serve as powerfully symbolic benchmarks that can be shared with others. Fellow site users comment on these posts, offer praise and encouragement, and sometimes respond by sharing their own successful experiences of the daily. This is what sets Pink Essence apart from other websites serving the transgender community: its communication platforms validate and provide evidence for the everydayness of transgender while underscoring how difficult it can be to achieve. Sharing one's accomplishment of the ordinary is profoundly legitimating and enjoyable. As Linda reminisced, "The first time I had a great day dressing as me, I went there [Pink Essence] after and posted all about it. Lots of us do that. It's nice just to talk about your day with other people. It's fun."

My Day Out posts also affirm the public character of ordinariness and the everyday, as both are things we achieve with (and can be taken away by) others. The act of going out, of being in public and placing oneself in a relationship with others confers feelings of ordinariness.

Sitting at the bar at Applebee's and receiving that silent recognition and confirmation, Rachel had a sense of belonging to the everyday world. As Rubin (2003) argues, this kind of mutual recognition is both a fundamental rhythm of everyday life and at stake for transgender individuals. Recognition, Rubin maintains, revolves around two axes: one of distinction (a divide between self and other) and one of integration (a synthesis and reciprocity between self and other). Both are at play in daily interactions, but for transgender individuals, integration is the greater feat, and as I argued in chapter 2, can be a potent object of desire. In particular, integration requires intelligibility and understanding. Extending Butler's question of what requires a livable life, Lennon suggests that it is "mutual intelligibility within everyday practices" that makes life livable (2006, 28). My Day Out posts are testaments to recognition, integration, and intelligibility as the transgender self enters public circulation and the communication circuits that define everyday life. For all of their ordinariness, these kinds of posts are inspirational and aspirational texts that communicate the very possibility of everyday life, of a livable life, to participants like Linda. As she put it, "I just love seeing and you know hearing about their day . . . Who knew good days like this were possible?"

Remediating Trans Lore

When Wren decided to transition gender in his early twenties, one of his most pressing challenges was managing his healthcare. Like many in the transgender community, Wren occupied a precarious state, a "condition in which certain populations suffer from failing social and economic networks of support and become differentially exposed to injury, violence, and death" (Butler 2009, 25). Wren lived in a moderately sized town in the suburban Midwest and was concerned that the medical professionals in his area, specifically his own general practitioner, would be unfamiliar with transgender bodies and health. He experienced "major anxiety" about participating in routine doctor's visits, unsure of how to talk about himself in ways that would translate to a nurse or physician. Wren also wanted to begin altering his physical body, taking hormones, and perhaps have surgical procedures. Wanting to learn as much as he could about this process, he questioned whether to address it with his primary care provider. He was also unsure about how to locate the kinds of specialists he needed.

In looking for guidance, Wren visited transgender websites, personal blogs, and listservs. He recalled, "The Internet helped with finding out general information and familiarizing myself with all the different identities that there are. Certain websites would teach you how to find and negotiate with doctors . . . and how to acquire all these different things. There are hard questions and decision you have to make. You have to decide whether to tell them that you're trans or not." To learn about healthcare and medical needs, he frequently visited two websites: FTM International, an organization that offers support and information specifically for female-to-male transgender people, and Transsexual Roadmap, which offers abundant resources and diverse streams of information for the larger transsexual community. After consulting these virtual resources, Wren began to find the clarification and direction he needed.

Synthesizing the collective advice he gleaned from these sites, Wren decided not to discuss his transition with his general practitioner. Rather, he sought out a therapist specializing in gender identity in a town within an hour's drive. Moreover, the websites taught him a crucial litany of questions to ask new potential therapists, such as "How many transsexual patients do you have?"—an important inquiry because it speaks to experience. However, the most important question he learned to ask was "What is your educational background?" This is vital because sexual reassignment surgeries require letters of recommendation, one of which must come from a clinical professional with a doctorate degree. These websites also informed Wren about other potential specialists he might want to locate, ones he had not previously considered such as hair removal practitioners and legal advisers. Finally, the best advice he culled from these websites—as well as from the personal blogs of transgender identifying people he routinely read—was "to take things slowly." More experienced transgender individuals, and folks who already transitioned, urged their readers to thoughtfully make each decision. From telling family and friends about his identity to deciding on hormone treatments and surgical procedures, Wren explains that he "needed to hear that I should take my time."

In reading through this vast archive of user-generated content created by and for transgender people on the Internet, Wren was accessing what

Bolin (1988) refers to as "'transsexual lore" (64). In her anthropological account of gender transition, Bolin explored the tightly knit communities and specialized bodies of knowledge that transsexuals form. She analyzed the ways they help each other survive, passing down lessons about transsexual life from the experienced to the less experienced through word of mouth. She delineated this in-group communicative exchange as transsexual lore. Bolin's work heavily focuses on transsexual lore that concerns access to medical services. This kind of knowledge base consists of a practical "how-to" guide that helps transsexuals get what they want such as hormone therapies or sexual reassignment surgeries from clinical gatekeepers. These "'recipes' for dealing with caretakers" instructed them what to say and, as importantly, what not to say when talking about their experiences with clinicians (64).

But transsexual lore (or what I will call "trans lore" from here on out to be inclusive of a wider range of transgender experiences) also has other key concerns, ones that more broadly involve the successful management of everyday life. Experiences of everyday trans lore routinely surfaced during my fieldwork with Trans Chat. During one meeting, a member discussed using a Yahoo! group to tap into the collective intelligence of the local transgender community to learn about nightclubs and bar culture. New to the area, she wanted to get a sense of which establishments were queer and transgender friendly. The Yahoo! group supplied this information with a surprising amount of anonymity and specificity. Within hours of joining the group, she received several suggestions about local bars, including the best time to arrive and where to park safely. She was also given advice about how to dress and how much money to bring.[7]

Since Bolin's study, the content of trans lore has remained primarily about everyday survival, but its primary medium of expression has shifted. Whereas trans lore was formerly rooted in modes of oral culture such as gossip and word of mouth, it has increasingly migrated to platforms of digital culture including websites, blogs, and chat forums. In this way, trans lore has undergone "remediation" (Bolter and Grusin 2000), a process of technological conversion wherein newer media forms "honor, rival, and revise" older ones (15). While transgender support groups and gay bars, for example, are still important mechanisms for the oral transmission of transgender-related knowledge and advice, they are now rivaled by digital culture. Trans individuals are increasingly turning to digital technologies to create, archive, and disseminate trans lore. From therapists to support group leaders, individuals who work with trans communities all commented on this digital migration toward virtual platforms of communication and assistance.

However, the process of remediation is not simply one of replacement. Rather, the digitalization of trans lore also supports the more traditional in-person sources of its transmission. For instance, many of the members at Trans Chat learned about it through online communities and platforms. Other participants, such as Linda, found other "real world" conveyors of trans lore using digital technology. A trans woman in her thirties from a Midwestern suburb, Linda was searching one night for online trans resources, and stumbled upon the website for "Janet's Closet."

Janet's Closet is a Michigan-based retail company that has both a "brick and mortar" and an online store offering a wide range of cross-dressing related products and services. One of their services is called "Queen For a Night," in which specialists at the store perform a makeover for clients and then organize a night out for them. The store provides makeup, clothing, and shoes, after which the store owner accompanies the client to a gay club for the evening, offering interpersonal support and guidance. Typically, pictures are taken of the outing and uploaded onto social media. The entire occasion is a conduit for trans lore. According to the store's website, Queen For a Night is intended

> for you girls that seek an experience out in the real world. We will work with utmost attention geared to your comfort; and to help bring out the woman you see within you. We keep things as relaxed as possible for these fun evenings (outings) . . . The timing and whole evening is formed around you and how much you would like to do and experience. (Janets Closet.com)

Linda explained that the makeover portion taught her how to do the kinds of everyday things such as styling one's hair and applying makeup she wished she had learned in adolescence. "I didn't know where to go to learn about things like hair, makeup, clothes, and all that. I heard about a place, in fact I looked it up on the Internet, called Janet's Closet. I went down and got a makeover thing with Janet the first time. I was really impressed."

Figure 5.2. Janet's Closet advertises "Queen For a Night" services on social media.

While the makeover helps with presenting the self, the critical component of Queen for a Night is the outing, which cultivates a social self and secures a sense of ordinariness in public with others. As the website states, "Sometimes we need others to help share an important event." For Margie, who I discussed earlier in the chapter, the outing was especially transformative. Margie also found Janet's Closet by searching for transgender resources online. She visited the site several times before visiting the store in person. For her, the website served as a steppingstone, a safe intermediary space where she could experiment with its services and products from a distance. Finally, after a few weeks of becoming familiar with the website, she made the long drive to the store and signed up for Queen For a Night. The experience was a public declaration of self that allowed Margie, for the first time, to feel relaxed in a social setting. "Having never been to a bar before, I was afraid to go and didn't want to go by myself. So I went with her and I was like 'oh my god.' It was a place where I really felt comfortable." After visiting the nightclub as a Queen for the Night, Margie felt comfortable to return on her own in the future. She absorbed the trans lore that the experience is intended to offer, or as she puts it, "I finally learned the ropes and had to go back."

Conclusion

Like a transgender breakfast cereal, the ordinary and the everyday are elusive constructs—at once objects of desire and denial, freedom and discipline, and closeness and distance. Yet, in critical scholarship, they have too often been reduced to punitive and normative phenomena—manifestations of discipline, oppression, and loss. But participant experiences reveal that the story is far more complicated. They wanted the simple joys of the ordinary: to have a day or a night out, engage in small talk, secure a sense of commonality with others, and post about it on social media. Importantly, their ability to do so in part rests out of their hands.

Although this chapter focused primarily on the individual efforts of my participants, the ordinary is not one-sided. Rather, it is a collective endeavor. Not only did Margie and many of the participants in my study have to re-learn being ordinary, in many ways they had to re-*earn* it as well. The ordinary is very much granted by the social, political, economic, and—as I have been arguing throughout this book—media structures that organize the everyday world. The ordinary requires the active participation of third parties who are willing to offer recognition, legitimacy, and taken-for-grantedness. Callie's sense of ordinariness depends on others to offer her the "Midwestern hi." Cameron's sense of ordinariness requires others to recognize his right to use the bathroom consistent with his gender identity—a right that may have to be encoded into law and policy. Steve's sense of ordinariness is contingent on others not gawking and gazing at him when he cross-dresses in public. Even as participants remain resilient and struggle for the ordinary, their success depends on the malleability of the social contract and on the ability of everyday structures to stretch and expand to accommodate gender variance. Their success also depends on the availability of transgender care structures—in both the digital and physical worlds. Rachel's sense of ordinariness hinges on the semi-public nature of Pink Essence's forums and the way they organize fellow users as a ready-to-hand audience for her accomplishments.

Interestingly, for the participants in my study, even though the structures of everyday life were replete with ruthless realities and had much expanding to do, and even as the ideology of the normal was used to disparage them, they nevertheless held a profoundly nuanced view of what it means to be ordinary. Their sophisticated understanding and their struggle to accomplish it pose important questions: When everyday life is such a challenge, requiring constant effort and calculation, where and how does one deploy queer resistance? Is the desire for ordinariness antithetical to queerness? Can individuals both struggle for the ordinary and perform transformative social interventions? In other words, how do queerness and ordinariness co-exist? The final chapter attends to these Gordian knots and seeks to articulate a theoretical framework for thinking through them.

A Queerly Ordinary Conclusion

We All Put Our Skirts On One Leg at a Time

"There's an imagined boundary that exists between me and the people at my dad's church. They're thinking you're a tranny [sic]. You're so weird and I don't know how to talk to you. And I'm thinking you're an asshole and I can't believe you voted for Bush. But really those are just imagined boundaries. We could very easily have a conversation about baseball and be fine!" During our interview, Alex, a trans man in his mid-twenties, recalled the experience of walking through aisles of worshippers at his father's church. He remembered making his way to his seat and accidentally brushing up against those standing in the pews. Although he was physically close to the churchgoers, Alex felt a tremendous distance from them. He thought to himself that even though he must share *something* in common with the parishioners, they would only ever see his otherness, his queerness, and he would only ever see their conservatism and normality. Bumping up against an imagined binary, the two sides were locked in opposition. Ignoring the middle space hovering between them, they would never have that conversation about baseball.

Later in our interview, Alex's thoughts returned to this middle space. As we talked about transgender representation in media, he noted the two "faces" he most often saw portrayed. "I have been largely dissatisfied with trans folks who have been interviewed anywhere, or anything that I've read or seen by a trans person that gets wide attention . . . The biggest one I've seen is 'I'm just like everybody else. There's nothing different about me.' So, they eliminate difference. Ugh! . . . It's like I want to erase this queerness. Others tend to be sort of isolationist, and sort of an extremism that I don't think is beneficial to a movement . . . you're telling people you don't understand this or you don't understand that and you're ridiculous for treating me like crap. I wouldn't want to interact with someone like that." For Alex, these two representational paradigms, the "I'm just like everybody else" and the "extremist" frame, created another inflexible binary, similar to the one he felt between the churchgoers at his father's parish and himself.

Alex wondered about the middle space, a space where transgender media figures were "not extreme but still held onto their queerness." He continued, "What about creating media that is just there and allows people to interface with it? What about art that is accessible and subtle, and underspoken so that it creates a space that is inviting and eliminates imagined boundaries that exists between people; like the imagined boundary that exists between me and the people at my dad's church? . . . Art that enables bringing people together is much better than art that distances everyone." This art occupied the same territory as that conversation about baseball: a middle space where seemingly oppositional elements are brought together.

This book has tracked the consequences of technological change and of transgender visibility's gradual move into America's cultural mainstream for the participants in my study. It has explored the ways they have engaged with media culture to construct identity, preserve self, and bring the ordinary and everyday within reach. Underlying these practices was an essential tension, one characterized by the pull of queerness and ordinariness, sameness and difference, closeness and distance, stability and instability, outsiderness and insiderness. The question about how to come to terms with and resolve these contradictory forces was ever-present throughout my fieldwork.

In this final chapter, I explore this tension and attend to the middle space that Alex and others forged in trying to resolve it. This is a negotiated space, one where queerness and ordinariness are not diametrically opposed, but rather layered on top of one another, remixed and combined in unpredictable and even contradictory ways. I call this the "queerly ordinary," which is a hybrid form of self- and life-making that combines components of queerness and ordinariness.

The queerly ordinary is a "grounded" (Glaser and Strauss 1967) concept that inductively emerged throughout my fieldwork and data analysis. Flashes of it appeared as participants narrated their life stories, articulated their identities, and discussed their encounters with media culture. I saw it in how they lived their everyday lives and navigated a society created without them in mind. Some had more of a choice in combining queerness and ordinariness. Having the privileges that come with whiteness, passing, education, and/or belonging to a higher socioeconomic position provided them the freedom to combine the two dynamics in ways they saw fit. Others, who were not white, could not pass, were less educated, or belonged to a lower socioeconomic position had less of an option in how they composed their queerly ordinary life. Some had little choice but to inhabit a place of instability and marginality. Whereas many embraced this marginal space, finding pleasure and empowerment there, others felt trapped, wanting to add more ordinariness into the mix.

In what follows, I develop the concept of the queerly ordinary. I interrogate what I call the "ideal queer subject," a figure who embodies the apex of queer theoretical aspiration, and then shift focus toward what I call "lived queerness," or how individuals mobilize and enact queerness in ways that work for them within the limitations and structures of their world. Finally, I theorize the queerly ordinary as an expression of lived queerness and explore how it can help us understand trans experiences with media and everyday life.

From the "Ideal Queer Subject" to "Lived Queerness"

One of the aims of this book is to advance an alternative and more nuanced conceptualization of the ordinary and everyday, to understand them as more than disciplinary operations of normalization and oppression. Clearly everyday life is, as scholars such as Foucault and Lefebvre have argued, fundamentally circumscribed within relations of power, a "brutally objective power" that "holds sway over all social life; according to its different aspects, we have named it: money, fragmented division of labour, market, capital, mystification and deprivation" (Lefebvre 1991, 166). To this list we can add patriarchy, heteronormativity, white supremacy, and the gender binary system.[1] From its inception, queer theory mobilized a much-needed critique of these normalizing forces that structure everyday life's dominant order. One of its foundational texts, Michael Warner's (1999) *The Trouble with Normal*, bears this association in its title. A trenchant polemic, the book targets normality as an assimilationist aspiration, a sort of "antipolitical politics" (Warner 1999, 60).

More recent queer scholarship has amplified the anti-normative impulse by positioning queerness as "anti-social," theorizing it as the absolute rejection of collective life, identity, and cultural intelligibility (Edelman 2004). Clarifying this idea, Halberstam (2008) wonders that if within history and culture the queer figure "has been bound epistemologically, to negativity, to nonsense, to anti-production, to unintelligibility," rather than protest these linkages why not "embrace the negativity that we anyway structurally represent?" (141). This kind of queer anti-sociality is a controversial concept and certainly has its critics. Some scholars, such as Jose Muñoz (2009), question the anti-social turn in theory, urging us to privilege an "understanding of queerness as collectivity" (11). Nonetheless, queer scholars by and large retain a view of the ordinary and the everyday as complacency with a "corrupt and bankrupt social order" (20), and contend, "being ordinary and being married are both antiutopian wishes, desires that automatically rein themselves in" (21).

I was an undergraduate at New York University in the late 1990s, a time when queer theory was flourishing in certain sectors of the academy and had a significant presence in the classes I took. As a young and newly out gay man, I was instantly drawn to its convictions, finding them new and exciting. I still do. I have relied on queer theoretical insight throughout my academic career and this book would be impossible without it. Yet, I also find it problematic for the ways it harbors a rote suspicion—sometimes warranted, sometimes not—of anything related to the ordinary and the everyday. Queer thought leaves little room for exploring desires that involve commonality, familiarity, orderliness, stability, and routine. It has little to say about the longing to "fit in," to be social, and to be seen as "an ordinary person" outside the lens of disciplinarity and normalization.

Even though queer theory is a moving target—an interdisciplinary and multivocal enterprise—it nevertheless conjures the specter of an "ideal queer subject," a figure who embodies the ultimate fulfillment of the queer project. The ideal queer subject harbors queer theory's canonical stances: ideological opposition, political resistance, anti-normativity, identity transgression, and cultural disruption. Perhaps most clearly articulated in Sycamore's (2004) book, *That's Revolting: Queer Strategies for Resisting Assimilation*, the ideal queer subject works against the "monster of assimilation" (7), pledges allegiance to "freaks, fruits, perverts, and whores" (7), and champions "queers striving to live outside conventional norms" (5). Above all, ideal queer subjects are characterized by and manifested in resistance: resistance to established political, cultural, and social orders. They are against domestication, marriage, ideological moderation, and white, middle-class values. Ideal queer subjects strategically position themselves against the "normal" because normality creates a hierarchy that awards conformity and generates a "betrayal of the abject and the queer in favor of a banalized respectability" (Warner 1999, 66). Profoundly political and eager to confront injustice, the ideal queer subject wages "an ongoing engagement with contentious, cantankerous queer politics" (Duggan 2002, 189). They repudiate capitalist, heteronormative models of success and embrace failure as liberation (Halberstam 2011). They are engaged with the present (but not occupied by "presentism"), understand the past (and refuse to recreate its mistakes), and are continually gazing toward the future (excited about its indeterminacy and potentiality) (Muñoz 2009).

The transgender figure in particular is often held up as the quintessential ideal queer subject, one that is situated at the vanguard of the movement. As Crawley (2002) maintains, "the existence of transgender people creates a purposeful critique to the rigidity of the binary gender paradigm" (19). Celebrated for harboring a "dangerous magic" (Paglia, as cited in Phillips 2006, 4), transgender people are heralded for challenging the gender binary and for resisting all that is normative. Transgender writer and cultural critic, Julia Serano (2007), calls this "subversivism," or "the practice of extolling certain gender and sexual expressions and identities simply because they are unconventional or nonconforming" (346).

Ideal queer subjects are not only discursive formations of queer theory, but also media studies where they are rearticulated as "ideal queer viewers." As with queer theory, critical media studies have also made significant investments in the concept of resistance (Hall 1980; Fiske 1987; Sholle 1991). In particular, queer subcultures have often been conceptualized as paragons of resistance (Doty 1993). Within these subcultures, the ideal queer viewer challenges, troubles, and "queers" encounters with media. For example, in Muñoz's (1999) analysis of queer cultural production and reception, he highlights the ways in which queer audiences of color "disidentify," a practice of investing "new life" into cultural products not intended for them and of constructing "oppositional counter publics" thereby engaging in what he calls "queer worldmaking" (195–196).

Ideal queer subjects and viewers, like the ones Muñoz analyzed, are compelling figures because they promote a model of active citizenship and critical media literacy. They recognize queer and trans authority, and open space for talking back to and reclaiming power. Nevertheless, these figures are in many ways ideal types. They ultimately lie beyond the bounds of full realization. As Puar (2007) argues, queer liberal thought creates "an impossible transcendent subject who is always already conscious of the normativizing forces of power and always ready and able to subvert, resist, or transgress them" (24). This is not to suggest we do away with ideal queer subjects—I love them for being so badass—but rather that we understand them as aspirational, as muses that guide and animate us but are essentially unattainable. "We may never touch queerness," Munoz (2009) argues, for it is "an ideality" (1). Similarly, Berlant and Warner (1995) suggest that queerness is "more a matter of aspiration than it is the expression of an identity or a history" (344). Any attempt to fully embody it will ultimately fall short, for the best anyone can do is to "live" queerness within the parameters of their everyday life. This is what I call "lived queerness," and it is exactly the kind of queerness that the participants in my study embodied.

"Lived queerness" refers to how the principles of queer theory are enacted, negotiated, undermined, and/or ignored within daily experiences of self, work, family, home, leisure, friendship, community, and politics. Within these domains, a life defined by radical queer resistance, an anti-social politics that enacts "the primacy of a constant no" (Edelman 2004, 5), or an outlook forever gazing into a utopian future (Muñoz 2009), is essentially unlivable in its purest form. "Lived queerness" is informed by McGuire's (2008) conceptualization of "lived religion." According to McGuire, the term "lived religion" intends to capture how religiosity is performed by actual practitioners—apart from the idealized and prescribed versions advanced by official religious institutions and structures. Lived religion shifts attention from institutional logics to social practices; from the need for ideological consistency to the embrace of inconsistency and the paradoxical; and from a clear sacred/secular divide toward more boundary blurring and porousness. Lived religion speaks to experiences that are "subjectively grounded" (12) and embodied, and affirms imperfect and improvised expressions of holy doctrine.

Lived queerness accomplishes much of the same. Crucially, it challenges the queer/normal binary, blurring the boundaries between the two. There is ordinariness in queerness, and queerness in ordinariness. Neither concept is hermetically sealed and safe from incursion by the other. As Raymond Williams (1989) argues, the ordinary "is always both traditional and creative" (4), and it has the capacity to fill, expand, and stretch. To speak about the ordinary and the queer in these ways is to advance a more capacious and nuanced understanding of each concept. It is to preserve queerness as "an open and flexible space," one that may risk seeming "blandly democratic" (Doty 1993, xv) but can accommodate processes of "intersecting or combining" (xvi).

Lived queerness is also subjectively grounded and embodied, what Johnson (2005) has called a "theory in the flesh" (144). In his formulation of "quare theory," Johnson has called on queer thinkers to more rigorously interrogate the material realities of race and to have a deeper understanding of the queer black experience in everyday life. According to Johnson, quare theory is "a theory of and for gays and lesbians of color," one that foregrounds "the ways in which lesbians, bisexuals, gays, and transgendered people of color come to sexual and racial knowledge" (127). This kind of situated and embodied theorizing must be "bidirectional," facilitating a meeting of the "ivory tower and front porch" (148). At one and the same time, it gazes upward toward the insights of theory and the academic imagination, but also downward toward the practice of everyday life.

Lived queerness shares the bidirectional orientation of "quare studies." It is both informed by the vision of queer theory and deeply concerned with how people *actually* (rather than *should*) live. As a result, lived queerness is neither inherently progressive nor regressive, but an imperfect, improvised, and ideologically impure expression of the ideal queer subject.

The Queerly Ordinary

Throughout my research process—from data collection to analysis—I have tried not to impose a set of preferred, a priori theoretical paradigms and interpretations onto data. Letting the data speak on their own terms led me into complicated territory. I encountered an entanglement of divergent life events, attitudes, opinions, and political points of view. This at times made my research journey difficult and frustrating. But the blessing and the curse of qualitative inquiry is that it rarely generates a neat and orderly picture. In trying to understand the wide field of audience discourses, practices, and strategies deployed by the participants in my study, the classic queer/normal frame seemed inadequate. The analytical optics of normalization and discipline—so central to queer and cultural critique—failed to fully capture the ontological or experiential nature of my participants' engagements with media in everyday life.

The binary opposition that set queerness against the normal seemed too finite and left little room for mixture, for the ways I saw people variably and creatively compose their subjectivities and realities. It also devalued desires for commonality, order, and everydayness that the participants in my study expressed. As Biddy Martin (1997) suggests, queer theory unnecessarily circulates an "enormous fear of ordinariness" and pays "too little attention to the dilemmas of the average people that we also are" (133).

In trying to balance the scale, I argue that the "queerly ordinary"—a state of being a little bit queer and a little bit ordinary—can offer a nuanced and grounded way to understand transgender people, and queer people more generally. It positions them as unique—defined by a difference that warrants recognition and affirmation, and fully average—defined by everyday concerns and mundane experiences. As Alex exclaimed, "I never wanted to look like I was trans. I don't want to be another kind of different. It doesn't mean I want to eliminate my difference! I just want to be 'me' . . . I mean, yes I'm trans, queer, anti-capitalist, but I'm also a person and not insanely different from the people at my father's church."

As Alex's statements illustrate, the queerly ordinary is a form of "lived queerness" that is fully anchored in "hybridity" (Bhabha 1994) and blurs the queer/normal divide. It is located at "the interstices—the overlap and displacement of domains of difference" and resolves "complex figures of difference and identity, past and present, inside and outside, inclusion and exclusion" (2). As a hybrid form, the queerly ordinary "entertains difference without an assumed or imposed hierarchy" (5). Being queer and ordinary are equally worthy, and the extent to which a person can be one or the other, or a mixture of both, depends on the context within which they find themselves.

Although they did not use the term "queerly ordinary," the participants in my study spoke about their experiences and practiced everyday life in line with its hybridity. Online and in the "real world," they socialized and built coalitions across queer and non-queer communities. They both resisted and complied with media power. When they could not queerly resist, they remained ordinarily resilient. They desired representations of transgender everydayness and of people who "happen to be transgender," but simultaneously wanted these representations to retain a queer difference. They spoke of transgender breakfast cereal. They articulated a desire for ordinary life to only moments later critique one. For example, during our interview Callie said she wanted an "ordinary life" and clarified: "The American picture of ordinary is married with kids and the white picket fence. And I would very much like to just have that, although not necessarily the white picket fence, five children, and a dog." At the same time, later in our discussion she renounced a "normal life," maintaining, "I think I've become more or less disenchanted with the idea of a normal life." She called such a life "boring" and "empty."

In this way, participants longed for the predictability of the mundane and were simultaneously suspicious of its normative leanings. They relished in fucking with gender while simultaneously sitting at the bar at Applebee's, having a cocktail and chatting with others. They used communications technologies to cultivate their differences and wage gender trouble but to also create legible identities and participate in the common rhythms of everyday life.

Upon first glance, this may appear to be a confusing and contradictory matrix, but the queerly ordinary life participants weaved made sense to them within the specific contexts of their life situations. They mixed and matched the incongruous, composing life and subjectivity in ways that recombined and integrated seemingly opposed cultural elements. Moreover, they looked for this hybrid dynamic in media culture.

In considering media representations of transgender identity, Josh expressed a desire to see simultaneous expressions of sameness and difference: "I don't agree with media just pointing out the difference and how we're different from everyone else. I don't think we're all the same and we have all the same pressures, but I do think that it does help for people to feel more comfortable with difference when they think we're not that different. Like, I don't want people to think they can't relate to me at all because I'm so different. You don't have to show me any kind of sympathy and respect." For Josh, media representations of sameness served as a sort of social thread. They allowed others to grow comfortable with transgender difference. They humanized transgender subjectivity and had the potential to generate empathy and respect. But at the same time, Josh insisted on the queerly ordinary, noting that people are not all the same and that they do experience different "pressures."

Linda also endorsed the queerly ordinary, locating it in transgender-themed teledocumentaries. She explained, "Whenever I get a chance to, I watch them. They show the good, the bad, the whole picture. And I think that's the way it should be. It should make us seem like ordinary people . . . They show daily life, which is what I think we need to see more of to prove we're no different than anybody else. We feed, we bathe, we clothe, just like everybody else does. They also show the different things we have to deal with on an everyday basis. I mean we are different, we dress differently, we have different needs sometimes . . . but we all put our skirts on one leg at a time." Linda's understanding of herself and of transgender life more generally involved "the good" and "the bad," sameness and difference coexisting in a "middle space." It was a place where common everyday rituals met the specificities of living as a transgender person. Putting a skirt on "one leg at a time" certainly is a common and mundane act, but for Linda, a person who defies gender expectations and encounters the pleasures and risks of doing so, it is a queerly ordinary act. It is private, occurring in the secluded space of her bedroom, but also public, for she wears the skirt outside the confines of the home. It is conforming, in that the goal is to "pass" as a woman, but also transgressive, for she challenges the gender binary and runs a real risk for doing so. It comes from a place of privilege, in that Linda is a white woman with a full-time job, but also marginality, as she is a big person who does not always pass successfully and lives in a small, rural working-class community.

The queerly ordinary always involves this kind of patchwork, this give and take. For some, living a queerly ordinary life means leaning heavily toward one side over the other, or even having to flat out choose a side. For Blake, a transgender man in his twenties, leading a queerly ordinary life meant forgoing a more fluid gender identity. He explained, "There is all this gender in society. I mean even just walking around, "excuse me sir, excuse me ma'am" . . . The people you see on television who are transgender, on talk shows for example, the most successful people are not in the middle. Those who are in the middle are ridiculed. It never ends well for them. I really don't want to make my life harder." Considering the challenges of securing employment, he conceded, "There is no point in me doing something that is only going to make life harder for me . . . I was trying to think about where I fit in to the professional world as an adult in society. That's really where it changed, once I started thinking about my professional future. People address you as male or female. You have to at least conform to one or the other in *some* aspects of life . . . In college, I could be in the middle and I could be fine. In the real world, when you're applying for jobs it's not that easy."

Blake's queer ordinariness shifted in response to the changing circumstances of his life and as he set new goals. To live in what he called "the adult world," he had to make painful compromises and his gender identity had to become more (although not fully) readable. Yet Blake never completely abandoned his queerness. He volunteers for multiple transgender advocacy groups. He uses his Facebook page as a forum to post about and debate queer and transgender politics. He is neither fully "out" nor "in," but rather, depending on the social context within which he finds himself, decides when and where to disclose his trans identity. As Blake's story makes clear, even as participants crafted queerly ordinary lives and identities, they had to make continual adjustments to the mix.

It is also important to note that there are boiling points, lines of demarcation, and risks to the queerly ordinary. Queerness can only accommodate so much ordinariness before it loses its character and bite. At a time when gender play and queerness have become increasingly visible and common in popular culture, Jenna Wortham (2016) of the *New York Times* recently asked: "When everyone can be 'queer,' is anyone?" At stake here is queer erasure—the total absorption of queerness into some watered-down mainstream aesthetic. Similarly, the ordinary can only stretch so far, can only be queered so much before it begins to retract or break. House Bill 2 in North Carolina, forcing transgender people to use the bathroom that aligns with their birth sex, represents just one of many reactions against the queering of the center.

These risks in part account for why there is so much resistance to the hybridity of queerness and ordinariness. More radical queers lament the increasingly "assimilationist" thrust of LGBTQ people and politics, whereas social conservatives warn about the perilous queering of American values. Indeed, when queerness and ordinariness collide, each does in fact change. As McKee (1999) argues,

> How believable is a model of cultural interaction which posits a complete transfer of power in one direction, and suggests a dominant culture so static, so powerful and yet so *absorbent*, that it can completely soak up another without making any changes to itself? (243)

The stories of the participants in my study are hinting at exactly this dynamic, one where there is a queering of the center and a centering of the queer. Of course, this process will be uneven and favor the powerful. But if we look at our contemporary media environment, our political landscape, and our social discourse, we see a culture coming to terms with transgender individuals, communities, and movements. We see the "dominant culture" itself changing—albeit gradually and unevenly. Facebook's nearly 60 gender options. The rise of gender-neutral language and the singular pronoun "they." The fight over access to public restrooms. Trans people demanding the rights of full citizenship and gaining access to the taken-for-granted rhythms and affordances of everyday life. As trans individuals continue to elbow their way into the center, they will change its composition. As they struggle for it, they will ask us to rethink the ordinary—what it is, why it is important, and who should have access to its gifts. In this way, the struggle for the ordinary is not mindlessly defeatist, assimilationist, or a form of "selling out." Rather, it takes on the ideology of impossibility and requires the strength, resilience, and creativity to move into the cultural center while retaining one's queerness, and to endure and fight the backlash for doing so. And, as people like Linda continue to put their skirts on "one leg at a time," the struggle for the ordinary will carry on . . . queerly.

ACKNOWLEDGMENTS

This book was a collective project from beginning to end. It was a labor of love and I am fortunate for the help I received while researching and writing it. I first have to thank the participants who took part in my study and whose voices you hear in this book. Their honesty and willingness to share their lives with me are the reason *Struggling for Ordinary* exists. I hope I have done justice to their experiences.

This book would also not exist without the unconditional support of Robin Means Coleman at the University of Michigan—my mentor, colleague, and friend. She taught me how to do qualitative research and audience studies, and has been one of my strongest advocates throughout my academic journey. She has been kind and generous with her time and energy. She has always led me in the right direction and encouraged me to continuously ask: "What's the story here?" I will never forget leaving her office after hours of conversation about this book feeling renewed and energized. Another intellectual mentor of mine worthy of immediate recognition is Paddy Scannell. As a PhD student at the University of Michigan, I was a faithful disciple. He opened my eyes to the study of everyday life, to the pleasure of the ordinary, and to the gifts of phenomenology. His body of work will always help ground my scholarship.

I am also forever grateful to Susan Douglas, who was the Chair of the Department of Communication Studies at University of Michigan while I was there. Her sage advice, steadfast encouragement, and sheer fabulousness helped me immeasurably. She too has been an exceptional mentor and friend, and was fully behind my efforts to write this book. Aswin Punathambekar at the University of Michigan has also been a pillar of support for me in writing this book. I love the way he thinks and the way he makes me think. Throughout, he has helped me focus and consider the issues addressed in this book in deeper ways. I also have to thank Gayle Rubin for helping me think through many of the knots my research uncovered. Your scholarship is fearless and an inspiration for me.

Along these lines, I owe a shout-out to everyone at Michigan who had a hand in supporting my work: Megan Ankerson, Sonya Dal Cin, Kristen Harrison, Rowell Huesmann, Shazia Iftkhar, Nojin Kwak, Russell Neuman, Michael Traugott, and Derek Vailliant. I also must acknowledge the generosity of Rackham Graduate School at U of M for all the resources and financial support they gave me. I also would not have successfully earned my PhD without the love and warmth of my chosen family in Ann Arbor: Dan Berebitsky, Lok-Sze Wong, Christy Byrd, Rossie Hutchinson, Jon Baugh, Emily Bellile, Shanta Robinson, Katie Brown, Gina Fedock-Robinson, and Liz Davis. Thank you to Old Town Tavern, the Old Town Crew, and Liz Davis for being there every Thursday night. Andrea McDonnell, a fellow Long Islander and gender studies scholar, was my partner in crime in grad school. Elliott Panek was the first friend I made in grad school and made surviving it an absolute joy. Finally, Clerky (Cathleen Clerkin) was my best friend and still is. She was sitting shotgun from the beginning of my research for this book until completion and has offered excellent advice. This section would not be complete without also thanking my Detroit family: Tim Tarbell, Manny Gilmer, and all my friends from Detroit Together Men's Chorus.

When I began working at the University of Virginia in 2013, I was incredibly lucky to join an amazing team of scholars in the Media Studies Department and the Women, Gender and Sexuality Department. Generous and enduring material, professional, and social support from the University of Virginia and from both my academic departments have made this book possible. After endless conversations about my book, after reading drafts many times, and after your golden best friendship, I must thank Chris Ali from the bottom of my heart. He helped sustain me throughout this entire process. Nora Draper at the University of New Hampshire also deserves my deepest thanks for reading a draft of the entire book and offering such thoughtful advice. I am so lucky that Chris introduced us. I also have to individually thank Siva Vaidhynathan, Charlotte Patterson, Hector Amaya, and Bruce Williams for being excellent chairs and for giving me the resources to thrive at University of Virginia. Thank you to Hector Amaya and Jennifer Peterson for taking time out of your very busy lives to read my chapter drafts. I also have to thank Allison Pugh in the Department of Sociology for her superb mentorship. I have cherished our many talks. Andrea Press too has been a guiding light for me in pursuing feminist audience research. Many thanks also go out to my wonderful colleagues in the Media Studies and Women, Gender and Sexuality Departments at UVa: Siva Vaidhyanathan, Hector Amaya, Aniko Bodroghkozy, Chris Ali, Shilpa Dave, Jack Hamilton, Aynne Kokas, William Little, Jennifer Petersen, Andrea Press, Nick Rubin, Francesca Tripodi, Bruce Williams, Charlotte Patterson, Denise Walsh, Cory Field, Bonnie Hagerman, Farzaneh Milani, Lisa Speidel, Lanice Avery, Karlin Leudtke, Geeta Patel, Doug Meyer, Alberto McKelligan Hernandez, and Amanda Davis. Barbara Gibbons also deserves special mention for being an excellent administrator and friend. Her behind-the-scenes work warrants my deepest gratitude. I also must deeply thank my Charlottesville chosen family: Augusta Reel, Jon Kropko, Cypress Walker, Ben Blackman, Chris Ali, Aynne Kokas, Chris Aukstikalnis, Clerky, Grey, Mike Hill, Tim Lyons, Lisa, Andy and Elena. You all have made Charlottesville feel truly like home.

I also must thank my students who have challenged, inspired, and taught me so much. I love teaching and I wrote this book with you all in mind.

NYU Press and Lisha Nadkarni have been a pleasure to work with and I am grateful they chose to work with me. I did my undergraduate and Masters work at NYU and it seems like things have come full circle. I particularly want to thank David Valentine and acknowledge the course he taught at NYU about transgender politics and identity, which served as an excellent introduction to the topic. During my time doing the "adjunct shuffle" on Long Island, it was Princess Williams who took a chance on me, hiring me to teach communications at Suffolk County Community College. So much of this starts with her. Jennifer Cooper also deserves recognition for our talk at Starbucks where she and I decided my path forward was an academic career. Thank you to Leah Serrano (Schmelzy), Marcie Silver, and Brendan Neff-Hall.

But the foundation upon which this book and my academic career rests is my family. I would not be where I am today without the brilliant love and unwavering support of my parents: Janet and Jay Rogove. From day one you encouraged me to pursue my dream of becoming a professor. My mom taught me to listen to people, to have empathy, and to show kindness, skills that have helped me immensely in my research. Jay was the one who talked me out of bouts of anxiety and self-doubt.

Even though at times they have not always been 100% sure of what exactly I do, they have supported me completely and have always had faith in me—which helped me have faith in myself. Giving me strength, my brothers and sisters also deserve mention: Steven and Kristina Cavalcante, Josh and Staci Rogove, Adam Rogove, and David and Ali Rogove.

Last, but certainly not least, I must thank my husband, Stephen Ninneman (Ninny Face). More than anyone, you have stuck beside me throughout the book-writing process with grace and a fabulous sense of humor. You have given me unbounded love and patience, even when I probably did not necessarily deserve them. WE did this. I love you.

NOTES

INTRODUCTION

1 The following work represents some of the first steps in scholarship examining the relationship between media and transgender life. See Gagné and Tewksbury (1999); Hegland and Nelson (2002); Ringo (2002); Hill (2005); Shapiro (2004); Gray (2009).

2 For more on audience research traditions, see Grossberg and Wartella (1996); Moores (1993); Brooker and Jermyn (2003); Nightingale (2014); Morley (1992).

3 According to Lefebvre (1991, 2002), it is only with the diffusion of capitalist modes of production, the acceleration of urban migration, and the rise of middle-class societies that the everyday became a historic reality. Under capitalism, the everyday was "upside-down." Individuals feel free, but are ultimately shackled to their job and to a world they did not create.

4 For a discussion of media environments, see Press and Williams (2010).

5 This approach widens the book's analytic optic and avoids lapsing into "media centrism," which artificially centers and exaggerates media influence and power. For a more in-depth exploration of media centrism, see Couldry (2012); Morley (2009, 2007); Moores (2012).

6 For more information on transgender taxonomies, see Stryker (2008). For an ethnography of the category "transgender," see Valentine (2007). Notably, the language of transgender and the development of non-binary identities are always changing and in constant negotiation. Much of this activity is currently happening online, particularly among youth on queer and transgender-themed Tumblr pages.

7 For a comprehensive analysis of the politics of transgender erasure, see Namaste (2000).

8 See National Center for Transgender Equality and the National Gay and Lesbian Task Force (2009).

9 See National Coalition of Anti-Violence Programs (2014).

10 Bonner (2003) argues that television specifically offers "an illusion of normality" (32).

11 For an interesting discussion of this process, see Doty (1993) and Lugowski (1999).

12 For example, see the foundational work of Laura Mulvey (1975). Also consult Dyer (1993) and Straayer (1990).

13 Practices of media use and consumption are complex, and can function in creative and transformative ways. De Certeau identifies media reception as an active

practice, a "silent production" where "a different world (the reader's) slips into the author's place," transforming the media text into an "inhabitable" and "rented" space (1984, xxi). For de Certeau, the dynamics of everyday life mirror ordinary language usage. The creativity that individuals express in constructing sentences and words from a predetermined language structure is akin to the creative and agentic moves and practices performed in daily life. In both instances individuals create their own collages and montages from materials already fixed in the world. With respect to media, it is the reappropriation, the ability to combine elements in new and unexpected ways, a form of drawing outside the lines while still remaining on the page, that bears witness to tactical assertions of power, agency, and creativity.

14 For an excellent description of queerness as a strategic position, see Halperin (1995). He argues that queerness is a "positionality vis-à-vis the normative . . . available to anyone who is or feels marginalized because of his or her sexual practices" (62). Queerness turns against the normal because on the macro-level, the regime of the normal serves the interests of larger formations of power, such as the modern neoliberal state and global capitalist institutions, which require stability and predictability to survive. On the micro-level, the normal encourages individuals to, in the name of conformity, "*freely and spontaneously* police both their own conduct and the conduct of others" (19; emphasis in original).

15 For more scholarship about the notion of queer anti-sociality, see Bersani (1996) and Edelman (2004).

16 As Ashley Love, a transgender blogger, explains, "so many 'transsexual' women selectively choose when to stay 'in the closet' . . . And I don't think they should be called cowards or sell outs" (Love 2010). Love (2010) takes issue with critics "who disagree with the group of trans people who just live their lives as the gender they are, with out using every chance they get to say how 'different' they are." Love's comments highlight an unnecessary and ethically loaded opposition between "the normal" (a harmful, "sellout" position) and "the queer" (a worthy celebrated one) erected in much critical and politically minded thought.

17 Rosen continues, "A life devoted to getting things wrong is inconceivable, since if it succeeded, it would destroy itself" (2002, 263). Rosen also argues that ordinariness is defined by a dynamic of regularity and predictability, which allows us to thrive and connects us with natural rhythms. Defined by cyclical phenomenon and routine, like day turning into night turning into day, and so on, Rosen argues that "the unity and regularity of praxis, the domain of intentional human activity . . . is itself dependent upon the unity and regularity of existence, to which we sometimes refer, not with complete accuracy, as the order of nature" (266).

18 The affordances of everyday life are not given or equally available. Rather, they are, in the words of sociologist Harold Garfinkel (1984), "an endless, ongoing, contingent accomplishment" (1). Garfinkel (1996) was one of the founders of a subfield in sociology called ethnomethodology that studied everyday life as

an "achieved phenomena of order" made possible by the perpetual work of its members (11). Although everyone is involved in the work of achieving everyday life, Garfinkel noted that for some it is a harder struggle and the stakes are higher.

CHAPTER 1. WE CAN NO LONGER HIDE IN PLAIN SIGHT

1 For more about the history of transgender media representations and communication networks, see Stryker (2008); Meyerowitz (2002); and Phillips (2006).

2 For a detailed analysis of this, see Downing, Morland, and Sullivan (2014).

3 For a great documentary about this event, see Susan Stryker and Victor Silverman's film *Screaming Queens* (2005, Frameline).

4 Martin Duberman's (1994) *Stonewall* does an excellent job covering the pre-and post-Stonewall moment.

5 There is a great publication about Rivera and Johnson worth reading titled *Street Transvestite Action Revolutionaries: Survival, Revolt and Queer Antagonist Struggle* (Untorelli Press) at www.untorellipress.noblogs.org/catalog/.

6 Information about the Tiffany Club of New England and the magazine *Transgender Tapestry* can be found at www.tcne.org/club-history.

7 This tension had always been brewing. In their case study of the alliance between the "ONE Institute for Homophile Studies" in Los Angeles, a gay rights group, and the "Erikson Educational Foundation" that championed transgender advocacy, Devor and Matte (2006) testify to the historically rooted challenges of this uneasy collaboration. Although the collaboration successfully advanced the acceptance of LGBT individuals, it suffered "partly from longstanding concerns about the relationship between trans and gay politics" and from vexing decisions about who deserves inclusion within an organization's mission and the allocation of its limited resources (399).

8 For a discussion of the issues at stake in the "transgender umbrella," see Davidson (2007).

9 Importantly, transgender life-writing provides a narrative framework for individuals looking to articulate their identities. It helps transgender individuals transform gender transformation "from private fantasy to realizable identity" (Prosser 1998, 124), allowing them to understand their own journey as a story with a beginning, middle, and end.

10 This history came to a head in a bizarre moment during the 1993 MTV Video Music Awards. RuPaul and Milton Berle were paired to present an award, but before doing so apparently had an off-stage squabble. The conflict spilled over on-stage during the live telecast of the show: RuPaul called Berle a "queen," Berle groped RuPaul's breasts, to which she responded, "So you used to wear gowns and now you're wearing diapers." In that moment, television's cross-dressing past met its present and the two worlds clashed.

11 In 2005, *Rent* is released as a movie.

12 Indeed, the logic of the long tail changed the economics of the entertainment and media industries. Whereas an older business model relied upon blockbuster hits and mass appeal products for attracting a large audience, Anderson (2006) contends that, "the hits now compete with an infinite number of niche markets, of any size" (5). Within this new formation of media economics, it became not only possible, but also commercially advantageous for media producers to cater to increasingly segmented markets. This changed the relative size and availability of transgender-themed media content.

13 For example, in their study, McKenna and Bargh (1998) concluded that individuals with marginalized and concealable identities want to belong to groups of like-minded others in the "actual" world, but struggle to do so because they hide their true selves out of embarrassment. As a result, these individuals rely on the Internet and its virtual communities more than those without marginalized and concealable identities. The researchers also found that the longer someone participated in an online group, the more important and meaningful their marginalized identity became for them, which was associated with higher levels of self-acceptance and an increased likelihood of coming out to important others. In an oral history project with Toronto's trans community, Hill (2005) finds that the Internet and more traditional communications technologies offered transgender participants a feeling of connectedness with others and worked to alleviate loneliness and social isolation. Crucially, media depictions showed that a transgender life was possible and offered "new perspectives and options for living a trans life" (Hill 2005, 43). At the same time, respondents were critical of problematic media portrayals of transgender and took issue with the limitations of computer-mediated communications in social interaction. Shapiro (2004) notes that the Internet has been a crucial asset in advancing the transgender rights movement by facilitating education, and easing the distribution of information and collective social and political action.

14 The more recent (and now canceled) VH1 reality makeover TV series *Transform Me* is also emblematic of this. The show's website frames the trans women as a trio of magical saviors:

> TRANSform Me is a makeover show in which a team of three transgender women . . . rescues women from personal style purgatory. Laverne and her ultra-glam partners in crime have undergone the ultimate transformation, so they're the perfect women for the job. . . . They'll travel the country in their tricked out fashion ambulance, siren blaring, and swoop into scenes of fashion disaster. They'll not only make women look better but feel a whole lot better about themselves . . . Then they hop in their fashion ambulance, and it's on to the next style crisis." (*Transform Me*)

This promotional text illustrates Brookey and Westerfelhaus's (2001) argument that popular film often achieves acceptance of queer characters through a "discourse of deification," portraying characters as morally and "unrealistically superior," as selflessly superhuman who harbor magic-like qualities (143–144).

CHAPTER 2. I SORT OF REFUSED TO TAKE MYSELF SERIOUSLY

1 In 2010, the non-discrimination legislation was attached to a budget bill as an amendment, yet failed to pass.

2 You can find the full text of the "Transmissions classic: The transgender documentary drinking game" in an article that appeared in the online version of the *Bay Area Reporter*. The article was written by Gwendolyn Ann Smith and can be found at *Bay Area Reporter*, www.ebar.com.

3 As I explained in chapter 1, we can also locate associations of gender variance with pathology in a science of sexuality that emerged at the turn of the twentieth century. At this time, the field of sexology and its practitioners characterized same-sex attraction and cross-gendered desires as sick and deviant, grouping them together in a strange brew of perversion. These associations were simultaneously alive and well in the popular culture of the time and have endured.

4 Butler (1990) further argues that "the very notion of 'the person' is called into question by the cultural emergence of those 'incoherent' or 'discontinuous' gendered beings who appear to be persons but who fail to conform to the gendered norms of cultural intelligibility" (17).

5 Transgender delegitimization and dehumanization are what Blumer (1954) refers to as "sensitizing concepts" (7), interpretive devices that help individuals make sense of the world. They were meaningful starting points to my participants that offered ways of seeing the world.

6 The cultural association of transgender women and sex work—particularly transgender women of color and sex work—is endemic. Recently, the ACLU took on the case of Meagan Taylor, who was arrested in Iowa under suspicion of being sex worker. She was not a sex worker. She was visiting Iowa with a friend to attend a funeral. The full story, Meagan Taylor, "I Was Arrested Just for Being Who I Am," *American Civil Liberties Union*, November 10, 2015, can be found at www.aclu.org.

7 For example, in the popular film *The Crying Game*, the main transgender character's performance harkens a "transgender deceiver" (Ryan 2009) stereotype, one that positions trans folks as perpetrators of deceit and duplicity. The character's gender identity is not revealed to her lover (and subsequently to the viewing audience) until the middle of the movie. During the moment of revelation, the film is shot so the audience joins in feelings of shock and betrayal with Dil's lover, who reacts by vomiting.

8 Crucially, possible selves motivate individuals to perform the work of identity. In this way, the formation of self is a process of attaining, accomplishing, and/or rejecting specific possible selves, which suggests that individuals are "active producers of their own development" (Markus and Nurius 1986, 955). In addition to incentivizing, possible selves offer "an evaluative and interpretive context for the now self," a frame of reference for understanding and giving meaning to one's identity, value, and potential at the current moment (962). Possible selves are

"distinctly social," in that they emerge through both mediated and unmediated interpersonal interaction and communication. The possible self is often the result of social comparison (954). Social comparisons allow individuals to engage in and develop self-understanding and knowledge, in that, through comparing ourselves with others, we learn about our own skills, abilities, feelings, and subjectivities (Festinger 1954). In contemporary society, social comparison has increasingly been done with mediated images.

CHAPTER 3. I WANT TO BE LIKE A REALLY BADASS LADY

1 Weibel (1996) also notes, "The primacy of the eye . . . as the dominant sense organ of the twentieth century is the consequence of a technical revolution that put an enormous apparatus to the service of vision. The rise of the eye is rooted in the fact that all of its aspects (creation, transmission, reception) were supported by analog and digital machines" (339).

2 That Jen came across transgender visibility on daytime television talk shows is not surprising. They have long offered a very public platform for non-normative displays of sexuality and gender, particularly "trash" and "tabloid"' varieties (Gamson 1999). *The Jerry Springer Show* is the most notorious exemplar of this genre. Many participants in my study mentioned the show by name, referring to it as a highly visible and potent symbol of transgender representation—if not blatant and intentional *mis*representation. Talk shows are, according to Gamson (1999), a "monster with two heads" (29–65). Capable of offering minorities visibility and a platform for raising sociopolitical topics, talk shows can also further marginalize the disenfranchised and reinscribe dominant social values (Gamson 1999; Grindstaff 2002; Manga 2003; Shattuc 1997).

3 Given the trends in social media, *XX Boys* has since migrated to Facebook and Tumblr. It does not seem to be active or renewing content today.

4 Cis gender refers to non-transgender identities and describes individuals that accept and have an affinity with the gender to which they were assigned at birth. A prefix from Latin that means "on this side of," cis emerged out of queer and transgender activist circles and academic communities. Within the past few years it has gained widespread popularity—so much so that Comedy Central's animated TV comedy series *South Park* parodied the concept ("The Cissy," Season 18, episode 3). The success of the word is related to transgender-themed websites and online, social networking platforms such as Tumblr, Facebook, and Reddit. It has made its way onto the online version of the *Oxford English Dictionary* and stands as one of the many gender identifications now available on Facebook.

5 I see this firsthand teaching the language of gender variance to undergraduates unfamiliar with it. At the beginning of the semester, many struggle with the language, stumbling over pronouns, and have difficulty thinking beyond the gender binary. Yet, as the semester advances, they become increasingly articulate and appreciate the ways their newly acquired vocabulary enriches their awareness and understanding of the world.

6 Although Sebastian includes intersex under the transgender umbrella, this is not a universal designation. These categorizations of "transgender" and "intersex" are contested and highly personal matters. Nonetheless, for Sebastian this film was a transgender representation.

CHAPTER 4. YOU HAVE TO BE REALLY STRONG

1 See the work of the following scholars: Hall (1980); Morley (1980); Ang (1985); Radway (1991); Press (1991); Coleman (2000).
2 See Ekman (1972); Shouse (2005). Brian Massumi (2002) specifies an emotion is "the conventional, consensual point of insertion of intensity into semantically and semiotically formed progressions" (28).
3 Stewart (2007) continues about "ordinary affects": "The question they beg is . . . what potential modes of knowing, relating, and attending to things are already somehow present in them in a state of potentiality and resonance" (3).
4 Hochschild further states, "Beneath the difference between physical and emotional labor there lies a similarity in the possible cost of doing the work: the worker can become estranged or alienated from an aspect of self—either the body or the margins of the soul—that is *used* to do the work" ([1983] 2003, 7).
5 Similarly, discussing resilience in the context of global communities and international politics, Carnes (2011) conceptualizes resilience as "an arc that runs from destruction and devastation, from diminishment in all its forms, to restoration and renewal and rebirth" (3). More pointedly, it entails "the capacity of individuals and communities to react, respond, rebuild, and begin again on firmer foundations" (3).

    Confronting current and impending global climate change and energy deficiencies, ecological scholars are researching how natural environments can absorb shocks without collapsing. In characterizing environmental resilience, Cox (2008) notes it is "the capacity of an ecosystem to tolerate disturbance without collapsing into a qualitatively different state that is controlled by a different set of processes" (6a). In other words, it is about sustaining and upgrading fundamental ecological principles and networks in order to rebuild when needed. This practice of rebuilding is also relevant in urban studies and urban planning, which have emphasized the necessity of resilience for the sustainability of the world's growing cities. For example, cities as complex systems must be flexible in order to effectively respond to external forces and threats. When faced with any adverse situation, the desirable outcome is the retention and integrity of vital social, governmental, and physical structures and organizations. As Dudley (2011) contends, urban resiliency is not dependent on a single element in a city—such as police, fire departments, or transportation networks. Rather, it is "the nature of the relationship between the elements. These elements need to be connected to others, but not so rigidly that they can't also operate independently" (376–380).
6 Masten (2001) maintains that resilience is in play when a phenomenon threatens to undermine the development of one's self and potential, and one's process of

adaptation is successful in sustaining continued personal growth and maturation. Notably, in coming to terms with distress, resilience is a dynamic process that manifests *over time*.

7 For an excellent discussion of queer representation on talk shows, see Gamson (1999).

8 For an interesting examination of parasocial relationships, media, and queer characters, see Schiappa, Gregg, and Hewes (2006). Their work shows that our relationships to media characters produce similar kinds of learning and affect as relationships with "real" people and groups.

9 According to Henri Lefebvre (1991), the everyday is a historically contingent phenomenon made possible by the diffusion of capitalist modes of production, the acceleration of urban migration, and the rise of the middle class and bourgeois society.

CHAPTER 5. WE'RE JUST LIVING LIFE

1 In further theorizing the everyday, Felski (1999) affirms: "Everyday life simply is the process of becoming acclimatised to assumptions, behaviours, and practices which come to seem self-evident and taken for granted . . . it is a lived process of routinisation . . . the quotidian is not an objectively given quality but a lived relationship" (31). Felski (1999) makes sure to underscore that although the everyday's process of routine may be politically problematic or hazardous, it fails to embody "an intrinsic political content" and its ideological orientation is not "intrinsically reactionary" (31).

2 Ontological security is a cognitive modality defined by a sense of security and continuity with respect to one's life and life course. See Anthony Giddens (1991, 1990).

3 Along these lines, the philosopher Stanley Rosen (2002) has argued that elusiveness is one of the primary features of the ordinary and everyday. It has become this way, he contends, because scholars and laymen alike have lost sight of it and have used the wrong tools to understand it. Rosen (2002) faults the dominance of an overtly rational, scientific, and quantitative paradigm in contemporary thought for marshaling the everyday under an "elaborate technical machinery" (1). As a result, ordinary life has become overdetermined, reduced to formulas and laws, and transformed into a theoretical relic. Rosen also suggests that the ordinary is elusive not only because we have made it that way, but because to some degree it has always been that way. Deeply complex and contradictory, ordinary life is often experienced as a bewildering heterogeneity. As Lefebvre (1991) argues, it is a dialectic that can only come to light through "an opposition and 'contrast' between a certain number of terms" (251).

Rosen's notion of "elusiveness" is particularly useful to work through the way participants in this study articulate their relationship to the ordinary and the everyday. However, whereas Rosen is primarily concerned with how the ordinary is *epistemologically* elusive, I focus on its *experiential* elusiveness as articulated by participants.

4 According to de Certeau (1984), everyday life is defined by a human agency that works within the limits of social, political, and economic power structures; it is an act of improvisation with the found materials and preexisting conditions of modern life. He identifies these practices of "agency within limits" as "tactics." Tactics work on and against power. To maintain and reinforce a dominant order, the powerful impose "strategies" or "actions which, thanks to the establishment of a place of power (the property of a proper), elaborate theoretical places (systems and totalizing discourses) capable of articulating an ensemble of physical places in which forces are distributed" (38). Strategies control, measure, delimit, transform, and define via the purposeful deployment of knowledge, in which "*a certain power is the precondition of this knowledge* and not merely its effect or its attribute" (36). Strategies are characteristically visible, spectacular, and totalizing. In many ways, mainstream American media may be considered "strategic." As instruments of power, they author a discursively spectacular space, a "totalizing discourse," via the encoding and marketing of media texts. They define domains of their own, as well as those that comprise an exterior (audiences) or those "targets or threats" that must be "managed" (36).

In negotiating and resisting the disciplinary logic of strategies, individuals employ an ensemble of "tactics," which "use, manipulate, and divert" the imposed order (de Certeau 1984, 30). As "an art of the weak" (37), a tactic "creates surprises" within "cracks that particular conjunctions open in the surveillance of the proprietary powers" (ibid.). Tactics are creative, local, and surreptitious "ways of making do" (29) within structures. When compared to the spectacle of the strategy, tactics represent "silent itineraries" (47), everyday practices and discourses unrecorded by history and authority. As a result, scholars are tasked with unearthing these silent itineraries, providing the backlighting for the tactical in everyday life.

5 The bathroom problem and the website "Safe2Pee" evidence what Garfinkel (1996) calls everyday society's "achieved phenomena of order," a continuous accomplishment made possible by the perpetual work of its members in locally defined contexts (11).

6 At another Trans Chat meeting, one participant talked about tapping into trans lore to learn about applying makeup. She routinely watched makeup tutorials posted by younger transgender women on YouTube to learn how to buy cosmetics and best practices for applying them. YouTube houses an immense archive of makeup tutorials made by and for transgender people.

7 Queerness as anti-sociality opposes the future-oriented, reproductive, and utopian politics of a heteronormative mainstream. As an example of the ultimate fulfillment of these politics, Edelman (2004) references mainstream cultural discourses surrounding the child. When employed in popular, political, and social conversation, the child is routinely portrayed as the pristine symbol of a future temporality, and a vulnerable, impressionable, and "pure" figure worth defending. Protecting the child and her innocence is then used as a justification to suppress

the "corrupting" and "troubling" force of queer life, desire, and otherness: "on every side, our enjoyment of liberty is eclipsed by the lengthening shadow of a Child whose freedom to develop undisturbed by encounters, or even by the threat of potential encounters, with an 'otherness' of which its parents, its church, or the state do not approve, uncompromised by any possible access to what is painted as alien desire, terroristically holds us all in check" (2004, 21). In opposition to a heteronormative futurity represented by the image of the child, to whom queer adults are in constant service, Edelman suggests queerness embrace the perversity of the "death drive," "the negativity opposed to every form of social viability" (9).

Edelman offers a radical, compelling, and trenchant polemic (much of which I am sympathetic toward). His critique of heteronormative futurity and the utopian politics in the name of the child is theoretically daring and necessary. Yet, as Halberstam (2008) notes, this theorization of queerness essentially promotes "a nihilism which always lines up against women, domesticity and reproduction" (154).

A QUEERLY ORDINARY CONCLUSION

1 To witness subversivism in action, see Bolin (1998); Hale (1996); Stone (1991). Stone's (1991) "The Empire Strikes Back," a seminal text that authenticates and legitimizes transgender subjectivity, argues for the expression of gender ambiguity as a political strategy. She advocates that transgender individuals refuse to pass, urging them to employ their bodies and identities in a radical, transformative politics. Moreover, she critiques those "normal" transgender folks who want to remain invisible.

BIBLIOGRAPHY

Aaron, Michele. 2004. "New Queer Cinema: An Introduction." In *New Queer Cinema: A Critical Reader*. Edited by Michele Aaron, 3–14. New Brunswick, NJ: Rutgers University Press.

Ahmed, Sara. 2004. *The Cultural Politics of Emotion*. New York: Routledge.

———. 2006a. "Orientations: Towards a Queer Phenomenology." *GLQ: A Journal of Lesbian and Gay Studies* 12, no. 4: 543–574.

———. 2006b. *Queer Phenomenology: Orientations, Objects, Others*. Durham, NC: Duke University Press.

Alasuutari, Pertti. 1999. "Introduction: Three Phases of Reception Studies." In *Rethinking the Media Audience*. Edited by Pertti Alasuutari, 1–21. London: Sage Publications.

Anderson, Benedict. 2006. *Imagined Communities: Reflections on the Origin and Spread of Nationalism*. London & New York: Verso.

Anderson, Chris. 2006. *The Long Tail: Why the Future of Business Is Selling Less of More*. New York: Hyperion.

Ang, Ien. 1985. *Watching Dallas: Soap Opera and the Melodramatic Imagination*. London: Methuen & Co.

———. 1996. "Ethnography and Radical Contextualism in Audience Studies." In *The Audience and Its Landscape*. Edited by J. Hay, L. Grossberg, and E. Warrtella, 247–262. Boulder, CO: Westview Press.

Anonymous Queers. 1990/1999. "Queers Read This: I Hate Straights." In *The Columbia Reader on Lesbians & Gay Men in Media, Society, and Politics*. Edited by L. Gross and J. D. Woods, 588–594. New York: Columbia University Press.

Aslinger, Ben. 2009. "Creating a Network for Queer Audiences at Logo TV." *Popular Communication* 7: 107–121.

Becker, Ron. 2006. *Gay TV and Straight America*. New Brunswick, NJ: Rutgers University Press.

Bell-Metereau, Rebecca. 1993. *Hollywood Androgyny*. New York: Columbia University Press.

Benjamin, Harry. 1966. *The Transsexual Phenomenon*. New York: Julian Press.

Bennett, Tony. 1996. "Figuring Audiences and Readers." In *The Audience and Its Landscape*. Edited by J. Hay, L. Grossberg, and E. Wartella, 145–159. Boulder, CO: Westview Press.

Bensman, Joseph. 2014. "Max Weber's Concept of Legitimacy." In *Essays on Modern Society*. Edited by Robert Jackall and Duffy Graham, 325–371. Knoxville: Newfound Press, University of Tennessee.

Berlant, Lauren. 2010. "Cruel Optimism." In *The Affect Theory Reader*. Edited by M. Gregg and G. J. Seigworth, 93–117. Durham, NC: Duke University Press.

———. 2011. *Cruel Optimism*. Durham, NC: Duke University Press.

Berlant, Lauren and Michael Warner. 1995. "What Does Queer Theory Teach Us About X?" *PMLA* 110, no. 3: 343–349.

Bersani, Leo. *1996. Homos*. Cambridge, MA: Harvard University Press.

Bhabha, Homi K. 1994. *The Location of Culture*. New York: Routledge.

Biocca, Frank A. 1988. "Opposing Conceptions of the Audience: The Active and Passive Hemispheres of Mass Communication Theory." *Communication Yearbook* 11: 51–80.

Bird, Elizabeth. 2003. *The Audience in Everyday Life: Living in a Media World*. Batavia, IL: Taylor & Francis Group.

Blaze, Alex. 2010a. "Facebook Will Assign You a Gender, and You'll Like It." *Bilerico Project*. January 15. Retrieved from www.bilerico.com.

———. 2010b. "YouTube Removes Man's Video for Going Shirtless." *Huffington Post*. May 12. Retrieved from www.huffingtonpost.com.

———. 2010c. "Dominic's YouTube Video Is Back Up." *Bilerico Project*. May 14. Retrieved from www.bilerico.com.

Blumer, Herbert. 1954. "What Is Wrong with Social Theory?" *American Sociological Review* 19, no. 1: 3-10.

Boag, Peter. 2011. *Re-dressing America's Frontier Past*. Berkeley: University of California Press.

Bob, M. 2012. "Female Mimics Magazine—Part 1, The Early Years." *TG Forum*. Retrieved from www.tgforum.com.

Bogle, Donald. 2001. *Toms, Coons, Mulattoes, Mammies, and Bucks: An Interpretive History of Blacks in American Films*, 4th edition. London: Bloomsbury Academic.

Bolin, Anne. 1988. *In Search of Eve: Transsexual Rites of Passage*. New York: Bergin & Garvey Publishers.

———. 1998. "Transcending and Transgendering: Male-to-Female Transsexuals, Dichotomy, and Diversity." In *Current Concepts in Transgender Identity*. Edited by D. Denny, 63–96. New York: Garland Publishing.

Bolter, Jay David and Richard Grusin. 2000. *Remediation: Understanding New Media*. Cambridge, MA: MIT Press.

Bonner, Frances. 2003. *Ordinary Television: Analyzing Popular TV*. London: Sage Publications.

Bornstein, Kate. 1995. *Gender Outlaw: On Men, Women and the Rest of Us*. New York: Vintage Books.

Brooker, Will and Deborah Jermyn. 2003. *The Audience Studies Reader*. London: Routledge.

Brookey, Robert A. and Robert Westerfelhaus. 2001. "Pistols and Petticoats, Piety and Purity: To Wong Fu, the Queering of the American Monomyth, and the Marginalizing Discourse of Deification." *Critical Studies in Media Communication* 18, no. 2: 141–156.

Brown, Wendy. 2005. *Edgework: Critical Essays on Knowledge and Politics*. Princeton: Princeton University Press.

Butler, Judith. 1988. "Performative Acts and Gender Constitution: An Essay in Phenomenology and Feminist Theory." *Theatre Journal* 40, no. 4: 519–531.

———. 1990. *Gender Trouble: Feminism and the Subversion of Identity*. New York: Routledge.

———. 2004. *Undoing Gender*. New York: Routledge.

———. 2009. *Frames of War: When Is Life Grievable?* London: Verso.

Califia, Pat. 1994. *Public Sex: The Culture of Radical Sex*. Berkeley: Cleis Press.

Cameron, Loren. 1996. *Body Alchemy: Transsexual Portraits*. Berkeley: Cleis Press.

Carey, James. 1992. *Communication as Culture: Essays on Media and Society*. New York: Routledge.

Carnes, Matthew. 2011. "Resilience." *Georgetown Journal of International Affairs*, Summer/Fall: 3–5.

Cascio, Jamais. 2009. "Resilience." *Foreign Policy*, May/June 172: 92.

Castells, Manuel. 1996/2000. *The Rise of the Network Society*. Malden, MA: Blackwell Publishers.

Cavalcante, Andre. 2015. "Anxious Displacements: The Representation of Gay Parenting on Modern Family and the New Normal and the Management of Cultural Anxiety." *Television & New Media* 16, no. 5: 454–471.

———. 2016. "'I Did It All Online': Transgender Identity and the Management of Everyday Life." *Critical Studies in Media Communication* 33, no. 1: 109–122.

Cavell, Stanley. 1984. *Themes Out of School: Effects and Causes*. San Francisco: North Point Press.

———. 1988. *In Quest of the Ordinary: Lines of Skepticism and Romanticism*. Chicago: University of Chicago Press.

Clark, Cedric. 1969. "Television and Social Controls: Some Observations on the Portrayal of Ethnic Minorities." *Television Quarterly* (Spring): 18–22.

Clough, Patricia. 2007. *The Affective Turn: Theorising the Social*. Durham, NC: Duke University Press.

Coleman, Robin Means. 2000. *African American Viewers and the Black Situation Comedy: Situating Racial Humor*. New York: Garland Publishing.

Couldry, Nick. 2012. *Media, Society, World: Social Theory and Digital Media Practice*. Cambridge, UK: Polity.

Cox, Craig. 2008. "Resilience." *Journal of Soil and Water Conservation* 63, no. 1: 6A.

Crawley, Sara L. 2002. "Prioritizing Audiences: Exploring Differences Between Stone Butch and Transgender Selves." *Journal of Lesbian Studies* 6, no. 2: 11–24.

Creed, Barbara. 2005. "The End of the Everyday: Transformation, Sexuality and the Uncanny." *Continuum: Journal of Media & Cultural Studies* 19, no. 4: 483–494.

Crowder, Austen. 2009. "Transgender Comics: Interview with Lauren Lindsey." *Bilerico Project*. August 3. Retrieved from www.bilerico.com.

Currah, Paisley. 2008a. "Expecting Bodies: The Pregnant Man and Transgender Exclusion from the Employment Non-Discrimination Act." *Women's Studies Quarterly* 36, no. 3/4: 330–336.

———. 2008b. "Stepping Back, Looking Outward: Situating Transgender Activism and Transgender Studies—Kris Hayashi, Matt Richardson, and Susan Stryker Frame the Movement." *Sexuality Research & Social Policy* 5, no. 1: 93–105.

Cvetkovich, Ann. 2003. *An Archive of Feelings: Trauma, Sexuality, and Lesbian Public Cultures*. Durham, NC: Duke University Press.

Davidson, Megan. 2007. "Seeking Refuge Under the Umbrella: Inclusion, Exclusion, and Organizing Within the Category Transgender." *Sexuality Research and Social Policy* 4, no. 4: 60–80.

de Certeau, Michel. 1984. *The Practice of Everyday Life*. Berkeley: University of California Press.

Denny, Dallas. 2006. "Transgender Communities of the United States in the Late Twentieth Century." *Transgender Rights*. Edited by Paisley Currah, Richard Juang, and Shannon Price Minter, 171–191. Minneapolis: University of Minnesota Press.

Deuze, Mark. 2012. *Media Life*. Cambridge, UK: Polity Press.

Devor, Aaron and Nicholas Matte. 2006. "ONE Inc. and Reed Erickson: The Uneasy Collaboration of Gay and Trans Activism, 1964–2003." In *The Transgender Studies Reader*. Edited by Susan Stryker and Stephen Whittle, 387–406. New York: Routledge.

———. 2007. "Building a Better World for Transpeople: Reed Erickson and the Erickson Educational Foundation." *International Journal of Transgenderism* 10, no. 1: 47–68.

Diffrient, David Scott. 2013. "'Hard to Handle': Camp Criticism, Trash-Film Reception, and the Transgressive Pleasures of *Myra Breckinridge*." *Cinema Journal* 52, no. 2: 46–70.

Doty, Alexander. 1993. *Making Things Perfectly Queer: Interpreting Mass Culture*. Minneapolis: University of Minnesota Press.

Dow, Bonnie. 2001. "Ellen, Television, and the Politics of Gay and Lesbian Visibility." *Critical Studies in Media Communication* 18, no. 2: 123–140.

Downing, Lisa, Iain Morland, and Nikki Sullivan. 2014. *Fuckology: Critical Essays on John Money's Diagnostic Concepts*. Chicago: University of Chicago Press.

Drag. 1976. Volume 6, no. 24. New York: Lee's Mardi Gras Enterprises.

Duberman, Martin. 1994. *Stonewall*. New York: Plume.

Dudley, Michael Q. 2011. "Resilience." In *Green Cities: An A-to-Z Guide*. Edited by Nevin Cohen and Paul Robbins, 376–380. Thousand Oaks, CA: SAGE Publications.

Duggan, Lisa. 2002. "The New Homonormativity: The Sexual Politics of Neoliberalism." In *Materializing Democracy: Toward a Revitalized Cultural Politics*. Edited by D. D. Nelson and R. Castronovo, 175–194. Durham, NC: Duke University Press.

———. 2003. *The Twilight of Equality? Neoliberalism, Cultural Politics, and the Attack on Democracy*. Boston, MA: Beacon Press.

Duits, Linda. 2010. "The Importance of Popular Media in Everyday Girl Culture." *European Journal of Communication* 25, no. 3: 243–257.

Dyer, Richard. 1993. *A Matter of Images: Essays on Representation*. London: Routledge.

Ebert, Roger. 1977. "Outrageous!" *Rogerebert.com.* August 26. Retrieved from www.rogerebert.com.

Edelman, Lee. 2004. *No Future: Queer Theory and the Death Drive.* Durham, NC: Duke University Press.

Ekins, Richard and David King. 1996. "Introduction." In *Blending Genders: Social Aspects of Cross-Dressing and Sex Changing.* Edited by Richard Ekins and Dave King, 49–52. London: Routledge.

———. 2005. "Virginia Prince: Transgender Pioneer." In *Virginia Prince: Pioneer of Transgendering.* Edited by Richard Ekins and Dave King, 5–16. Binghamton, NY: Haworth Medical Press.

Ekman, Paul. 1972. "Universal and Cultural Differences in Facial Expression of Emotion." In *Nebraska Symposium on Motivation.* Edited by J. R. Cole, 207–283. Lincoln: University of Nebraska Press.

Epstein, Steven. 1996. "A Queer Encounter: Sociology and the Study of Sexuality." In *Queer Theory/Sociology.* Edited by S. Seidman, 145–167. Cambridge, MA: Blackwell Publishers.

Fawaz, Ramzi. 2016. *The New Mutants: Superheroes and the Radical Imagination of American Comics.* New York: New York University Press.

Feinberg, Leslie. 1992. *Transgender Liberation: A Movement Whose Time Has Come.* New York: World View Forum.

———. 1996. *Transgender Warriors: Making History from Joan of Arc to Dennis Rodman.* Boston, MA: Beacon Press.

Felski, Rita. 1999. "The Invention of Everyday Life." *New Formations: A Journal of Culture/Theory/Politics* 39: 15–31.

Female Impersonators. 1969. Issue 1. New York: Health Knowledge.

Festinger, Leon. 1954. "A Theory of Social Comparison Processes." *Human Relations* 7, no. 2: 117–140.

Fetterman, David. 1989. *Ethnography: Step by Step.* London: Sage.

Fiske, John. 1987. *Television Culture.* New York: Routledge.

Foucault, Michel. 1980. *Power/Knowledge: Selected Interviews and Other Writings 1972–1977.* New York: Pantheon Books.

———. 1990. *The History of Sexuality: An Introduction.* New York: Vintage/Random House.

———. 1995. *Discipline and Punish: The Birth of the Prison.* 2nd edition. New York: Vintage Books.

Gagné, Patricia and Richard Tewksbury. 1999. "Knowledge and Power, Body and Self: An Analysis of Knowledge Systems and the Transgendered Self." *Sociological Quarterly* 40, no. 1: 59–83.

Gamson, Joshua. 1999. *Freaks Talk Back: Tabloid Talk Shows and Sexual Nonconformity.* Chicago: University of Chicago Press.

———. 2005. *The Fabulous Sylvester: The Legend, the Music, the Seventies in San Francisco.* New York: Picador.

Garber, Eric. 1989. "A Spectacle in Color: The Lesbian and Gay Subculture of Jazz Age Harlem." In *Hidden from History: Reclaiming the Gay and Lesbian Past.* Edited by

Martin Duberman, Martha Vicinus, and George Chauncey, Jr., 318–331. New York: New American Library.

Garber, Marjorie. 1992. Vested Interests: Cross-dressing and Cultural Anxiety. New York: Routledge.

Garfinkel, Harold. 1964. "Studies of the Routine Grounds of Everyday Activities." Social Problems 11, no. 3: 225–250.

———. [1967] 1984. Studies in Ethnomethodology. Cambridge: Polity Press.

———. 1996. "Ethnomethodology's Program." Social Psychology Quarterly 59, no.1: 5–21.

Garvin, Glenn. 2003. "Breaking Boundaries." Miami Herald, March 15. Retrieved from www.miamiherald.com.

Geertz, Clifford. 1973. Interpretation of Cultures: Selected Essays. New York: Basic Books.

Gibbs, Anna. 2002. "Disaffected." Continuum: Journal of Media & Cultural Studies 16, no. 3: 335–341.

———. 2014. "Affect Theory and Audience." In The Handbook of Media Audiences. Edited by Virginia Nightingale, 251–266. Malden, MA: John Wiley & Sons.

Giddens, Anthony. 1990. The Consequences of Modernity. Oxford: Polity Press.

———. 1991. Modernity and Self-Identity: Self and Society in the Late Modern Age. Cambridge: Polity Press.

GLAAD. 2010. "Network Responsibility Index 2009–2010." GLAAD. Retrieved from www.glaad.org.

Glaser, Barney and Anselm Strauss. 1967. The Discovery of Grounded Theory: Strategies for Qualitative Research. Chicago: Aldine.

Goffman, Erving. 1959. The Presentation of Self in Everyday Life. New York: Anchor Books.

Grant, Jaime M., Lisa A. Mottet, Justin Tanis, Jack Harrison, Jody L. Herman, and Mara Keisling. 2011. Injustice at Every Turn: A Report of the National Transgender Discrimination Survey. Washington, DC: National Center for Transgender Equality and National Gay and Lesbian Task Force.

Gray, Mary. 2009. Out in the Country: Youth, Media, and Queer Visibility in Rural America. New York: New York University Press.

Green, Melanie C., Timothy C. Brock, and Geoff F. Kaufman. 2004. "Understanding Media Enjoyment: The Role of Transportation into Narrative Worlds." Communication Theory 14, no. 4: 311–327.

Greenspun, Roger. 1970. "Movie Review: The Christine Jorgensen Story" in "Screen: 'You Can't Win 'Em All' Proves a Cliché: Collinson's Caper Film Written by Gordon." New York Times, July 25. Retrieved from www.nytimes.com.

Grindstaff, Laura. 2002. The Money Shot: Trash, Class, and the Making of TV Talk Shows. Chicago: University of Chicago Press.

Gross, Larry. 1998. "Minorities, Majorities and the Media." In Media, Ritual, & Identity. Edited by T. Liebes, J. Curran, and E. Katz, 87–102. London and New York: Routledge.

———. 2005. "The Past and the Future of Gay, Lesbian, Bisexual, and Transgender Studies." Journal of Communication 55, no. 3: 508–528.

Grossberg, Lawrence. 1992. *We Gotta Get Out of This Place: Popular Conservatism and Postmodern Culture*. New York: Routledge.

Halberstam, Judith. 1998. *Female Masculinity*. Durham, NC: Duke University Press.

———. 2005. *In a Queer Time & Place: Transgender Bodies, Subcultural Lives*. New York: New York University Press.

———. 2008. "The Anti-Social Turn in Queer Studies." *Graduate Journal of Social Science* 5, no. 2: 140–156.

———. 2011. *The Queer Art of Failure*. Durham, NC: Duke University Press.

Hale, Jacob. 1996. "The Political Power of Transgender." *Lesbian Review of Books* 11, no. 4: 23.

Hall, Stuart. 1980. "Encoding/Decoding." In Centre for Contemporary Cultural Studies, ed., *Culture, Media, Language: Working Papers in Cultural Studies 1972–79* (pp. 128–138). London: Hutchinson.

———. 1990. "Cultural Identity and Diaspora." In *Identity: Community, Culture and Difference*. Edited by J. Rutherford, 222–237. London: Lawrence and Wishart, Ltd.

Halperin, David. 1995. *Saint Foucault: Towards a Gay Hagiography*. New York: Oxford University Press.

———. 2012. *How to Be Gay*. Cambridge, MA: Belknap Press.

Hausman, Bernice. 2006. "Body, Technology, and Gender in Transsexual Autobiographies." In *The Transgender Studies Reader*. Edited by Susan Stryker and Stephen Whittle, 335–361. New York: Routledge.

Hay, James, Lawrence Grossberg, and Ellen Wartella. 1996. *The Audience and Its Landscape*. Boulder, CO: Westview Press.

Hegland, Jane E. and Nancy J. Nelson. 2002. "Cross Dressers in Cyberspace: Exploring the Internet as a Tool for Expressing Gendered Identity." *International Journal of Sexuality and Gender Studies* no. 7: 139–161.

Heidegger, Martin. 1962. *Being and Time*. Oxford: Basil Blackwell.

Highmore, Ben. 2002. *Everyday Life and Cultural Theory: An Introduction*. New York: Routledge.

Hill, Darryl. 2005. "Coming to Terms: Using Technology to Know Identity." *Sexuality & Culture* 9, no. 3: 24–52.

Hill, Robert. 2013. "Before Transgender: *Transvestia*'s Spectrum of Gender Variance, 1960–1980." In *The Transgender Studies Reader 2*. Edited by S. Stryker and A. Z. Aizura, 364–379. New York: Routledge.

Hillier, Lynne, Chyloe Kurdas, and Philomena Horsley. 2001. "'It's just easier': The Internet as a Safety-Net for Same Sex Attracted Young People." December 1. Australian Research Centre in Sex, Health, and Society, La Trobe University, Melbourne, Commonwealth Department of Health & Aged Care. *Australian Policy Online*. Retrieved from www.apo.org.au. DOI: 10.4225/50/557E600573DC8

Hoberman, J. 2010. "'Psycho' is 50: Remembering Its Impact, and the Andrew Sarris Review." *Village Voice*, June 15. Retrieved from www.villagevoice.com.

Hochschild, Arlie. [1983] 2003. *The Managed Heart: Commercialization of Human Feeling*. Berkeley: University of California Press.

hooks, bell. 1992. *Black Looks: Race and Representation*. Boston: South End Press.

Horak, Laura. 2016. *Girls Will Be Boys: Cross Dressed Women, Lesbians, and American Cinema*. New Brunswick, NJ: Rutgers University Press.

Horton, Donald and R. Richard Wohl. 1956. "Mass Communication and Para-social Interaction." *Psychiatry* 19: 215–229.

Howe, Alyssa. 2001. "Queer Pilgrimage: The San Francisco Homeland and Identity Tourism." *Cultural Anthropology* 18, no. 1: 35–61.

Hurd, Ian. 2015. "Legitimacy." In *Princeton Encyclopedia of Self-Determination*. Princeton: Princeton University Press. Retrieved from *Encyclopedia Princetoniensis: The Princeton Encyclopedia of Self-Determination*. www.pesd.princeton.edu.

Inniss, Leslie and Joe Feagin. 2002. "*The Cosby Show*": The View From the Black Middle Class." In *Say It Loud!: African American Audiences, Media and Identity*. Edited by Robin Means Coleman, 187–204. New York: Routledge.

Jenkins, Henry. 1992. *Textual Poachers: Television Fans and Participatory Culture*. New York: Routledge.

———. 2002. "Interactive Audiences?: The 'Collective Intelligence' of Media Fans." In *The New Media Book*. Edited by Dan Harries, 57–70. London: British Film Institute.

———. 2006. *Convergence Culture: Where Old and New Media Collide*. New York: New York University Press.

Johnson, E. Patrick. 2005. "'Quare' Studies, or (Almost) Everything I Know About Queer Studies I Learned From My Grandmother." In *Black Queer Studies: A Critical Anthology*. Edited by E. Patrick Johnson and Mae G. Henderson, 124–189. Durham, NC: Duke University Press.

Kama, Amit. 2002. "The Quest for Inclusion: Jewish-Israeli Gay Men's Perceptions of Gays in the Media." *Feminist Media Studies* 2, no. 2: 195–212.

Kaplan, Alice and Kristin Ross. 2002. "Introduction to Everyday Life: *Yale French Studies*." In *The Everyday Life Reader*. Edited by Ben Highmore, 76–82. New York: Routledge.

Keller, J. 2009. "Ad Campaign Fights Transgender 'Bathroom Bill.'" *WBZ, MA*. July 2. Retrieved from *CBS Boston*. www.wbztv.com.

Kissell, Rick. 2015. "Bruce Jenner Interview Ratings: 17 Million Watch ABC Special." *Variety*, April 25. Retrieved from www.variety.com.

Kulick, Don. 1999. "Transgender and Language: A Review of the Literature and Suggestions for the Future." *GLQ* 5, no. 4: 605–622.

Lamb, Jonah Owen. 2013. "New Numbers Show San Francisco Has Nation's Highest Rents." *San Francisco Examiner*, November 14. Retrieved from www.sfexaminer.com.

Lefebvre, Henri. 1987. "The Everyday and Everydayness." *Yale French Studies* no. 73: 7–11.

———. 1991. *The Critique of Everyday Life, Volume 1*. London: Verso.

———. 2002. Work and Leisure in Everyday Life. In *The Everyday Life Reader*. Edited by Ben Highmore, 225–236. New York: Routledge.

Lennon, Kathleen. 2006. "Making Life Livable: Transsexuality and Bodily Transformation." *Radical Philosophy* 140: 26–34.

Leonard, Tom. 2008. "Pregnant Man Thomas Beatie Gives Birth to Baby Girl." *Telegraph*, July 3. Retrieved from www.telegraph.co.uk.

Leys, Ruth. 2011. "The Turn to Affect: A Critique." *Critical Inquiry* 37: 434–472.

Livingstone, Sonia. 2003. "The Changing Nature of Audiences: From the Mass Audience to the Interactive Media User." In *The Blackwell Companion to Media Research*. Edited by A. Valdivia, 337–359. Oxford: Blackwell.

Lotz, Amanda. 2007. *The Television Will Be Revolutionized*. New York & London: New York University Press.

Love, Ashley. 2010. "Thoughts on Transsexual (not to be confused with CD/TV/GQ) Inequality in a Diverse 'Transgender' Umbrella." *Transforming Media (tfm)*, January 22. Retrieved from www.transformingmedia.blogspot.com.

Lowder, J. Bryan. 2014. "Listen to Leelah Alcorn's Final Words." *Slate.com*. December 31. Retrieved from www.slate.com.

Lugowski, David M. 1999. "Queering the (New) Deal: Lesbian and Gay Representation and the Depression Era Cultural Politics of Hollywood's Production Code." *Cinema Journal* 38, no. 2: 3–35.

Lunt, Peter and Sonia Livingstone. 1996. "Rethinking the Focus Group in Media and Communications Research." *Journal of Communication* 46, no. 2: 79–98.

Luthar, Suniya, Dante Cicchetti, and Bronwyn Becker. 2000. "The Construct of Resilience: A Critical Evaluation and Guidelines for Future Work." *Child Development* 71, no. 3: 543–562.

MacAulay, Maggie and Marcos Daniel Moldes. 2016. "Queen Don't Compute Reading and Casting Shade on Facebook's Real Names Policy." *Critical Studies in Media Communication* 33, no. 1: 6–22. DOI: 10.1080/15295036.2015.1129430

Manga, Julie Engel. 2003. *Talking Trash: The Cultural Politics of Daytime TV Talk Shows*. New York: New York University Press.

Markus, Hazel and Paula Nurius. 1986. "Possible Selves." *American Psychologist* 41, no. 9: 954–969.

Martin, Biddy. 1997. "Extraordinary Homosexuals and the Fear of Being Ordinary." In *Feminism Meets Queer Theory*. Edited by E. Weed and N. Schor, 109–135. Bloomington: Indiana University Press.

Massumi, Brian. 2002. *Parables for the Virtual*. Durham, NC: Duke University Press.

Masten, Ann S. 2001. "Ordinary Magic: Resilience Processes in Development." *American Psychologist* 56, no. 3: 227–238.

McGuire, Meredith B. 2008. *Lived Religion: Faith and Practice in Everyday Life*. Oxford: Oxford University Press.

McKee, Alan. 1999. "Resistance Is Hopeless: Assimilating Queer Theory." *Social Semiotics* 9, no. 2: 235–249.

McKenna, Katelyn Y. A. and John A. Bargh. 1998. "Coming Out in the Age of the Internet: 'Demarginalization' Through Virtual Group Participation." *Journal of Personality and Social Psychology* 75: 681–694.

Mediamatic. "Interview Kael T. Block: On XX Boys and More." *Mediamatic*. Retrieved from www.mediamatic.net.

Meeker, Martin. 2006. *Contacts Desired: Gay and Lesbian Communications and Community, 1940s–1970s*. Chicago: University of Chicago Press.

Meyer, Doug. 2015. *Violence Against Queer People: Race, Class, Gender, and the Persistence of Anti-LGBT Discrimination*. New Brunswick, NJ: Rutgers University Press.

Meyerowitz, Joanne. 2002. *How Sex Changed: A History of Transsexuality in the United States*. Cambridge, MA: Harvard University Press.

Mitchell, W.J.T. 1996. "What Do Pictures *Really* Want?" *October 77*, Summer: 71–82.

Moores, Shaun. 1993. *Interpreting Audiences: The Ethnography of Media Consumption*. Thousand Oaks, CA: Sage Publications.

———. 2012. *Media, Place and Mobility*. New York: Palgrave Macmillan.

Moraes, Lisa de. 2015. "TLC Jumps on Transgender Series Bandwagon with 'All That Jazz.'" *Deadline Hollywood*, March 12. Retrieved from www.deadline.com.

Morley, David. 1980. *The Nationwide Audience: Structure and Decoding*. London: British Film Institute.

———. 1983. "Cultural Transformations: The Politics of Resistance." In *Language, Image, Media*. Edited by Howard Davis and Paul Walton, 104–17. Oxford: Basil Blackwell.

———. 1992. *Television, Audiences and Cultural Studies*. New York: Routledge.

———. 2007. *Media, Modernity and Technology: The Geography of the New*. New York: Routledge.

———. 2009. "For a Materialist, Non-Media-centric Media Studies." *Television & New Media* 10, no. 1: 114–116.

Mulvey, Laura. 1975. "Visual Pleasure and Narrative Cinema." *Screen* 16, no. 3: 6–18.

Muñoz, Jose Esteban. 1999. *Disidentifications: Queers of Color and the Performance of Politics*. Minneapolis: University of Minnesota Press.

———. 2009. *Cruising Utopia: The Then and There of Queer Futurity*. New York: New York University Press.

Namaste, Viviane. 2000. *Invisible Lives: The Erasure of Transsexual and Transgender People*. Chicago: University of Chicago Press.

National Center for Transgender Equality and the National Gay and Lesbian Task Force. 2009. "National Transgender Discrimination Survey." Washington, DC. Retrieved from *National Center for Transgender Equality*, www.transequality.org.

National Coalition of Anti-Violence Programs. 2014. "Lesbian, Gay, Bisexual, Transgender, Queer, and HIV-Affected Hate Violence in 2013: A Report from the National Coalition of Anti-Violence Programs (2014 release edition)." New York: 2014. Retrieved from *Anti-Violence Project*. www.avp.org.

Nesteroff, Kliph. 2015. *The Comedians: Drunks, Thieves, Scoundrels, and the History of American Comedy*. New York: Grove Press.

Newton, Esther. 1979. *Mother Camp: Female Impersonators in America*. Chicago and London: University of Chicago Press.

Ng, Eve. 2013. "A 'Post-Gay' Era? Media Gaystreaming, Homonormativity, and the Politics of LGBT Integration." *Communication, Culture & Critique* 6, no. 2: 258–283.

Nightingale, Virginia. 2014. *The Handbook of Media Audiences*. Malden, MA: Wiley Blackwell.

Nightingale, Virginia and Karen Ross. 2003. "Introduction." In *Critical Readings: Media and Audiences*. Edited by V. Nightingale and K. Ross, 1–11. Maidenhead, UK: Open University Press.

Palmer, Neal, Joseph Kosciw, Emily Greytak, Michele Ybarra, Josephine Korchmaros, and Kimberly Mitchell. 2013. "Out Online: The Experiences of Lesbian, Gay, Bisexual and Transgender Youth on the Internet." *Gay, Lesbian and Straight Education Network (GLSEN)*. New York. Retrieved from www.glsen.org.

Perkins, Roberta. 1996. "'The Drag Queen Scene:' Transsexuals in Kings Cross." In *Blending Genders: Social Aspects of Cross-Dressing and Sex Changing*. Edited by Richard Ekins and Dave King, 53–62. London: Routledge.

Perloff, Richard. 1993. "Third-Person Effect Research 1983–1992: A Review and Synthesis." *International Journal of Public Opinion Research* 5, no. 2: 167–184.

Phillips, John. 2006. *Transgender on Screen*. New York: Palgrave Macmillan.

Press, Andrea. 1991. *Women Watching Television: Gender, Class, and Generation in the American Television Experience*. Philadelphia: University of Pennsylvania Press.

Press, Andrea and Bruce Williams. 2010. *The New Media Environment: An Introduction*. Hoboken, NJ: Wiley-Blackwell.

Prosser, Jay. 1998. *Second Skins: The Body Narratives of Transsexuality*. New York: Columbia University Press.

Puar, Jasbir. 2007. *Terrorist Assemblages: Homonationalism in Queer Times*. Durham. NC: Duke University Press.

Radway, Janice. 1991. *Reading the Romance: Women, Patriarchy, and Popular Literature*. Chapel Hill: University of North Carolina Press.

Rich, B. Ruby. 2013. *New Queer Cinema: The Director's Cut*. Durham, NC: Duke University Press.

Richards, Renée, with John Ames. 2007. *No Way Renée: The Second Half of My Notorious Life*. New York: Simon & Schuster.

Ringo, Peter. 2002. "Media Roles in Female-to-Male Transsexual and Transgender Identity Formation." *International Journal of Transgenderism* 6, no. 3. Retrieved from https://www.atria.nl/ezines/web/IJT/97-03

Riva, Maria. 1993. *Marlene Dietrich*. New York: Alfred A. Knopf.

Rivera, Sylvia. 2007. "Sylvia Rivera's Talk at LGMNY, June 2001 Lesbian and Gay Community Services Center, New York City." *Centro Journal* 6, no. 1: 116–123.

Robinson, A. 2010. "Xbox Live: 'Gay', 'Transgender' Now OK." *Computer and Videogames*, March 5. Retrieved from www.computerandvideogames.com.

Rosen, Stanley. 2002. *The Elusiveness of the Ordinary: Studies in the Possibility of Philosophy*. New Haven, CT: Yale University Press.

Rosenberg, D. 2007. "(Rethinking) Gender." *Newsweek*, May 21. Retrieved from www.thedailybeast.com.

Ross, Karen. 2012. *The Handbook of Gender, Sex and Media*. Malden, MA: Wiley-Blackwell.

Rubin, Henry. 2003. *Self-Made Men: Identity and Embodiment among Transsexual Men*. Nashville, TN: Vanderbilt University Press.

Ruddy, Jenn. 2010. "Facebook "Re-evaluates" Decision to Censor Trans Man's Post-Op Chest Pics." *Daily Xtra*, January 14. Retrieved from www.dailyxtra.com.

Ryan, Joelle. 2009. "Reel Gender: Examining the Politics of Trans Images in Film and Media." Doctoral Dissertation. Bowling Green State University. *American Culture Studies Ph.D. Dissertations*. 62. Retrieved from http://scholarworks.bgsu.edu

Sacks, Harvey. 1984. "On Doing 'Being Ordinary.'" In *Structures of Social Action: Studies in Conversation Analysis*. Edited by J. M. Atkinson and J. Heritage, 413–429. Cambridge, UK: Cambridge University Press.

Scannell, Paddy. 1996. *Radio, Television & Modern Life: A Phenomenological Approach*. Oxford: Blackwell Publishing.

———. 2014. *Television and the Meaning of Live: An Inquiry into the Human Situation*. Cambridge, UK: Polity Press.

Schiappa, Edward, Peter Gregg, and Dean Hewes. 2006. "Can One TV Show Make a Difference?: *Will & Grace* and the Parasocial Contact Hypothesis." *Journal of Homosexuality* 51, no. 4: 15–37.

Schilt, Kristen. 2009. "Jorgensen, Christine (1926–1989)." *Encyclopedia of Gender and Society, Volume 1*. Edited by Jodi O'Brien, 474. Los Angeles: Sage Publications.

Sedgwick, Eve Kosofsky. 2003. *Touching Feeling: Affect, Pedagogy, Performativity*. Durham, NC: Duke University Press.

Seigworth, Gregory and Melissa Gregg. 2010. "An Inventory of Shimmers" In *The Affect Theory Reader*. Edited by Gregory Seigworth and Melissa Gregg, 1–25. Durham, NC: Duke University Press.

Sender, Katherine. 2002. "Business, Not Politics: Gays, Lesbians, Bisexuals, Transgender People and the Consumer Sphere." *Annenberg School for Communication Departmental Papers (ASC)*. Retrieved from www.repository.upenn.edu.

———. 2004. *Business, Not Politics: The Making of the Gay Market*. New York: Columbia University Press.

Serano, Julia. 2007. *Whipping Girl: A Transsexual Woman on Sexism and the Scapegoating of Femininity*. Emeryville, CA: Seal Press.

Shapiro, Eve. 2004. "'Trans'cending Barriers: Transgender Organizing on the Internet." *Journal of Gay and Lesbian Social Services* 16: 165–179.

Shattuc, Jane. 1997. *The Talking Cure: TV Talk Shows and Women*. New York: Routledge.

Sheringham, Michael. 2000. "Attending to the Everyday: Blanchot, Lefebvre, Certeau, Perec." *French Studies* 54, no. 2: 187–199.

Sholle, David. 1991. "Reading the Audience, Reading Resistance: Prospects and Problems." *Journal of Film and Video* 43, no. 1: 80–89.

Shouse, Eric. 2005. "Feeling, Emotion, Affect." *M/C Journal* 8, no. 6. December. Retrieved from www.journal.media-culture.org.au.

Silverman, Victor and Susan Stryker. 2005. *Screaming Queens*. Documentary. San Francisco: Frameline.

Silverstone, Roger. 1994. *Television and Everyday Life*. New York: Routledge.

Simmel, Georg. 1971. *On Individuality and Social Forms*. Chicago: University of Chicago Press.

Simon, Max. 2010. "Apple Originally Thought 'Peekaboo Tranny' Would Be a Great App Store Addition." *Queerty*, October 29. Retrieved from www.queerty.com.

Skidmore, Emily. 2011. "Constructing the 'Good Transsexual': Christine Jorgensen, Whiteness, and Heteronormativity in the Mid-Twentieth-Century Press." *Feminist Studies* 37, no. 2: 270–300.

Smith, Gwendolyn Ann. 2015. "Transmissions Classic: The Transgender Documentary Drinking Game." *Bay Area Reporter*, June 11. Retrieved from www.ebar.com.

Steinmetz, Katy. 2014. "The Transgender Tipping Point." *Time*, May 29. Retrieved from www.time.com.

Sterling Brands. 2014. "On the Future: A Forecast of Near-Future Trends." Annual Trends Report. Retrieved from www.sterlingbrands.com.

Stewart, Jacqueline. 2003. "Negroes Laughing at Themselves?: Black Spectatorship and the Performance of Urban Modernity." *Critical Inquiry* 29, no. 4: 650–677.

Stewart, Kathleen. 2007. *Ordinary Affects*. Durham, NC: Duke University Press.

Stone, Sandy. 1991. "The Empire Strikes Back: A Posttranssexual Manifesto." In *Body Guards: The Cultural Politics of Gender Ambiguity*. Edited by K. Straub and J. Epstein, 280–304. New York: Routledge.

Straayer, Chris. 1990. "The Hypothetical Lesbian Heroine." *Jump Cut* no. 35: 50–57.

———. 1996. *Deviant Eyes, Deviant Bodies: Sexual Re-orientations in Film and Video*. New York: Columbia University Press.

Stryker, Susan. 1998. The Transgender Issue: An Introduction. *GLQ: A Journal of Lesbian and Gay Studies* 4: 145–158.

———. 2008. *Transgender History*. Berkeley, CA: Seal Press.

Stryker, Susan and Paisley Currah. 2014. "Introduction." *TSQ: Transgender Studies Quarterly* 1, no. 1–2: 1–18.

Stryker, Susan and Aren Z. Aizura. 2013. "Introduction: Transgender Studies 2.0." In *The Transgender Studies Reader 2*. Edited by Susan Stryker and Aren Z. Aizura, 1–12. New York: Routledge.

Sullivan, K. E. 2000. "Ed Gein and the Figure of the Transgendered Serial Killer." *Jump Cut: A Review of Contemporary Media* 43: 38–47.

Sweet, L. 2009. "Critic: Flush Bathroom Bill." *Boston Herald*, April 8. Retrieved from www.bostonherald.com.

Sycamore, Matt Bernstein. 2004. *That's Revolting: Queer Strategies for Resisting Assimilation*. Berkeley: Soft Skull Press.

Taylor, Melanie. 1998. "'The Masculine Soul Heaving in the Female Bosom': Theories of Inversion and *The Well of Loneliness*." *Journal of Gender Studies* 7, no. 3: 287–296.

Turkle, Sherry. 2011. "What Makes an Object Evocative?." In *Evocative Objects: Things We Think With*. Edited by Sherry Turkle, 307–326. Cambridge, MA: MIT Press.

———. 2012. *Alone Together: Why We Expect More from Technology and Less from Each Other*. New York: Basic Books.

Valentine, David. 2006. "'I Went to Bed with My Own Kind Once': The Erasure of Desire in the Name of Identity." In *The Transgender Studies Reader*. Edited by S. Stryker and S. Whittle, 407–419. New York: Routledge.

———. 2007. *Imagining Transgender: An Ethnography of a Category*. Durham, NC: Duke University Press.

Walters, Suzanna Danuta. 2001. *All the Rage: The Story of Gay Visibility in America*. Chicago: University of Chicago Press.

Warner, Michael. 1999. *The Trouble with Normal: Sex, Politics, and the Ethics of Queer Life*. New York: Free Press.

Weibel, Peter. 1996. "The World as Interface: Towards the Construction of Context-Controlled Event-Worlds." In *Electronic Culture: Technology and Visual Representation*. Edited by Timothy Druckrey, 338–351. New York: Aperture.

Weinreb, Michael. 2011. "Renée Richards Wants to Be Left Alone." *Grantland*, July 7. Retrieved from www.grantland.com.

Wellman, Barry, Anabel Quan-Haase, Jeffrey Boase, Wenhong Chen, Keith Hampton, Isabel Diaz, and Kakuko Miyata. 2003. "The Social Affordances of the Internet for Networked Individualism." *Journal of Computer-Mediated Communication* 8, no. 3. DOI: 10.1111/j.1083–6101.2003.tb00216.x

Wilchins, Riki. 1997. *Read My Lips: Sexual Subversion and the End of Gender*. Ithaca, NY: Firebrand Books.

———. 2004. *Queer Theory, Gender Theory: An Instant Primer*. Los Angeles: Alyson Books.

Williams, Raymond. 1983. *Keywords: A Vocabulary of Culture and Society*. New York: Oxford University Press.

———. 1989. *Resources of Hope: Culture, Democracy, Socialism*. New York: Verso.

Wortham, Jenna. 2016. "When Everyone Can Be 'Queer,' Is Anyone?" *New York Times*, July 12. Retrieved from www.nytimes.com.

Zeigler, Cyd. 2010. "Kye Allums: First Transgender Man Playing NCAA Women's Basketball." *Outsports.com*. November 1. Retrieved from www.outsports.com.

Zoonen, Liesbet Van. 1995. "Gender, Representation, and the Media." In *Questioning the Media: A Critical Introduction*. Edited by John Downing, Ali Mohammadi, and Annabelle Sreberny, 311–328. Thousand Oaks, CA: Sage.

INDEX

ABOUT THE AUTHOR

Andre Cavalcante is Assistant Professor of Media Studies and Women, Gender & Sexuality at the University of Virginia. His research and teaching specialize in the study of media audiences; lesbian, gay, bisexual, transgender, and queer issues in media culture; and the practice of everyday life.